.NET
Interview Questions

Sixth Revised & Updated Edition

(Around 600 plus Interview questions from real C# .NET Interviews)

By
Shivprasad Koirala

BPB PUBLICATIONS
B-14 Connaught Place, New Delhi-110 001

FIRST EDITION 2005

6TH REVISED & UPDATED EDITION 2013   **Reprint 2015**

Copyright © 2011 BPB PUBLICATIONS, INDIA

ISBN: 978-81-8333-147-0

Distributors:

COMPUTER BOOK CENTRE
12, Shrungar Shopping Centre, M.G. Road,
BENGALURU-560001
Ph: 25587923, 25584641

MICRO BOOKS
Shanti Niketan Building, 8, Camac Street,
KOLKATA-700017 Ph: 22826518, 22826519

BUSINESS PROMOTION BUREAU
8/1 Ritchie Street, Mount Road,
CHENNAI-600002, Ph: 28410796, 28550491

MICRO MEDIA
Shop No. 5, Mahendra Chambers, 150 DN Rd.
Next to Capital Cinema, V.T. (C.S.T.) Station,
MUMBAI-400001, Ph: 22078296, 22078297

BPB PUBLICATIONS
B-14, Connaught Place, New Delhi-110001
Ph: 23325760, 43526249

DECCAN AGENCIES
4-3-329, Bank Street,
HYDERABAD-500195
Ph: 24756967, 24756400

BPB BOOK CENTRE
376 Old Lajpat Rai Market, DELHI-110006
Ph: 23861747

INFOTECH
G-2, Sidhartha Building,
96 Nehru Place, New Delhi-110019
Ph: 26438245

INFOTECH
Shop No. 2, F-38, South Extension Part-1
New Delhi-110049
Ph: 24691288

Published by Manish Jain for BPB Publications, B-14, Connaught Place, New Delhi-110001 and Printed by him at Adinath Printers Delhi.

Introduction

The team behind the book

Author: Shivprasad Koirala.

Supporting author: Shaam Sheikh / Ajay / Amrita

Publisher: Manish Jain

BPB publication and me

I still remember the struggling days when I wanted to print this book and no publisher wanted to take risk on a new comer. Many publishers even mocked at the idea of an interview question book series.

One lucky day I got in touch with Manish Jain from Bpb and this book got life. I am thankful to Bpb publication to make this author and putting forward a great interview question book series.

Thanks to Special people

I would like to first start by thanking the two old eyes who made this person without any expectations, my dad and mom.

I have been very selfish to steal time from my kids (Sanjana, Simran and Aditya) and my wife (Vishna) to complete this book. So a big thanks to stand by me to ensure that this book comes alive.

I am blessed to have Raju as my brother who always keeps my momentum moving on. I am grateful to Mr. Bhavnesh Asar who initially conceptualized the idea, i believe concept thinking is more important than execution.

Special thanks to Mr Sukesh marla with whom I had long fruitful technical discussion which has flown in the book and made the book stronger.

Thanks to Mr. Shaam, Mr. Ajay and Miss Amrita for all the effort they have put in. It was their tiresome three months of support that we have finally made it.

About the Author

Author currently runs a training firm www.questpond.com where he teaches Microsoft technologies for beginners and advanced level. Writing is something I do extra and I love doing it.

No one is perfect and same holds true for me .So anything you want to comment, suggest, and point typo / grammar mistakes or technical mistakes regarding the book you can mail me at shiv_koirala@yahoo.com. Believe me guys your harsh words would be received with love and treated to the top most priority. Without all you guys I am not an author. Writing an interview question book is really a great deal of responsibility. I have tried to cover maximum questions for the topic because I always think probably leaving one silly question will cost someone's job there. But huge natural variations in an interview are something difficult to cover in this small book. So if you have come across such questions during interview which is not addressed in this book do mail at shiv_koirala@yahoo.com .Who knows probably that question can save some other guys job.

Foreword

Changing job is one of the biggest event for any IT professional. When he starts the search he realizes that he needs much more than actual experience. Working on a project is one thing and cracking an interview is a different ball game, many may differ on this but that's my personal opinion. When you work on a project you are doing a routine job and you tend to forget the basic fundamentals. For instance you are working on a highly technical project which uses remoting majorly in the project,it'svery much possible that you can fail in simple ADO.NET questions because you are completely out of touch with it. We all know failing in simple ADO.NET questions will not even clear your first round. It does not mean you do not know the fundamentals;it's only that you need to revise the same.

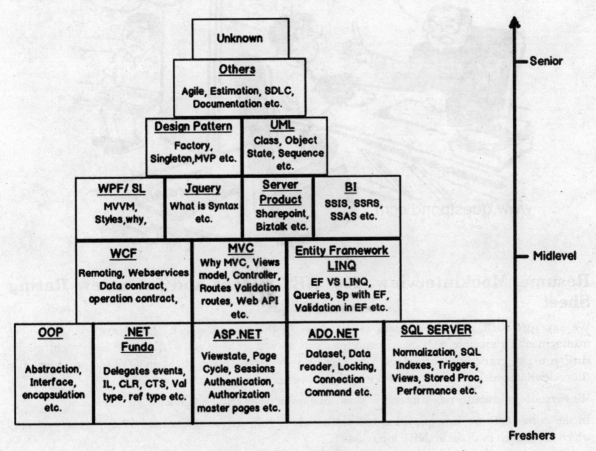

Figure: Road map for .NET preparation

This book will give you bird eye view of what is needed in .NET interviews. It will help you in doing quick revision so that you can be ready for the interview in day or two. The best way to read this book is not from start to end rather just read the index and then go in details if needed.

Before you start preparing for .NET interviews, one golden advice, keep a bigger picture in mind. Do not concentrate on topics which you love. Every company is different, every interviewer is different, so prepare in a holistic way rather than specifics. Please see image (Road map for .net preparation) which shows road map of how to prepare in .NET interviews.

It's really good to see emails saying 'We got a job', just makes us feel better, please do write to us on shiv_koirala@yahoo.com about your success. I hope this book takes you to a better height and gives you extra confidence boost during interviews.

Best of Luck and Happy Job-Hunting.............

Resume, Mockinterview, 100 .NET Videos and Interview Rating Sheet

We have provided a self-assessment rating sheet in the book for .NET,Java,Networking, Project management,Architecture, SQL Server and lot more. If you are able get 80 % in the assessment we are sure you can crack any Interview. You can find the assessment sheet in DVD as an excel file (InterviewRating.xls). So take the self-test again and again to improve your confidence.

We have also provided a mock interview video of how actually .NET interviews are conducted.

In the same DVD we have provided 100 videos which help to you understand 50 important concepts which are probed in detail in .NET interviews.

A sample resume to help you understand how a good resume is made.

Below is a simple sample screen shot of interview preparation assessment sheet.

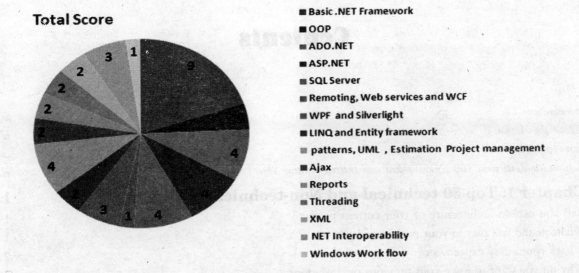

Total Score

- ■ Basic .NET Framework
- ■ OOP
- ■ ADO.NET
- ■ ASP.NET
- ■ SQL Server
- ■ Remoting, Web services and WCF
- ■ WPF and Silverlight
- ■ LINQ and Entity framework
- ▨ patterns, UML , Estimation Project management
- ■ Ajax
- ▨ Reports
- ▨ Threading
- ▨ XML
- ■ NET Interoperability
- ▨ Windows Work flow

Figure: Rating Sheet

Contents

Chapter 2: Basic .NET Framework   **18**

Chapter 3: OOPS   **38**

Chapter 4: ADO.NET   **50**

Chapter 8: Remoting, Web services and WCF   143

Chapter 9: WPF and Silverlight   **159**

Chapter 10: LINQand Entity framework   175

Chapter 11: Design patterns,UML, Estimation and Project management   184

Chapter 16: NET Interoperability   264

Chapter 17: Windows workflow Foundation   274

1
Top 50 Technical and Non-technical Questions

> **Note:** This is a challenge from me, you should atleast get 15 questions from my top 50 most asked question.

Can you explain architecture of your current project?

> **Note:** I think 40% (the percentage can be higher) .NET interview starts with this question. Below is a sample answer and will differ from developer to developer.

My current architecture is an 3 tier architecture with UI made in ASP.NET, middle tier having the business logic and the data access layer uses enterprise data application blocks. It uses MVC architecture to keep the UI code clean.

We also have a common library which is shared in our project and for external customer we have exposed some service via WCF.

What role did you play in your project and company?

> **Note:** Do not answer in one liner like I am developer, project manager, talk end to end. This will help interviewer to understand much better about you completely. Below is a simple sample answer how professionals reply.

My role was end to end. I was involved right from the requirement phase where I was a part of requirement gathering and creating use cases.

I was also actively involved in design phase to conceptualize the technical aspect of the project.

My main role was then in development / coding phase where I was involved in coding and unit testing.

I also played an important role in system and acceptance testing to fix defects and issues raised by testers and end users.

So my role was end to end with main focus on coding and unit testing.

I am also partly involved with the COE group where I help developers in the company to upgrade to new technologies.

> ***Note:*** *If you are a part of other activities like training, quality, pre-sales team, estimation etc speak about the same during interview.Companies now a day's look out for multitasking capabilities rather than specific capabilities.*

What's your salary expectation?

This is a very complex question at the end of the book we have a complete chapter which discusses specifically on current .NET developer salary packages and some tips for negotiation.

One golden tip from me, if you really want the job and you do not want salary to be a hurdle, add the word "NEGOTIABLE" after the salary amount.

Why do you want to leave your previous organization?

This is a subjective answer and varies from individual to individual. Some answers which can explain your current situations:

- For better prospects.
- Expecting a salary rise.
- Relocation.
- Looking for a better position.
- Had a kid (For women's)

> ***Note:*** *Do not give answers like company was not good, there was too much politics, it was a maintenance job etc etc. These answers can lead to more cross questions making the interviewer uncomfortable.*

How much do you rate yourself between 1 to 10?

> ***Note:*** *This questions comes in different forms like, How much do you rate yourself in ASP.NET, How much do you rate yourself in SQL Server etc.*

Answer for this question is again very subjective but some important tricks here to avoid any traps.

- Even if you are really good in that topic do not rate yourself 10 or 9, just shows that you are overconfident. If you are extremely good put 8. Let your technical answers talk about your rating.
- If you know the topic averagely, rate yourself 5.
- If you are bad in the topic or have never done anything do not put any rating. Probably it's better to say you have not worked rather than trying to attempt and create more problems.

Can you speak about yourself?

> ***Note:*** *Many people become emotional here and talk personal. Most of the time interviewer is expecting to talk about your role you played, technological skills and which path you want to grow. Below is a sample answer and it varies from person to person.*

I have 8 years of experience, in the first 4 years I worked as a developer in Microsoft technologies. The next 2 years after that I worked as a team lead guiding the team, helping them resolve problems. Currently

I am working in Microsoft server products like SharePoint,BizTalk. My main technical skills revolve around C#, Visual studio, SQL Server, .NET and ASP.NET.

I would like to see myself as technical lead in further coming times.

> **Note:** *The last sentence is very important, let the interviewer know where you want to see yourself in the later stages.*

How can we improve performance of .NET?

> **Note:** *This question can have various other forms like How can we improve performance of ASP.NET, How can we improve performance of SQL Server etc. Remember 5 best points of each category. You can pick your favorite ones. But whatever you pick, should be commonly used by every one.*

Below are some common points you can remember. List is endless but I do not want to make it long, so that you can remember important ones.

- Use string builder for concatenation rather than string when concatenation huge string values.
- Avoid boxing / unboxing, use generics.
- Avoid writing in line SQL queries use stored procedures.
- Choose your indexes (clustered and non-clustered) properly.
- Use Caching for data which will not change frequently.
- In ASP.NET use output cache directive for page level caching.

What is the difference between .NET 1.X,2.0,3.0, 3.5 and 4.0?

Below is the list of top differences between the framework versions. Please remember the list is much bigger than what I have put down. But for interview perspective I have taken top 5 in each one of them so that we can remember the important ones.

.NET 2.0	.NET 3.0	.NET 3.5	.NET 4.0
Support for 64 bit application.Generics SQL cache dependency Master pagesMembership and roles	WCF WPF WWF WCS (card space)	LINQAjax inbuilt ADO Entity frameworkADO data servicesMulti targeting	MEFParallel computing DLR dynamic Code contract language runtime Lazy initialization Background GC

What is ILcode, JIT, CLR, CTS, CLS and CAS?

- IL code is a partially compiled code.
- JIT (Just in time compiler) compiles IL Code to machine language.
- CLR (Common language run time) is the heart of.NET framework and it does 4 primary important things Garbage collection, CAS (Code Access security), CV (Code verification) and IL to Native translation.

- CTS (Common types system) ensure that data types defined in two different languages get compiled to a common data type.

- CLS is a specification or set of rules or guidelines. When any programming language adheres to these set of rules it can be consumed by any .NET language.

- CAS is the part of .NET security model which determines whether or not a particular code is allowed to run and what kind of resources can the code access.

> **Note:** *Do have a look at the video What is IL code, CLR, CTS, CLS and JIT? There are two parts to this video in the first part we have discussed the theory in the next part we have discussed practically how these terminology come to life in .NET environment.*

What is a garbage collector?

Garbage collector is a feature of CLR which cleans unused managed (it does not clean unmanaged objects) objects and reclaims memory. It's a back ground thread which runs continuously and at specific intervals it checks if there are any unused objects whose memory can be claimed.

> **Note:** *Do have a look at the video What is Garbage collector, Gen 0, 1 and 2, which is in the DVD?*

What is GAC?

GAC (Global Assembly Cache) is where all shared .NET assembly resides. GAC is used in the following situations:

- If assemblies have to be shared among several application which resides in the same computer.

- If the assembly has some special security, requirements like only administrators can remove the assembly. If the assembly is private then a simple delete of assembly the assembly file will remove the assembly.

> **Note:** *Do have a look at two classic videos shipped in the DVD which shows how garbage collector works internally.*
>
> *What is Garbage Collector, Gen 0, 1 & 2 ?*
>
> *What is IDisposable interface & finalize dispose pattern in GC?*

What are stack,heap,value, reference types, boxing and unboxing?

Stack and heap are memory types in an application. Stack memory stores data types like int, double, Boolean etc. While heap stores data types like string and objects.

For instance when the below code runs the first two variables i.e. "i" and "y" are stored in a stack and the last variable "o" is stored in heap.

```
void MyFunction()
{
        int i = 1; // This is stored in stack.
        int y = i; // This is stored in stack.
```

```
      object o = null; // This is stored in heap.
} // after this end the stack variable memory space is reclaimed while //
the heap memory is reclaimed later by garbage collector.
```

Value types contain actual data while reference types contain pointers and the pointers point to the actual data.

Value types are stored on stack while reference types are stored on heap. Value types are your normal data types like int, bool, double and reference types are all objects.

When value type is moved to a reference type it's called as boxing. The vice-versa is termed as unboxing.

> **Note:** *Watch indepth videos given in the DVD What is a stack, Heap, Value types and Reference types and What is boxing and unboxing?. These videos example explain step by step concept of boxing, unboxing, value, reference types, stack and heap.*

How are exceptions handled in .NET?

Exceptions are handled by "System.Exception" base class. If you want raise an error from source you need to create the exception object with below code snippet.

> *throw new Exception("Customer code cannot be more than 10");*

Once the exception is raised of you want to catch the same you need to use the try catch block as shown below.

```
try
{
     // This section will have the code which
     // which can throw exceptions.
}
catch(Exception e)
{
     // Handle what you want to
     // do with the exception
     label.text = e.Message;
}
```

What are different types of collections in .NET?

There are five important collections in .NET Arrays, Lists, Hashtable, stacks and queues .

What are generics?

Generics help to separate logic and data type to increase reusability. In other words you can create a class whose data type can be defined on run time.

> **Note:** *Watch the video shipped in the DVD What is generics ?.*

Explain Abstraction, encapsulation, inheritance and polymorphism?

Abstraction

Abstraction means show only what is necessary. Example color is abstracted to RGB. By just making the combination of these three colors we can achieve any color in world. It is a model of real world or concept.

Encapsulation

It is a process of hiding all the complex processing from the outside world and make your objects simple.

Inheritance

This concept helps to define parent child relationship between classes.

Polymorphism

It's a property of object to act differently under different conditions. For instance a simple user object depending on conditions can act like a admin or like data entry object.

> **Note:** *Watch the video Can you define OOP and the 4 principles of OOP? for more detail explanation.*

How is abstract class different from aninterface?

	Abstract class	Interface
Implementation	Some methods in abstract classes can have implementation.	All methods, function, properties in interfaces are empty. They are simple signatures.
Scenario	Abstract classes are used when we want to share common functionality in parent child relationship.	Interfaces are used to define contract, enforce standardization, decoupling and dynamic polymorphism.
Variable declaration	We can declare variables	In interface we cannot declare variables.
Inheritance VS Implementation	Abstract classes are inherited.	Interfaces are implemented.

> **Note:** *Refer the below 3 videos to understand abstract classes and interfaces in more depth.*
>
> *What is an abstract class?*
>
> *Define Interface & What is the diff. between abstract & interface?*
>
> *Define Interface & Diff. between abstract & interface? - Part 2*

What are the different types of polymorphism?

There are 2 kinds of polymorphism static and dynamic. Many people also call them as runtime or compile time polymorphism. Static polymorphism is implemented by overloading while dynamic polymorphism is implemented by overriding and virtual keyword.

> **Note:** *Do watch the video "What is Polymorphism, overloading, overriding and virtual?" for in depth demonstration of how to implement polymorphism in .NET. The video also talks about two different types of polymorphism in depth.*

How does delegate differ from an event?

Delegate is an abstract strong pointer to a function or method while events are higher level of encapsulation over delegates. Events use delegates internally.

They differ for the below re(I) What is the difference between delegate and events?asons:

- Actually, events use delegates in bottom. But they add an extra layer on the delegates, thus forming the publisher and subscriber model.

- As delegates are function to pointers, they can move across any clients. So any of the clients can add or remove events, which can be confusing. But events give the extra protection / encapsulation by adding the layer and making it a publisher and subscriber model.

Just imagine one of your clients doing this

```
c.XyzCallback = null
```

This will reset all your delegates to nothing and you have to keep searching where the error is.

> **Note:** *Do watch the below three videos given in the DVD to get more insight on delegates and events.*
>
> *What problem does Delegate Solve? - Part1*
>
> *What is a Multicast delegate? - Part2*
>
> *What are events & what's the difference between delegates & events? - Part3*

What are different access modifiers?

There are 5 access modifiers. Access modifiers define scope for members.

- Private: Accessible only with in the class.
- Protected: Accessible with in the class and in derived classes.
- Friend (internal in C#):Accessible anywhere within the current project.
- Protected friend (protected internal in C#): Accessible with current project and derived classes.
- Public: Accessible everywhere.

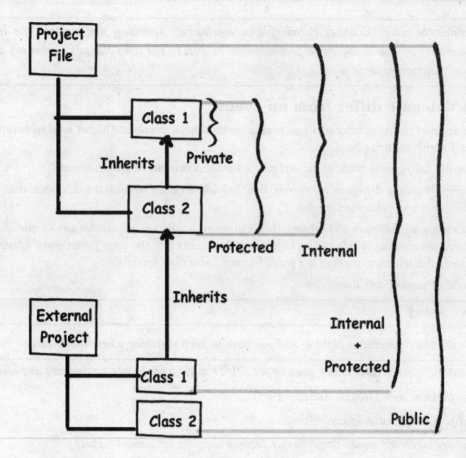

Figure 1.1: different access modifiers

Note: *Watch the video*

Can you explain encapsulation and abstraction? Where we have explained how encapsulation can be implemented using access modifiers.

Can you explain connection, command, datareader and dataset in ADO.NET ?

- Connection: This object creates a connection to the database. If you want to do any operation on the database you have to first create a connection object.

- Command: This object helps us to execute SQL queries against database. Using command object we can execute select, insert, update and delete SQL command.

- Data reader: This provides a recordset which can be browsed only in forward direction. It can only be read but not updated. Data reader is good for large number of records where you want to just browse quickly and display it.

- Dataset object: This provides a recordset which can be read back and in forward direction. The recordset can also be updated. Dataset is like a in memory database with tables, rows and fields.

- Data Adapter: This object acts as a bridge between database and dataset; it helps to load the dataset object.

How does "Dataset" differ from a "Data Reader"?

- "Dataset" is a disconnected architecture, while "Data Reader" has live connection while reading data. If we want to cache data and pass to a different tier "Dataset" forms the best choice and it has decent XML support.

- When application needs to access data from more than one table "Dataset" forms the best choice.

- If we need to move back while reading records, "data reader" does not support this functionality.

- However, one of the biggest drawbacks of Dataset is speed. As "Dataset" carry considerable overhead because of relations, multiple table's etc speed is slower than "Data Reader". Use "Data Reader" when you want to quickly read and display records on a screen.

- Dataset can manipulate data while data reader is only for reading purpose.

How is ASP.NET page life cycle executed?

Following is the sequence in which the events occur:

- Init
- Load
- Validate
- Event
- Render

Remember the word SILVER : SI (Init) L (Load) V (Validate) E (Event) R (Render) .

> **Note:** *Watch the complete video of Can you explain ASP.NET application and Page life cycle ?*

What are Httphandlers and HttpModules and difference between them?

Handlers and modules helps you inject pre-processing logic before the ASP.NET request reaches the website.

For instance before your request reaches any resource you would like to check if the user has been authenticated or not.

Httphandlers is an extension based processor. In other words the pre-processing logic is invoked depending on file extensions.

Httpmodule is an event based processor. In other words ASP.NET emits lot of event like BeginRequest, AuthenticateRequest etc, we can write logic in those events using Httpmodule.

> **Note:** *Watch the complete video of Can you explain ASP.NET application and Page life cycle ? where we have explained handlers and modules in depth.*

What are different kind of validator controls in ASP.NET ?

There are six main types of validation controls:

RequiredFieldValidator

It checks whether the control have any value. It is used when you want the control should not be empty.

RangeValidator

It checks if the value in validated control is in that specific range. Example TxtCustomerCode should not be more than eight lengths.

CompareValidator

It checks that the value in controls should match some specific value. Example Textbox TxtPie should be equal to 3.14.

RegularExpressionValidator

When we want the control, value should match with a specific regular expression.

CustomValidator

It is used to define User Defined validation.

Validation Summary

It displays summary of all current validation errors on an ASP.NET page.

How is 'Server.Transfer' different from 'response.Redirect' ?

'Response.Redirect' sends message to the browser saying it to move to some different page, while 'Server.Transfer' does not send any message to the browser but rather redirects the user directly from the server itself. So in 'server.transfer' there is no round trip while 'response.redirect' has a round trip and hence puts a load on server.

In "Response.Redirect" you can move cross domain. In other words let's say you want to move from www.questpond.com to www.yahoo.com that's possible by "Response.Redirect". "Server.Transfer" can redirect only within the server and not cross domain.

Can you explain windows, forms and passport authentication?

There are 3 major ways of doing authentication and authorization:

- Windows: In this mode the users are stored in windows local user groups.

- Forms: In this mode we create a login screen and use the forms authentication class to do validations. It's a ticket based authentication.

- Passport :In this mode the users are validated from Microsoft sites like hotmail, devhood, MSN etc, ticket is generated and that ticket can be used to do authentication and authorization in your web application.

Note: *Watch the 6 videos which talks in depth about the above concepts. Its possible that interviewer can get in to details.*

What is Authentication, Authorization, Principal & Identity objects? Part-1

ASP.NET Authentication and Authorization Video series Part-2

ASP.NET Authentication and Authorization Video series Part-3

ASP.NET Authentication and Authorization Video series Part-4

ASP.NET Authentication and Authorization Video series Part-5

ASP.NET Authentication and Authorization Video series Part-6

What is difference between Grid view, Data list, and repeater?

Grid view and data grid by default display all the data in tabular format i.e. in table and rows. Developer has no control to change the table data display of datagrid.

Data list also displays data in a table but gives some flexibility in terms of displaying data row wise and column wise using the repeat direction property.

Repeater control is highly customizable. It does not display data in table by default. So you can customize from scratch the way you want to display data.

Which are the various modes of storing ASP.NET session?

● **InProc:** In this mode Session, state is stored in the memory space of the Aspnet_wp.exe process. This is the default setting. If the IIS reboots or web application restarts then session state is lost.

● **StateServer:** In this mode Session state is serialized and stored in a separate process (Aspnet_state.exe); therefore, the state can be stored on a separate computer(a state server).

● **SQL SERVER**: In this mode Session, state is serialized and stored in a SQL Server database.

Session state can be specified in <sessionState> element of application configuration file. Using State Server and SQL SERVER session state can be shared across web farms but note this comes at speed cost as ASP.NET needs to serialize and deserialize data over network repeatedly.

How can we do caching in ASP.NET?

There are twoways of caching output cache directive and using the cache objects.

What is ViewState?

Viewstate is a built-in structure for automatically retaining values amongst the multiple requests for the same page. The viewstate is internally maintained as a hidden field on the page but is hashed, providing greater security than developer-implemented hidden fields do.

What are indexes and what is the difference between clustered and non-clustered?

Index makes your search faster by using B-Tree structure logic. Clustered and non-clustered indexes are two types of indexes. In clustered index the leaf node points to the actual data while in non-clustered index the leaf node uses the clustered index to locate data.

How is stored procedure different from functions?

● Function cannot affect the state of the database which means we cannot perform CRUD operation on the database. Stored Procedure can affect the state of the database by using CRUD operations.

● Store Procedure can return zero or n values whereas Function can return only one value.

● Store Procedure can have input, output parameters for it whereas functions can have only input parameters.

- Function can be called from Stored Procedure whereas Stored Procedure cannot be called from Function.

What's the difference between web services and remoting?

Remoting works only when both the ends i.e. server and client are in .NET technologies. Web services are useful when the client is not .NET like java etc.

What's the difference between WCF and Web services?

- WCF services can be hosted in multiple protocols like http, tcp etc. Web services can only be hosted on Http protocol.

- WCF has COM+ so you can call two different WCF services in a transaction, we can not call two different web services in one transaction.

- WCF integrates with MSMQ easily, but for web services we will need to write code to communicate with the MSMQ pool.

In simple words below equation shows the difference with simple equation.

WCF = Web services + Remoting + MSMQ + COM+

Web service = WCF – (Remoting + MSMQ + COM+)

Note: *Do watch the below 4 videos of WCF to get more insight in to WCF.*

What are basic steps to create a WCF service (Part I, Creating the Service)?

What are basic steps to create a WCF service (Part II, Consuming the Service)?

What are endpoints, address, contracts and bindings?

What are various ways of hosting WCF service?

What are end point, contract, address, and bindings?

When we want to host any WCF service we need to provide where to host it, how to host it and what to host.

- **Contract** (What)

  Contract is an agreement between two or more parties. It defines the protocol how client should communicate with your service. Technically, it describes parameters and return values for a method.

- **Address** (Where)

  An Address indicates where we can find this service. Address is a URL, which points to the location of the service.

- **Binding** (How)

  Bindings determine how the service can be accessed. It determines how communications is done. For instance, you expose your service, which can be accessed using SOAP over HTTP or BINARY over TCP. So for each of these communications medium two bindings will be created.

- **End point**: It's the combination of contract, address and binding.

In WCF web.config file we can specify end point, address, binding and contract as shown in the below code snippet.

```
<endpoint          address="http://www.questpond.com"          binding="wsHttpBinding"
contract="WcfService3.IService1">
```

> **Note:** *Do watch the below 4 videos of WCF to get more insight in to WCF.*
>
> *What are basic steps to create a WCF service (Part I, Creating the Service)?*
>
> *What are basic steps to create a WCF service (Part II, Consuming the Service)?*
>
> *What are endpoints, address, contracts and bindings?*
>
> *What are various ways of hosting WCF service?*
>
> *What is the difference of hosting a WCF service on IIS and Self hosting?*
>
> *What is the difference between BasicHttpBinding and WsHttpBinding?*

What is WPF and silverlight?

WPF (Windows Presentation foundation) is a graphical subsystem for displaying user interfaces, documents, images, movies etc. It uses XAML which is a XML descriptive language to represent UI elements.

Silver light is 16. Windows Presentation Framework (Vista Series)a web browser plug-in by which we can enable animations, graphics and audio video. You can compare silver light with flash. We can view animations with flash and it's installed as a plug-in in the browser.

> **Note:** *Do have a look at the below videos for WPF and silverlight.*
>
> *What is the need of WPF when we had GDI, GDI+ and DirectX?*
>
> *Can you explain how we can make a simple WPF application?*
>
> *Can you explain the architecture of Silverlight ?*
>
> *What are the basic things needed to make a silverlight application ?*

What is LINQ and Entity framework?

LINQ is a uniform programming model for any kind of data access. It is also an OR mapper which helps us to expedite our business object creation process.

ADO.NET entity is an ORM (object relational mapping) which abstracts data model by providing a simplified object model.

In other words the complete middle tier development is expedited using entity framework.

> **Note:** *Below simple video demonstration in the DVD will help your understand LINQ and entity framework in to great depth.*
>
> *What is LINQ and can you explain same with example?*
>
> *Can you explain a simple example of LINQ to SQL?*

What's the difference between LINQ to SQL and Entity framework?

- LINQ to SQL is good for rapid development with SQL Server. EF is for enterprise scenarios and works with SQL server as well as other databases.

- LINQ maps directly to tables. One LINQ entity class maps to one table. EF has a conceptual model and that conceptual model map to storage model via mappings. So one EF class can map to multiple tables or one table can map to multiple classes.

- LINQ is more targeted towards rapid development while EF is for enterprise level where the need is to develop loosely coupled framework.

If you are starting with fresh development using entity framework, in case you are in older version of framework where entity framework does not exist use linq to sql.

What are design patterns?

Design patterns are recurring solution to recurring problems in software architecture.

> **Note:** *Do watch the following videos for design pattern which is shipped with the DVD :*
>
> *Introduction*
>
> *Factory pattern*
>
> *Memento Pattern*
>
> *Singleton Pattern*

Which design patterns are you familiar with?

Left to the readers, pick any three patterns which you have used in your project and talk about it. In chapter "Design patterns, UML, Estimation and Project management" we have explained 3 design patterns.

> *Note : In DVD we have snipped 3 design pattern videos you can have a look at them.*
>
> *Factory pattern*
>
> *Memento Pattern*
>
> *Singleton Pattern*

Can you explain singleton pattern?

Singleton pattern helps us to create a single instance of an object which can be shared across project. Main use of singleton pattern is for global data sharing and caching.

> **Note:** *The DVD contains a video explanation with source code for "Singleton Pattern".*

What is MVC, MVP and MVVM pattern?

All the above design patterns come in presentation pattern category and help to remove any kind of cluttered code in UI like manipulation of user interfaces and maintaining state. Thus keeping your UI code cleaner and better to maintain.

MVC pattern divides the architecture in to 3 part model, view and controller. The first request comes to the controller and the controller then decides which view to be displayed and ties up the model with the view accordingly.

MVP (Model view presenter) has the same goals as MVC i.e. separating the UI from the model. It does the same by using a presenter class. The UI talks via an interface to the presenter class and the presenter class talks with the model.

MVVM is an architectural pattern with the focus of removing UI cluttered code. It does the same by using an extra class called as view model. MVVM is mostly suitable for Silverlight and WPF projects because of the rich bindings provided by the technologies.

> **Note:** *In the DVD we have shipped 4 videos which explains MVC, MVP and MVVM patterns. Below are the name of the videos :*
>
> *The basic of MVC HttpHandlers*
>
> *MVC using core ASP.NET and HttpHandler*
>
> *MVC using MVC ASP.NET*
>
> *Model View Presenter video*

What is UML and which are the important diagrams?

The Unified Modeling Language (UML) is a graphical language for visualizing, specifying, constructing, and documenting the artifacts of a software-intensive system.

UML provides blue prints for business process, System function, programming language statements, database schemas and reusable components.Some of the important UML diagrams are use case, class diagrams, sequence diagram, activity diagram, object diagrams, collaboration diagrams, state chart diagrams, component diagram and deployment diagram.

> **Note:** *We have shipped 5 videos which explains some important UML diagrams in detail. Below is the list.*
>
> *Introduction*
>
> *Use Case Diagrams*
>
> *Class Digrams*
>
> *Sequence Digrams*
>
> *Collaboration Diagrams*

What are different phases in a software life cycle?

There are six phases in software development:

- Requirement
- Design
- Coding and unit testing

- System testing
- Acceptance testing
- Go live

What is Ajax and how does it help?

Ajax stands for Asynchronous JavaScript and XML. There are two prime benefits of Ajax:

- It send's only necessary data to the server. For instance let's say you have 4 textboxes and on a submit button you want to only send two text box data, Ajax helps in the same.

- The second benefit is it's asynchronous. In other words when you click on submit button and until the server processes the request you can do other activities on the site. For instance when you click on send email and until the email is sent, you can start composing a new email at the back ground.

How did you do unit testing in your project?

From unit testing perspective there are two great tools "NUNIT" and "Visual studio unit test template". Talk about which you are comfortable with. Below are two videos in DVD which shows demo of how to use NUNIT and VSTS unit test template.

> **Note:** *In the DVD we have shipped four videos which explain unit testing using*
>
> *What is Unit Testing & can we see an example of the same?*
>
> *How can we write data driven test using NUNIT & VS Test?*

What is Agile?

Agile is a development methodology where we develop in incremental and iteratively. In agile weconsider software as the most important entity and accept user changes and deliver them in small releases. There are four important principle of agile:

- Individuals and interactions over processes and tools.
- Working software over comprehensive documentation.
- Customer collaboration over contract negotiation.
- Responding to change over following a plan.

How did you do code reviews?

Code reviews are either done manually i.e. peer review or automated review using tools like style cop and fxcop.

> **Note:** *We have shipped two videos in the DVD which explains how to use stylecop and fxcop tools for code reviews.*

How did you convert requirements to technical document?

> **Note:** *This is a subjective answer. Below goes my version.*

Requirements are normally available in use cases or free text. The first step is to identify the classes, properties for the classes, methods / functions and relationship between the classes.

As a general rule nouns become classes and verbs become actions for the classes.

Once the classes are identified we can use sequence or collaboration diagrams to detail out the interactions.

The database objects are later created using the class diagrams.

2

Basic .NET Framework

What is an IL code?

It's a CPU independent partially compiled code.

> **Note:** *Half compiled means this code is not yet compiled to machine/CPU specific instructions.*

Why IL code is not fully compiled?

We do not know in what kind of environment .NET code will run. In other words we do not know what can be the end operating system, CPU configuration, machine configuration, security configuration etc. So the IL code is half compiled and on runtime this code is compiled to machine specific using the environmental properties (CPU,OS, machine configuration etc).

Who compiles the IL code and how does it work?

IL code is compiled by JIT (Just in time compiler).

How does JIT compilationwork?

JIT compiles the code just before execution and then saves this translation in memory. Just before execution JIT can compile per-file, per function or a code fragment.

What are different types of JIT?

In Microsoft .NET there are 3 types of JIT compilers:

- **Normal-JIT (Default):** Normal-JIT compiles only those methods that are called at runtime. These methods are compiled the first time they are called, and then they are stored in cache. When the same methods are called again, the compiled code from cache is used for execution.

- **Econo-JIT:** Econo-JIT compiles only those methods that are called at runtime. However, these compiled methods are not stored in cache so that RAM memory can be utilized in an optimal manner.

- **Pre-JIT:** Pre-JIT compiles complete source code into native code in a single compilation cycle. This is done at the time of deployment of the application. We can implement Pre-jit by using ngen.exe.

Normal-jit is the default implementation and it produces optimized code. Econo-jit just replaces IL instruction with native counterpart. It does not do any kind of optimization. Econo-jit does not store the compiled code in cache so it requires less memory.

The choice of Normal-JIT and Econo-JIT is decided internally. Econo-JIT is chosen when devices have limitation memory and CPU cycle issues like windows CE powered device. When there is no memory crunch and CPU power is higher than Normal-JIT is used.

Pre-JIT is implemented by using ngen.exe which is explained in the next question.

What is Native Image Generator (Ngen.exe)?

Ngen stores full compiled.NET native code in to cache. In other words rather than dynamically compiling the code on run time a full image of native compiled code is stored in cache while installing the application. This leads to better performance as the assembly loads and execute faster.

In order to install full compiled native code in cache we can execute the below command line from your visual studio command prompt.

```
ngen.exe install <assemblyname>
```

So does it mean that NGEN.EXE will always improve performance?

No, it's not always necessary that ngen.exe produces optimized code because it uses the current environments parameters which can change over a period of time. For instance a code compiled in windows XP environment will not be the optimized code to run under windows 2008 server. So we need to once test with 'ngen' and without 'ngen' to conclude if really the performance increases.

What is a CLR?

CLR (Common language run time) is the heart of.NET framework and it does 4 primary important things:

● Garbage collection
● CAS (Code Access security)
● CV (Code verification)
● IL to Native translation.

Note: There are many other uses of CLR but I have kept it short from the interview point of view. In the further section we will go in depth of these questions.

What is the difference between managed and unmanaged code?

Code that executes under CLR execution environment is called as managed code. Unmanaged code executes outside CLR boundary. Unmanaged code is nothing but code written in C++, VB6, VC++ etc. Unmanaged codes have their own environment in which the code runs and it's completely outside the control of CLR.

What is a garbage collector?

Garbage collector is a feature of CLR which cleans unused managed (it does not clean unmanaged objects) objects and reclaims memory. It's a back ground thread which runs continuously and at specific intervals it checks if there are any unused objects whose memory can be claimed.

Note: GC does not claim memory of unmanaged objects.

> **Note:** *Garbage collector is one of the very important interview topics due to complexity of generations, double GC loop because of destructor and the implementation of finalize and dispose pattern. So please do go through the video of "What is Garbage collection, Generation, Finalize, Dispose and Idisposable?" to ensure that you understand the fundamentals well.*

What are generations in Garbage collector (Gen 0, 1 and 2)?

Generations defines age of the object. There are three generations:

- **Gen 0**: When application creates fresh objects they are marked as Gen 0.
- **Gen 1**: When GC is not able to clear the objects from Gen 0 in first round it moves them to Gen 1 bucket.
- **Gen 2**: When GC visits Gen 1 objects and he is not able to clear them he moves them gen 2.

Generations are created to improve GC performance. Garbage collector will spend more time on Gen 0 objects rather than Gen 1 and Gen 2 thus improving performance.

> **Note:** *More the objects in Gen 0, more your application is stable.*

Garbage collector cleans managed code, how do we clean unmanaged code?

Garbage collector only claims managed code memory. For unmanaged code you need to put clean up in destructor / finalize.

But when we create a destructor the performance falls down?

Yes, when we define a destructor, garbage collector does not collect these objects in the first round. It moves them to Gen 1 and then reclaims these objects in the next cycle.

As more objects are created in Gen 1 the performance of the application falls down because more memory is consumed.

So how can we clean unmanaged objects and also maintain performance?

We need to follow the below steps:

- Implement IDisposable interface and implement the dispose function.
- In Dispose function call the "GC.SuppressFinalize" method.
- At the client side ensure that the "Dispose" function is called when the object is no more required.

Below goes the code, this is also called as "Finalize and Dispose pattern". This ensures that your objects are created in Generation 0 rather than Generation 1. "GC.SuppressFinalize" tells the garbage collector to not worry about destructor and destroy the objects in the first call itself.

```
class clsMyClass: IDisposable
{
    ~clsMyClass()
    {
        // In case the client forgets to call
```

```
                // Dispose, destructor will be invoked for
                Dispose(false);
        }
        protected virtual void Dispose(bool disposing)
        {
                if (disposing)
                {
                        // Free managed objects.
                }
                // Free unmanaged objects
        }

        public void Dispose()
        {
                Dispose(true);
                // Ensure that the destructor is not called
                GC.SuppressFinalize(this);
        }
}
```

> **Note:** *Please do go through the videos of "What is IDisposable interface & finalize dispose pattern in GC?" in which we have actually showed how generation performance increases by using Finalize and Dispose pattern.*

Can we force garbage collector to run?

"System.GC.Collect ()" forces garbage collector to run. This is not a recommended practice but can be used if situations arise.

What is the difference between finalize and dispose?

- Finalize is a destructor and dispose is a function which is implemented via 'Idisposable' interface.
- Finalize is nondeterministic, since it's called by garbage collector. Dispose is a function and needs to be called by the client for clean up. In other finalize is automatically called by garbage collector while dispose needs to be called forcefully.

> **Note:** *As a good practice Finalize and dispose is used collectively because of double garbage collector loop. You can talk about this small note after you talk about the above 2 differences.*

What is CTS?

In .NET there are lots of languages like C#, VB.NET, VF.NET etc. There can be situations when we want code in one language to be called in other language. In order to ensure smooth communication between these languages the most important thing is that they should have a common type system. CTS (Common types system) ensures that data types defined in two different languages get compiled to a common data type.

So "Integer" data type in VB6 and "int" data type in C++ will be converted to System.int32, which is data type of CTS.

> **Note:** *If you know COM programming, you would know how difficult it is to interface VB6 application with VC++ application. As datatype of both languages did not have a common ground where they can come and interface, by having CTS interfacing is smooth.*

What is a CLS (Common Language Specification)?

CLS is a subset of CTS. CLS is a specification or set of rules or guidelines. When any programming language adheres to these set of rules it can be consumed by any .NET language.

For instance one of the rule which makes your application CLS non-compliant is when you declare your methods members with same name and with only case differences in C#. You can try this, create a simple class in C# with same name with only case differences and try to consume the same in VB.NET,it will not work.

What is an Assembly?

Assembly is unit of deployment like EXE or a DLL.

What are the different types of Assembly?

There are two types of assembly Private and Public assembly. A private assembly is normally used by a single application, and is stored in the application's directory, or a sub-directory beneath. A shared assembly is stored in the global assembly cache, which is a repository of assemblies maintained by the .NET runtime.

Shared assemblies are needed when we want the same assembly to be shared by various applications in the same computer.

What is Namespace?

Namespace does two basic functionalities:

● It logically groups classes, for instance System.Web.UI logically groups UI related features like textboxes, list control etc.

● In Object Oriented world, many times it is possible that programmers will use the same class name. Qualifying NameSpace with class names avoids this collision.

What is Difference between NameSpace and Assembly?

Following are the differences between namespace and assembly:

● Assembly is physical grouping of logical units, Namespace, logically groupsclasses.

● Namespace can span multiple assemblies while assembly is a physical unit like EXE, DLL etc.

What is ILDASM?

ILDASM is a simple tool which helps you to view IL code of a DLL or EXE. In order to view IL code using ILDASM, go to visual studio command prompt and run "ILDASM.EXE". Once ILDASM is running you can view the IL code by opening the DLL or EXE.

What is Manifest?

Assembly metadata is stored in Manifest. Manifest contains metadata which describes the following things:

- Version of assembly.
- Security identity.
- Scope of the assembly.
- Resolve references to resources and classes.

The assembly manifest is stored in the DLL itself.

Where is the version information stored of an assembly?

Version information is stored in assembly inside the manifest.

Is versioning applicable to private assemblies?

Yes, versioning is applicable to private assemblies also.

What is the use of strong names?

> **Note:** *This question can also be asked in two different ways, what are weak references and strong reference or how do you strong name a .NET assembly.*

When we talk about .NET application it has two parts one is the class library or the DLL and the other the consumer like windows UI etc using this DLL.

If the consumer identifies the DLL library by namespace and class names it's called as weak reference. It's very much possible in deployment environment someone can delete the original class library and fake a similar class library with the same class name and namespace name.

Strong name is a unique name which is produced by the combination of version number, culture information,public key and digital signature. No one can fake this identity or generate the same name.

So your consumer or UI will refer the class library with strong names rather than class and namespace names. In order to create strong name, right click on the class library, click on properties, click on signing tab and click on the new menu to generate strong names as shown in the below figure.

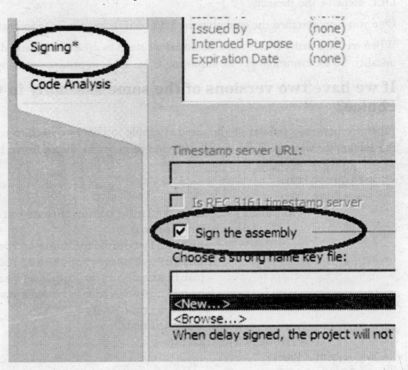

Figure 2.1: Strong names

What is Delay signing?

The whole point about strong names is to ensure that the clients (UI, External components etc) who is consuming the DLL knows that the DLL was published from a valid source. This authenticity is verified by using strong names. Strong name protection is good from external hackers but what if your own developers think of doing something mischievous.

That's where delay signing helps. The strong name key has two keys public key and private key. You only share the public key with your developers so that they can work seamlessly. The private key is stored in a secured location and when the DLL is about to be deployed on production the key is injected for further security.

What is GAC?

GAC (Global Assembly Cache) is where all shared .NET assembly resides. GAC is used in the following situations:

●   If the application has to be shared among several application which is in the same computer.

●   If the assembly has some special security, requirements like only administrators can remove the assembly. If the assembly is private then a simple delete of assembly the assembly file will remove the assembly.

How to add and remove an assembly from GAC?

You can use the 'GacUtil' tool which comes with visual studio. So to register an assembly in to GAC go to "Visual Studio Command Prompt" and type "gacutil –i (assembly name)", where (assembly name) is the DLL name of the project.

One you have installed the assembly the DLL can be seen in 'c:\windows\assembly\' folder.

When we have many DLL's to be deployed we need to create setup and deployment package using windows installer. So the common way of deploying GAC DLL in production is by using windows installer.

If we have two versions of the same assembly in GAC how to we make a choice?

When we have two version of the same assembly in GAC we need to use binding redirect tag and specify the version we want to use in the new version property as shown in the below "app.config" file.

```
<configuration>
    <runtime>
        <assemblyBinding xmlns="urn:schemas-microsoft-com:asm.v1">
            <dependentAssembly>
                <assemblyIdentity name="ComputerName"
                publicKeyToken="cfc68d722cd6a164" />
                <publisherPolicy apply="yes" />
                <bindingRedirect oldVersion="1.1.0.0"
                newVersion="1.0.0.0" />
            </dependentAssembly>
        </assemblyBinding>
    </runtime>
</configuration>
```

What is reflection?

Reflection helps us to browse methods, properties and function of a given class or assembly on run time. You can also invoke the methods and functions using reflection. Below is a simple sample code where we are browsing in run time through methods and function of "MyClass".

```
MyClass objMyClass = new MyClass();
// Get the class type
Type parameterType = objMyClass.GetType();
string name = parameterType.Name;
// Browse through members
foreach (MemberInfo objMemberInfo in parameterType.GetMembers())
{
      Console.WriteLine(objMemberInfo.Name);
}
// Browse through properties.
foreach (PropertyInfo objPropertyInfo in parameterType.GetProperties())
{
      Console.WriteLine(objPropertyInfo.Name);
}
```

If you want to invoke method and function you need to use the invoke member function as shown in the below code.

```
parameterType.InvokeMember("Display",BindingFlags.Public   |
BindingFlags.NonPublic | BindingFlags.InvokeMethod |
BindingFlags.Instance,null, objMyClass, null);
```

What are stack and heap?

Stack and heap are memory types in an application. Stack memory stores data types like int, double, Boolean etc. While heap stores data types like string and objects.

For instance when the below code run the first two variables i.e. "i" and "y" are stored in a stack and the last variable "o" is stored in heap.

```
void MyFunction()
{
      int i = 1; // This is stored in stack.
      int y = i; // This is stored in stack.
      object o = null; // This is stored in heap.
} // after this end the stack variable memory space is reclaimed while //
the heap memory is reclaimed later by garbage collector.
```

What are Value types and Reference types?

Value types contain actual data while reference types contain pointers and the pointers point to the actual data.

Value types are stored on stack while reference types are stored on heap. Value types are your normal data types like int, bool, double and reference types are all objects.

What is concept of Boxing and Unboxing?

When value type is moved to a reference type it's called as boxing. The vice-versa is termed as unboxing.

Below is sample code of boxing and unboxing where integer data type is converted in to object and then vice versa.

```
int i = 1;
object obj = i;       // boxing
int j = (int) obj;    // unboxing
```

How performance is affected due to boxing and unboxing?

When boxing and unboxing happens the data needs to jump from stack memory to heap and vice-versa which is a bit of memory intensive process. As a good practice avoid boxing and unboxing where ever possible.

How can we avoid boxing and unboxing?

First thing it's very difficult to avoid boxing and unboxing. For instance most of the time you will moving data from UI objects like text boxes etc to business objects and also vice versa which will demand boxing and unboxing. Below are some key points to remember:

- First thing is it really necessary to use boxing and unboxing. If it's unavoidable like moving data from UI text boxes to internal c# data types, then go for it.

- Try to see if you can use generics and avoid it.

How to prevent my .NET DLL to be decompiled?

By design, .NET embeds rich Meta data inside the executable code using MSIL. Any one can easily decompile your DLL back using tools like ILDASM (owned by Microsoft) or Reflector for .NET which is a third party. Secondly, there are many third party tools, which make this decompiling process a click away. So any one can easily look in to your assemblies and reverse engineer them back in to actual source code and understand some real good logic, which can make it easy to crack your application.

The process by which you can stop this reverse engineering is using "obfuscation". It is a technique, which will foil the decompilers. Many third parties (XenoCode, Demeanor for .NET) provide .NET obfuscation solution. Microsoft includes one that is Dotfuscator Community Edition with Visual Studio.NET.

> **Note:** *We leave this as homework to reader's compile, a DLL obfuscate it using "Dotfuscator Community Edition" which comes with Visual Studio.NET and try viewing the same using ILDASM.*

What is the difference between Convert.toString and .toString () method?

Just to give an understanding of what the above question means seethe below code.

```
int i =0;
MessageBox.Show(i.ToString());
MessageBox.Show(Convert.ToString(i));
```

We can convert the integer "i" using "i.ToString()" or "Convert.ToString" so what is the difference. The basic difference between them is "Convert" function handles NULLS while "i.ToString()" does not. It will throw a NULL reference exception error. So as a good coding practice using "convert" is always safe.

How can we handle exceptions in .NET?

Exceptions are handled by "System.Exception" base class. If you want to raise an error from source you need to create the exception object with below code snippet.

```
throw new Exception("Customer code cannot be more than 10");
```

Once the exception is raised if you want to catch the same you need to use the try catch block as shown below.

```
try
{
    // This section will have the code which
    // which can throw exceptions.
}
catch(Exception e)
{
    // Handle what you want to
    // do with the exception
    label.text = e.Message;
}
```

How can I know from which source the exception occurred?

"System.Exception.StackTrace"allows you to identify series of call which lead to this exception.

What if we do not catch the exception?

If you do not catch the error, .NET framework will handle the same and you will get a message box as shown in the below figure.

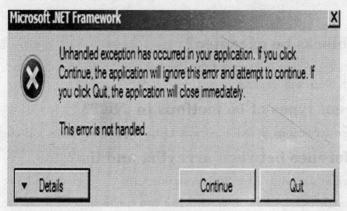

Figure 2.2: .Net framework handles the errors

What are system level exceptions and application level exceptions?

Exceptions that are thrown by .NET framework are called as system exceptions. These errors are non-recoverable or fatal errors like ArgumentOutOfRangeException, IndexOutOfRangeException, StackOverflowException etc.

Application exceptions are custom exceptions created for the application. Application exceptions are created by deriving from "ApplicationException" class as shown below. You can then create the object of the below exception and throw the same from the code and catch the same on the client side.

```
public class MyOwnException: ApplicationException
{
        private string messageDetails = String.Empty;
        public DateTime ErrorTimeStamp {get; set;}
        public string CauseOfError {get; set;}

        public MyOwnException(){}
        public MyOwnException(string message,
        string cause, DateTime time)
        {
                messageDetails = message;
                CauseOfError = cause;
                ErrorTimeStamp = time;
        }

        // Override the Exception.Message property.
        public override string Message
        {
                get
                {
                        return string.Format("This is my own error message");
                }
        }
}
```

Can two catch blocks be executed?

No, once the proper catch section is executed the control goes to the 'finally' block. So there no chance by which multiple catch block will 'execute'.

What are different types of collections in .NET?

There are five important collections in .NET Arrays, Lists, Hashtable, stacks and queues .

What is the difference between arraylist and list?

- Arrays are fixed in size while Arraylist is resizable.
- Arrays are strongly typed, in other words when you create an array it can store only one data type data. Arraylist can store any datatype.

Are Arraylist faster or Arrays?

Array list takes any data type which leads to boxing and unboxing. As arrays are strongly typed they do not do boxing and unboxing. So arrays are faster as compared to array list.

```
// Array definition
int[] str = new int[10];

// Array list definition
ArrayList MyList = new ArrayList();
```

What are hashtable collections?

In arraylist or array if we have to access any data we need to use the internal index id generated by the array list collection. For instance the below code snippet shows how the internal id is used to fetch data from array list.

In actual scenarios we hardly remember internal id's generated by collection we would like to fetch the data by using some application defined key. There's where hash table comes in to picture.

string str = MyList[1].ToString();

Hash table helps to locate data using keys as shown below. When we add data to hash table it also has a provision where we can add key with the data. This key will help us to fetch data later using key rather than using internal index id's generated by collections.

objHashtable.Add("p001","MyData");

This key is converted in to numeric hash value which is mapped with the key for quick lookup.

What are Queues and stack collection?

Queues are collection which helps us to add object and retrieve them in the manner they were added. In other word queues helps us to achieve the first in first out collection behavior.

Stack collection helps us to achieve first in last out behavior.

Can you explain generics in .NET?

Generics help to separate logic and data type to increase reusability. In other words you can create a class whose data type can be defined on run time.

For instance below is a simple class "class1" with a "compareme" function created using generics. You can see how the unknown data type is put in greater than and less than symbol. Even the compare me method has the unknown data type attached.

```
public class Class1<UNNKOWDATATYPE>
{

    public bool Compareme(UNNKOWDATATYPE v1, UNNKOWDATATYPE v2)
    {
```

```
            if (v1.Equals(v2))
            {
                    return true;
            }
            else
            {
                    return false;
            }
        }
}
```

During runtime you can define the datatype as shown in the below code snippet.

```
Class1<int> obj = new Class1<int>();
bool b = obj.Compareme(1,2); // This compares numeric
Class1<string> obj1 = new Class1<string>();
bool b1 = obj1.Compareme("shiv","shiv"); // This does string comparison
```

Can you explain the concept of generic collection?

Array List, Stack and Queues provide collections which are not type safe. This leads 2 problems first it's not type safe and second it leads to boxing and unboxing.

By using generics we can have type safety and also we can avoid boxing and unboxing. Below is a simple code snippet which shows a strong typed list of type integer and string.

```
List<int> obj;
obj.add(1); // you can only add integers to this list
List<string> obj;
obj.add("shiv"); // you can only add string to this list
```

What is the difference between dictionary and hashtable?

Dictionary collection is a generic collection equivalent for hashtable. Hashtable allows you to add key and value of any type (i.e. objects) . This leads to two problems one is boxing and unboxing issues and second it's not strongly typed.

```
// Creates a strongly typed dictionary with integer key and value
// pair
Dictionary<int,int> obj = new Dictionary<int,int>();
// We can only add integer value and key to the dictionary collection
Obj.Add(123,550);
```

What are the generic equivalent for array list,stack, queues and hashtable?

Below are the listed generic equivalents for each of them:

- Array list generic equivalent is List<int>.
- Stack generic equivalent is Stack<int>.
- Queue generic equivalent is Queue<int>.
- Hashtable generic equivalent is Dictionary<int,int>.

What is the use of IEnumerable, ICollection, Ilist and IDictionary?

The above 4 entities are nothing but interfaces implemented by collections:

IEnumerable: All collection classes use this interface and it helps to iterate through all the collection elements.

ICollection: This interface has the count property and it's implemented by all collection elements.

IList:This interface allows random access, insertion and deletion in to the collection.Itsimplemented by array list.

IDictionary:This interface is implemented by hashtable and dictionary.

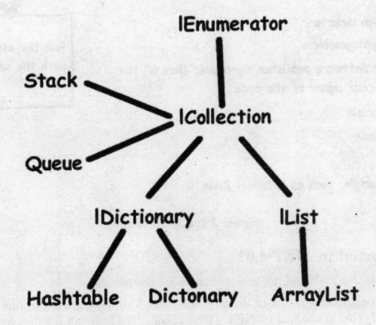

Figure 2.3: Interface collections

What is code access security (CAS)?

CAS is the part of .NET security model which determines whether or not a particular code is allowed to run and what kind of resources can the code access.

So how does CAS actually work?

It's a four step process:

- First Evidence is gathered about the assembly. In other words from where did this assembly come?, who is the publisher etc.

- Depending on evidences the assembly is assigned to a code group. In other words what rights does the assembly depending on the evidence gathered.
- Depending on code group security rights are allocated.
- Using the security rights the assembly is run with in those rights

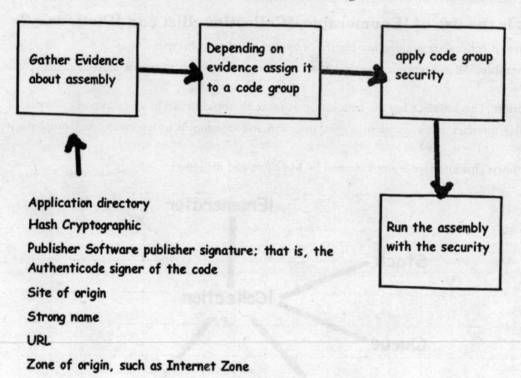

Figure 2.4: CAS in action

Is CAS supported in .NET 4.0?

CAS is deprecated in .NET 4.0 and two major changes are brought in:

- Permission granting is no more the work of CAS; it's now the work of the hosting model. In other words CAS is disabled in .NET 4.0 by default. The host will decide what rights to be given to the .NET assembly.
- A new security model i.e. Security transparent model is introduced. The security transparent model puts code in to separate compartments/ boxes as per the risk associated. If you know a code can do something wrong you can compartmentalizethe code as 'Security transparent' and if you have a code which you trust you can box them in to 'Security critical'.

What is sandboxing?

If you have want to execute an untrusted third party DLL, you can create your own 'appdomain' and assign permission sets so that your 3rd party DLL runs under a control environment.

How can we create a windows service using .NET?

Windows Services are long-running processes that runs at the background. It has the ability to start automatically when the computer boots and also can be manually paused, stopped or even restarted.

Following are the steps to create a service:

Create a project of type "Windows Service".

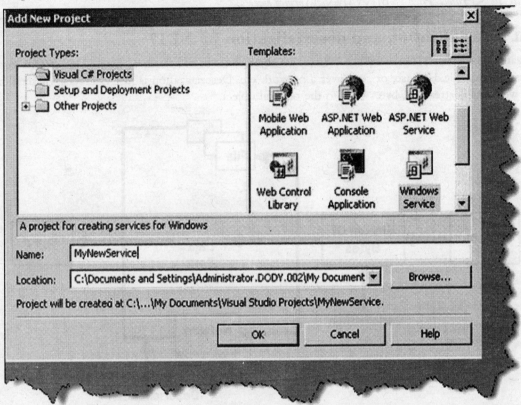

Figure 2.5: Windows service

If you see, the class created it is automatically inheriting from "System.ServiceProcess.ServiceBase".

You can override the following events provided by service and write your custom code. All the three main events can be used that is Start, stop and continue.

```
protected override void OnStart(string[] args)
{
}
protected override void OnStop()
{
}
```

```
protected override void OnContinue()
{
}
```

Now to install the service you need to do run the install util exe.

InstallUtil <Project Path>\BIN\MyNewService.exe

What is serialization and deserialization in .NET?

Serialization is a process where we can convert an object state in to stream of bytes. This stream can then be persisted in a file,database, or sent over a network etc. Deserialization is just vice-versa of serialization where we convert stream of bytes back to the original object.

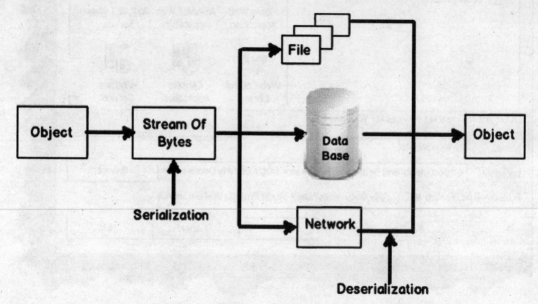

Figure 2.6: serialization and deserialization in .NET

Below is a simple code of how to serialize and de-serialize an object.

Let's first start with serialization.

Step 1: Create the object and put some values

```
// Serialization
Customer obj = new Customer(); // Create object
obj.CustomerCode = 123; // Set some values
```

Step 2: Create the file where to save the object.

```
using System.Runtime.Serialization;
```

```
using System.Runtime.Serialization.Formatters.Binary;

IFormatter i = new BinaryFormatter(); // Use the binary formatter
Stream stream = new FileStream("MyFile.txt", FileMode.Create,
FileAccess.Write, FileShare.None); // Give file name
```

Step 3: Use serialize method to save it to hard disk

```
i.Serialize(stream, o); // write it to the file
stream.Close(); // Close the stream
```

Let's also see a simple example of de-serialization.

Step 1: Read the file

```
// De-Serialization
IFormatter formatter = new BinaryFormatter(); // Use binary formatter
Stream stream = new FileStream("MyFile.txt", FileMode.Open, FileAccess.Read,
FileShare.Read); // read the file
```

Step 2: Recreate it back to the original object.

```
Customer obj = (Customer)formatter.Deserialize(stream); // take data back
to object
stream.Close(); // close the stream
```

If you want to save to XML or any other content type use the appropriate formatter.

Can you mention some scenarios where we can use serialization?

Below are some scenarios where serialization is needed:

- Passing .NET objects across network. For example .NET remoting, web services or WCF services use serialization internally.

- Copy paste .NET objects on clip board.

- Saving old state of the object and reverting back when needed. For example when the user hits the cancel button you would like to revert back to the previous state.

When should we use binary serialization as compared to XML serialization?

- Binary is smaller in size, so faster to send across network and also faster to process.

- XML is more verbose, but easy to understand and human readable. But due to the XMLstructure its complex to parse and can impact performance.

> **Note:** *Many people answer that XML serialization should be used when you have different platforms and binary serialization should be used when you same platforms. But this answer is actually not right as we have lot of binary serialization methodology like ASN, protbuf which are cross platform and widely accepted. So the important difference is that one is XML which readable by eyes and the binary is not.*

Can you explain the concept of "Short Circuiting"?

Short circuiting occurs when you do logical operations like 'AND' and 'OR'.

"When we use short circuit operators only necessary evaluation is done rather than full evaluation."

Let us try to understand the above sentence with a proper example. Consider a simple "AND" condition code as shown below. Please note we have only one "&" operator in the below code.

```
if(Condition1 & Condition2)
{
}
```

In the above case "Condition2" will be evaluated even if "Condition1" is "false". Now if you think logically, it does not make sense to evaluate "Condition 2", if "Condition 1" is false .It's a AND condition right?, so if the first condition is false it means the complete AND condition is false and it makes no sense to evaluate "Condition2".

There's where we can use short circuit operator "&&". For the below code "Condition 2" will be evaluated only when "Condition 1" is true.

```
if(Condition1 && Condition2)
{
}
```

The same applies for "OR" operation. For the below code (please note its only single pipe ("|").) "Condition2" will be evaluated even if "Condition1" is "true". If you think logically we do not need to evaluate "Condition2" if "Condition1" is "true".

```
if(Condition1 | Condition2)
{
}
```

So if we change the same to double pipe ("||") i.e. implement short circuit operators as shown in the below code, "Condition2" will be evaluated only if "Condition1" is "false".

```
if(Condition1 || Condition2)
{
}
```

What is the difference between "Typeof" and "GetType" ?

Both "TypeOf" and "GetType" help you to get the type. The difference is from where the information is extracted. "TypeOf" gets the type from a class while "GetType" gets type from an object.

Will the following c# code compile?

```
double dbl = 109.22;
int i = dbl;
```

No, the above code will give an error. Double size is larger than "int" so an implicit conversion will not take place. For that we need to do explicit conversion. So we need to something as shown in the below code. In the below code we have done an explicit conversion.

```
double dbl = 109.22;
int i =(int) dbl; // this is explicit conversion / casting
```

Also note after explicit conversion we will have data loss. In variable "i" we will get "109" value, the decimal values will be eliminated.

3

OOP

> **Note:** *We have come out with a exclusive book on 'OOP's with real project scenarios'. In this book we have tried to understand OOP's fundamentals and also tried to apply them on projects by simulating project scenarios.*

What is Object Oriented Programming?

OOP is software designing technique where we think in terms of real world objects.

What is a Class and object?

Class is a blue print / template. Objects are instances of classes, in other words they bring life in class. To use a class we need to create an object.

What are different properties provided by Object-oriented systems?

Following are characteristics of Object Oriented System's:

Abstraction

Abstraction means show only what is necessary. Example color is abstracted to RGB. By just making the combination of these three colors we can achieve any color in world. So rather than remembering each and every color we just use RGB.

Encapsulation

It is a process of hiding all the complex processing from the outside world and make's your objects simple.

Inheritance

This concept helps to define parent child relationship between classes.

Polymorphism

It's a property of object to act differently under different conditions. For instance a simple user object depending on conditions can act like a admin or like data entry object.

Remember the word **APIE (Abstraction,Polymorphism, Inheritance and Encapsulation)**.

How can we implement encapsulation in .NET?

Encapsulation can be achieved by using the below 5 access modifiers.

●   Private: Only members of class have access to the variables.

- Protected: All members in current class and in derived classes can access the variables.

- Friend (internal in C#): Only members in current project have access to the elements.

- Protected friend (protected internal in C#): All members in current project and all members in derived class can access the variables.

- Public: All members have access in all classes and projects.

> *Note: This question can also be tweaked by asking what are the different access modfiers in .NET .*

What's the difference between abstraction and encapsulation?

> *Note: This question is a bit confusing question. Abstraction says show only what is necessary and encapsulation says hide complexity. Does it look like talking the same thing's with different faces?.*

Abstraction and encapsulation complement each other. Encapsulation implements abstraction. Abstraction is design process while encapsulation happens during coding phase which is achieved by using access modifiers. Abstraction is done in design phase while encapsulation is implemented in execution phase using access modifiers.

How is inheritance implemented in .NET?

Inheritance is implemented by using the ":" symbol.

Below is a simple code snippet where we have "Customer" class which is the parent class. We have then created a child class called as "CustomerDiscount" which inherits all the properties and adds a "Discount" property.

```
class Customer
{
    public string customerName;
    public string customerCode;
}

class CustomerDiscount: Customer
{
    public double Discount;
}
```

What are the two different types of polymorphism?

There are 2 kinds of polymorphism static and dynamic. Many people also call them as runtime or compile time polymorphism.

How can we implement static polymorphism?

Static polymorphism is implemented by using method overloading. In compile time itself we come to know if there are mismatches. Below code snippet shows how method overloading is implemented. The add method can take either 2 inputs or 3 inputs.

Depending on the number of inputs the addition logic is executed.

```
// add method with 2 inputs.
objmaths.add(1,2);
// add method with 3 inputs.
objmaths.add(1,2,3);
```

How can we implement dynamic polymorphism?

Dynamic polymorphism is implemented by using overriding and virtual keyword.

Below is a simple code snippet which has three classes, Customer class is the parent class.CustomerDiscount10Percent and CustomerDiscount20Percent are child classes.

Customer parent class has a discount function which returns zero discounts. This function is defined as virtual and then overridden by both the child classes with 10 and 20% discount.

```
class Customer
{
      public string customerName;
      public string customerCode;
      public virtual int Discount()
      {
            return 0;
      }
}

class CustomerDiscount10Percent: Customer
{
      public override int Discount()
      {
            return 10;
      }

}

class CustomerDiscount20Percent: Customer
{
      public override int Discount()
      {
            return 20;
      }

}
```

Now on the client side on the fly your parent object can point to any child classes and invoke the child implementation accordingly. This is called as dynamic polymorphism; the parent object can point to any of the child objects and invoke the child function dynamically.

```
Customer obj;
obj = new CustomerDiscount10Percent();
obj = new CustomerDiscount20Percent();
```

What is the difference overriding and overloading?

> **Note:** *I am not sure why this question is asked frequently. It's like comparing apples with mangoes. Probably it's just the common word "over" which confuses developers.*

Overloading is a concept where we can have same method names with different input signature.

In overriding we have a parent class with virtual functions which are overridden in the child classes.

What is operator overloading?

Operator overloading is a concept of polymorphism where you can redefine operators like +, -, * etc with additional functionalities.

For instance we can redefine the + functionalities to add objects like obj1 + obj2. Below is simple code snippet which redefines + operator.

```
class SomeClass
{

      private int someValue;

      public SomeClass(int val)
      {
            someValue = val;
      }

      public static SomeClass operator +(SomeClass arg1, SomeClass arg2)
      {
            return new SomeClass(arg1.someValue + arg2.someValue);
      }

}
```

You can now use the + operator to add objects of type someclass as shown in the below code snipet.

> *Obj = obj1 + obj2;*

What are abstract classes?

Abstract class is a half defined parent class. The full implementation of abstract class is defined by the child classes.

For example below code snippet shows a simple abstract class / half defined class called "DatabaseCommon" and later the concrete classes i.e. "SQLServer" and "Oracle" inherit and define a complete implementation for the same.

To define an abstract class we need to use the abstract keyword.

```
public abstract class DatabaseCommon
{
}
public class SQLServer: DatabaseCommon
{
}
public class Oracle: DatabaseCommon
{
}
```

What are abstract methods?

Abstract classes can have abstract methods. Abstract methods when defined in a parent class have to be implemented in the child classes. If abstract methods are not implemented it will throw a error.

What is an Interface?

Interface is a contract that defines the signature of the functionality. It looks like a class but has no implementation. It has only empty definition of methods, functions, events, and indexer.

Interfaces provide forced implementation. For instance in the below code snippet we have created a simple interface called as "IDbCompulsory". The below classes who implement interface "IDbCompulsory" has to provide implementation for "ExecSql".

```
interface IDbCompulsory
{
     void ExecSql();
}
public class SQLServer: IDbCompulsory
{
     public void ExecSql()
     {
          // Here code for firing SQL Server SQL statements
          // are written
     }
}
public class Oracle: IDbCompulsory
{
     public void ExecSql()
     {
          // Here code for firing Oracle SQL statements
          // are written
     }
}
```

Do interface have accessibility modifier ?

All elements in Interface should be public. So no accessibility modifier is required.

Can we create an object of abstract class or an interface?

No.

What is difference between abstract classes and interfaces?

	Abstract class	Interface
Implementation	Some methods in abstract classes can have implementation.	All methods, function, properties in interfaces have to empty compulsorily.
Scenario	Abstract classes are used when we want to share common functionality in parent child relationship.	Interfaces are used to define contract, enforce standardization, decoupling and dynamic polymorphism.
Variable declaration	We can declare variables	In interface we cannot.
Inheritance VS Implementation	Abstract classes are inherited.	Interfaces are implemented.

An abstract with only abstract method, how is it different from interfaces?

If you define all methods, function, properties as abstract in abstract class it inhibits the same behavior as an interface.

If we want to update interface with new methods, what is the best practice?

The biggest use of interface is to ensure that strict CONTRACT is followed between clients and components. So that when changes happen on the components clients do not have to change too much. In real world CONTRACTS between two parties do not change which implies that interfaces should also not change.

So if you want to add new methods or change methods in interfaces the best practice is to create new interfaces by inheriting. With this approach your older client who are using the interface stay happy and the new clients who want those new or changed methods get the benefits of the new functionality.

Let's consider you have a simple interface called as "IView" which helps you to view data, below is the code for the same. Let's consider that this interface is consumed by many clients.

```
interface Iview
{
    public void View();
}
```

Over a period of time some users demand "Edit" functionality as well but the rest of the users are happy with the 'View" functionality and they do not want them to get affected by these changes. Now if you go and change this interface ("IView") a.k.a you will be disturbing everyone.

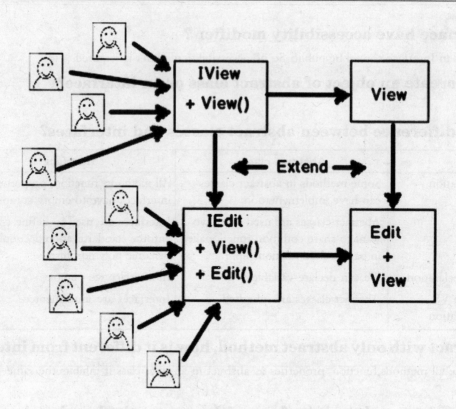

Figure 3.1: update interface with new methods

So the best option would be to add a new interface i.e. "IEdit" which inherits from "IView". So the "IEdit" will have the functionality for "Edit" as well as "View" because it's also inheriting from "IView". And the clients who are consuming "IView" do not need to update as "IView' is not changed at all.

```
interface IEdit: Iview
{
        public void Edit();
}
```

So putting this whole story in one single sentence for the interviewer.

Interface once fixed should not be changed. If we ever have to add new functions, new interfaces should be created so that we do not break compatibility with old clients.

What is a delegate?

Delegate is an abstract pointer to a function or method. In other words you can create a pointer which points to a method or function and then pass that pointer wherever you wish and invoke the function / method.

How can we create a delegate?

Creating a delegate is four step process:

- Declare a delegate.
- Create an object reference.
- Point the reference to the method.
- Invoke the method via the delegate.

Below is the code snippet for the same.

```
// Declare a delegate
public delegate int PointToAdd(int i, int y);

// Create a reference pointer
PointToAdd objpointer = null;

// Point to the method
objpointer = Add;

// Invoke the function/method
objpointer.Invoke(10,20);
```

What is a multicast delegate?

Normally when you create a delegate, your delegate points to only one function or method. In case you want to point multiple functions and invoke them sequentially, you need to use the multicast delegate.

To point to multiple function using delegate pointer we need to use "+=" sign as shown in the below code snippet.

```
ptrcall += Method1;
ptrcall += Method2;
```

What are Events?

Events are higher level of encapsulation over delegates. Events use delegates internally. Delegates are naked and when passed to any other code, the client code can invoke the delegate. Event provides a publisher / subscriber mechanism model.

So subscribers subscribe to the event and publisher then push messages to all the subscribers. Below is a simple code snippet for the same:

Create a delegate and declare the event for the same.

```
public delegate void CallEveryone();
public event CallEveryone MyEvent;
```

Raise the event.

```
MyEvent();
```

Attached client methods to the event are fired / notified.

```
obj.MyEvent += Function1;
```

What is the difference between delegate and events?

They can not be compared because one derives from the other.

- Actually, events use delegates in bottom. But they add an extra layer of security on the delegates, thus forming the publisher and subscriber model.

- As delegates are function to pointers, they can move across any clients. So any of the clients can add or remove events, which can be confusing. But events give the extra protection / encapsulation by adding the layer and making it a publisher and subscriber model.

Just imagine one of your clients doing this

```
c.XyzCallback = null
```

This will reset all your delegates to nothing and you have to keep searching where the error is.

Do events have return type?

No, events do not have return type.

Can events have access modifiers?

Yes.

Can we have shared events?

Yes, you can have shared events, do note only shared methods can raise shared events.

What is shadowing?

Shadowing replaces the complete element of the parent class. For instance you can see in the below sample code where the clsParent has a variable int "i", which is replaced by the child class clsChild by a method "i".

In other words when you refer the parent object "i" it is a variable and when you refer the child object"i" it is a method.

```
class clsParent
{
      public int i=0;
}
class clsChild: clsParent
{
      public new void i()
```

```
        {
            Console.WriteLine("Hey i became a method");

        }
}
```

What is the difference between Shadowing and Overriding?

Overriding redefines only the implementation while shadowing redefines the whole element.

If we inherit a class do the private variables also get inherited?

Yes, the variables are inherited.

How can we stop the class from further inheriting?

We can stop the class from further inheriting by using the "Sealed" keyword. For instance below is a simple sample code where we have a class called as "Human" which is further inherited to create a "Male" or "Female" class.

Now the below code is great, but we do not anyone to further inherit from "Male" or "Female" class. In simple words "Male" and "Female" are the last legs in this inheritance hierarchy. This can be done by using the "Sealed" keyword.

```
public class Human
{}
public sealed class Male: Human
{}
public sealed class Female: Human
{}
```

If anyone tries to inherit the sealed classes he will end with the below error "cannot derive from sealed type".

What is the use of "Must inherit" keyword in VB.NET?

If you want to create an abstract class in VB.NET it's done by using "Must Inherit" keyword. You cannot create an object of a class, which is marked as "Must Inherit". When you define "Must Inherit" keyword for class, you can only use the class by inheriting.

What are similarities between Class and structure?

Following are the similarities between classes and structures:

●   Both can have constructors, methods, properties, fields, constants, enumerations, events, and event handlers.

●   Structures and classes can implement interface.

●   Both of them can have constructors with and without parameter.

●   Both can have delegates and events.

What is the difference between Class and structure's?

Following are the key differences between them:

- Structures are value types and classes are reference types. So structures use stack and classes use heap.

- Structures members cannot be declared as protected, but class members can be. You cannot do inheritance in structures.

- Structures do not require constructors while classes require.

- Objects created from classes are terminated using Garbage collector. Structures are not destroyed using GC.

What does virtual keyword mean?

They signify that method and property can be overridden by the child classes.

What are shared (VB.NET)/Static(C#) variables?

When you define a variable as static or shared only one instance of the object or variable is created.

What is ENUM?

It is used to define constants.

What is nested Classes?

Nested classes are classes within classes.

If you create the child class object which constructor will fire first?

```
public class class1
{
        public class1(){}
}

public class class2: class1
{
        public class2(){}
}
```

Parent class constructor will fire first.

In what instances you will declare a constructor to be private?

When we create a private constructor, we cannot create object of the class. Private constructors are used when we want only a single instance of the class to be created and externally no one can use the 'new' keyword to create the object.

Can we have different access modifiers on get/set methods of a property?

Yes, we can have different access modifiers.

```
public string CustName
{
     get
     {
          return _Custname;
     }
     protected set
     {
          Custname = value;
     }
}
```

Will the finally run in this code?

In the below code in the try statement we have a return statement, will the finally block still run.

```
public static void Main()
{
     try
     {
          // Some code
          return;
     }
     finally
     {
          //Will this run
     }
}
```

Yes, the finally code will run even though there is a return statement in the try. Finally block will run irrespective what happens in try block. That's the reason why finally block is a good place to put clean up code.

What is Indexer?

An indexer is a member that enables an object to be indexed in the same way as an array.

Can we have static indexer in C#?

No.

4

ADO.NET

What are the different components in ADO.NET?

There are 6 important componentsin ADO.NET:

- Connection: This object creates a connection to the database. If you want to do any operation on the database you have to first create a connection object.

- Command: This object helps us to execute SQL queries against database. Using command object we can execute select, insert, update and delete SQL command.

- Data reader: This provides a recordset which can be browsed only in forward direction.It can only be read but not updated. Data reader is good for large number of records where you want to just browse quickly and display it.

- Dataset object: This provides a recordset which can be read back and in forward direction. The recordset can also be updated. Dataset is like a in memory database with tables, rows and fields.

- Data Adapter: This object acts as a bridge between database and dataset; it helps to load the dataset object.

- Data View: This object is used to sort and filter data in Data table of dataset.

> **Note:** *Remember (2C4D), 2C for connection and command, 4D for dataset,datareader, dataview and dataadapter.*

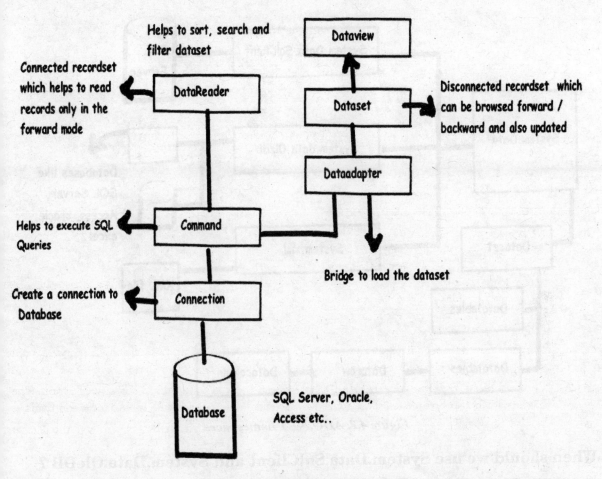

Figure 4.1: ADO.NET architecture

What is the namespace in which .NET has the data functionality class?

Following are the namespaces provided by .NET for data management:

System.Data

This namespace has the dataset object which helps us to access data in a data source independent manner.

System.Data.SqlClient:

This namespace has objects which helps us to connect to SQL Server database.

System.Data.OleDB

This namespace has objects which helps us to connect to other databases like Oracle, Access and also SQL Server database.

System.XML

This Contains the basic objects required to create, read, store, write, and manipulate XML documents.

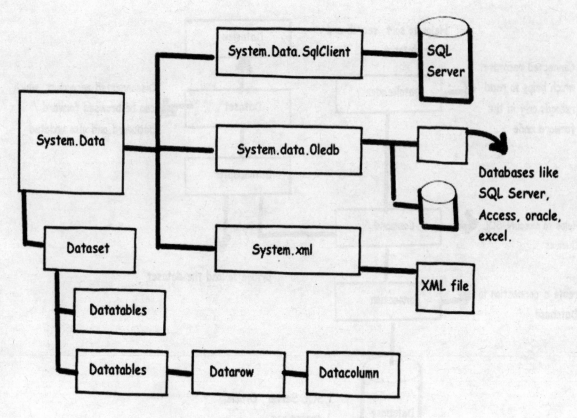

Figure 4.2: ADO.NET namespaces

When should we use System.Data.SqlClient and System.Data.OleDB ?

If you want to connect only to SQL Server use sqlclient or else use oledb. Oledb also connects to other database plus sql server .Sqlclient is meant specifically meant for SQL server so has better performance as compared to oledb.

What is difference between dataset and data reader?

Following are some major differences between dataset and data reader:

- Dataset is a disconnected architecture while data reader is connected architecture.
- Data Reader provides forward-only and read-only access to data, while dataset moves back as well as forward.
- Datasetobject is an in-memory database with tables, rows and columns while datareader is just simple table which can be read only in a forward direction.
- Dataset can persist contents while data reader cannot persist contents, they are read only and forward only.

What is the use of command objects?

Command object helps to execute SQL statements. Following are the methods provided by command object:

- **ExecuteNonQuery:** Executes insert, update and delete SQL commands. Returns an Integer indicating the number of rows affected by the query.

- **ExecuteReader:** Executes select SQL statements which can either be in your .NET code or in a stored procedure. Returns a "Datareader" object.

- **ExecuteScalar:** Executes SQL command and returns only a single value like count,sum, first record etc.

What are Dataset objects?

Dataset is an in memory object with data tables, rows and columns. You can visualize it as in-memory RDBMS.Dataset has the following features:

- The in memory RDBMS works in a disconnected manner. In other words even if the connection is closed the dataset is still there in memory.

- You can do modification in the in-memory database object and send the final changes to the database.

Below is a simple code snippet which shows how to access a column value. You can see how the full dataset object hierarchy is accessed to get the column value.

```
objDataset.Tables[0].Rows[0]["CustCode"]
```

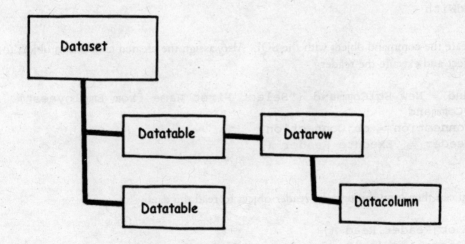

Figure 4.3: dataset an in-memory RDBMS representation

What is the use of data adapter?

Data adapter object acts like a bridge it helps to load the dataset object. Below is a simple code snippet which shows how the dataadapter object is created and then using the fill method the dataset object is loaded.

```
SqlDataAdapter objAdapter = new SqlDataAdapter(objCommand);
DataSet objDataset = new DataSet();
objAdapter.Fill(objDataset);
```

What are basic methods of Data adapter?

There are three most commonly used methods of Data adapter:

Fill: Executes the Select Command to fill the Dataset object with data from the data source. It can also be used to update (refresh) an existing table in a Dataset with changes made to the data in the original data source if there is a primary key in the table in the Dataset.

Fill Schema:Extracts just the schema for a table from the data source, and creates an empty table in the DataSet object with all the correspondingconstraints.

Update:Updates the original datasource with the changes made to the content of the DataSet.

How can we fire a simple SQL Statement using ADO?

- First imports the namespace "System.Data.SqlClient".

- Create a connection object and call the "Open" function.

```
With objConnection
      .Connection String = strConnectionString
      .Open()
EndWith
```

- Create the command object with the SQL. Also, assign the created connection object to command object and execute the reader.

```
ObjCommand = New SqlCommand ("Select First Name from Employees")
With objCommand
      .Connection = objConnection
      Breeder = .Execute Reader ()
EndWith
```

- You can then loop through the reader object to read the data.

```
Do while objReader.Read ()
lstData.Items.Add (objReader.Item ("First Name"))
Loop
```

- Do not forget to close the connection object.

```
objConnection.close*();
```

How do we use stored procedure in ADO.NET and how do we provide parameters to the stored procedures?

ADO.NET provides the SqlCommand object, which provides the functionality of executing stored procedures. In the command type we need to provide the command type as stored procedure as shown in the below code snippet.

```
SqlCommand objCommand = new SqlCommand("sp_Insert", objConnection);
objCommand.CommandType = CommandType.StoredProcedure;
objCommand.ExecuteNonQuery();
```

How can we force the connection object to close after my data reader is closed?

Command method Execute reader takes a parameter called as Command Behavior wherein we can specify saying close connection automatically after the Data reader is close.

PobjDataReader = pobjCommand.ExecuteReader (CommandBehavior.CloseConnection)

I want to force the data reader to return only schema of the data store rather than data.

PobjDataReader = pobjCommand.ExecuteReader (CommandBehavior.SchemaOnly)

How can we fine-tune the command object when we are expecting a single row?

Again, CommandBehaviour enumeration provides two values Single Result and Single Row. If you are expecting a single value then pass "CommandBehaviour.SingleResult" and the query is optimized accordingly, if you are expecting single row then pass "CommandBehaviour.SingleRow" and query is optimized according to single row.

Which is the best place to store connection string in .NET projects?

Config files are the best places to store connection strings. If it is a web-based application "Web.config" file will be used and if it is a windows application "App.config" files will be used.

How do you fill the dataset?

Create object ofdata adapterand call the fill command method of the adapter.

```
SqlDataAdapter objAdapter = new SqlDataAdapter(objCommand);
DataSet objDataset = new DataSet();
objAdapter.Fill(objDataset);
```

What are the various methods provided by the dataset object to generate XML?

- ReadXML

Read's a XML document in to Dataset.

- GetXML

  This is a function, which returns the string containing XML document.

- Writexml

  This writes a XML data to disk.

How can we save all data from dataset?

Dataset has "AcceptChanges" method, which commits all the changes since last time "Acceptchanges" has been executed.

How can we check which rows have changed since dataset was loaded?

For tracking down changes, Dataset has two methods, which comes to rescue "Get Changes "and "Has Changes".

Get Changes

Returns dataset, which are changed since it, was loaded, or since Accept changes was executed.

Has Changes

Or abandon all changes since the dataset was loaded use "Reject Changes This property indicates that has any changes been made since the dataset was loaded or accept changes method was executed.

> **Note:** *One of the most misunderstood things about these properties is that it tracks the changes of actual database. That is a fundamental mistake; actually the changes are related to only changes with in dataset and have nothing to with changes happening in actual database. Dataset are disconnected and do not know anything about the changes happening in actual database.*

How can we add/remove row is in "Data Table" object of "Dataset"?

"Data table" provides "NewRow" method to add new row to "Data Table". "Data Table" has "DataRowCollection" object that has all rows in a "Data Table" object. Following are the methods provided by "DataRowCollection" object:

Add

Adds a new row in Data Table

Remove

It removes a "Data Row" object from "Data Table"

Remove At

It removes a "Data Row" object from "Data Table" depending on index position of the "Data Table".

What is basic use of "DataView"?

"DataView" is used for sorting and finding data within "data table".

Data view has the following methods:

Find

It takes an array of values and returns the index of the row.

Find Row

This also takes array of values but returns a collection of "Data Row".

If we want to manipulate data of "Data Table" object create "Data View" (Using the "Default View" we can create "Data View" object) of the "Data Table" object and use the following functionalities:

Add New

Adds a new row to the "Data View" object.

Delete

Deletes the specified row from "Data View" object.

How can we load multiple tables in a Dataset?

```
objCommand.CommandText = "Table1"
objDataAdapter.Fill(objDataSet, "Table1")
objCommand.CommandText = "Table2"
objDataAdapter.Fill(objDataSet, "Table2")
```

Above is a sample code, which shows how to load multiple "Data Table" objects in one "Dataset" object. Sample code shows two tables "Table1" and "Table2" in object ObjDataSet.

lstdata.DataSource = objDataSet.Tables("Table1").DefaultView

In order to refer "Table1" Data Table, use Tables collection of Datasets and the Default view object will give you the necessary output.

How can we add relation between tables in a Dataset?

```
Dim objRelation As DataRelation
objRelation=New
DataRelation("CustomerAddresses",objDataSet.Tables("Customer").Columns("Custid")
,objDataSet.Tables("Addresses").Columns("Custid_fk"))
objDataSet.Relations.Add(objRelation)
```

Relations can be added between "Data Table" objects using the "Data Relation" object. Above sample, code is trying to build a relationship between "Customer" and "Addresses" "Data table" using "Customer Addresses" "Data Relation" object.

What is the use of Command Builder?

Command Builder builds "Parameter" objects automatically. Below is a simple code, which uses command builder to load its parameter objects.

> *Dim pobjCommandBuilder As New OleDbCommandBuilder(pobjDataAdapter)*
>
> *pobjCommandBuilder.DeriveParameters(pobjCommand)*

Be careful while using "Derive Parameters" method as it needs an extra trip to the Data store, which can be very inefficient

What's difference between "Optimistic" and "Pessimistic" locking?

In optimistic locking there is no locking actually. It only checks if the old values are changed, in case they are changed it means somebody has changed the data, so it raises exception.

In pessimistic locking you actually lock the record, depending on the type of lock no other process can make modifications to the record.

How many ways are there to implement optimistic locking in ADO.NET?

Following are the ways to implement optimistic locking using ADO.NET:

- When we call "Update" method of Data Adapter it handles locking internally. If the Dataset values are not matching with current data in Database, it raises concurrency exception error. We can easily trap this error using Try. Catch block and raise appropriate error message to the user.

- Define a Date time stamp field in the table. When actually you are firing the UPDATE SQL statements, compare the current timestamp with one existing in the database. Below is a sample SQL which checks for timestamp before updating and any mismatch in timestamp it will not update the records. This I the best practice used by industries for locking.

> *Update table1 set field1=@test where Last Timestamp=@Current Timestamp*

- Check for original values stored in SQL SERVER and actual changed values. In stored procedure check before updating that the old data is same as the current Example in the below shown SQL before updating field1 we check that is the old field1 value same. If not then some one else has updated and necessary action has to be taken.

> *Update table1 set field1=@test where field1 = @oldfield1value*

Locking can be handled at ADO.NET side or at SQL SERVER side i.e. in stored procedures. For more details of how to implementing locking in SQL SERVER read "What are different locks in SQL SERVER?" in SQL SERVER chapter.

How can do pessimistic locking?

Pessimistic locking is done by using transaction isolation levels like read committed, read uncommitted, repeatable read and serializable.

How can we perform transactions in .NET?

The most common sequence of steps that would be performed while developing a transactional application is as follows:

- Open a database connection using the Open method of the connection object.
- Begin a transaction using the Begin Transaction method of the connection object. This method provides us with a transaction object that we will uselater to commit or rollback the transaction. Note that changes caused by any queries executed before calling the Begin Transaction method will be committed to the database immediately after they execute. Set the Transaction property of the command object to the above mentioned transaction object.
- Execute the SQL commands using the command object. We may use oneormorecommand objects for this purpose, as long as the Transaction property of all the objects is set to a valid transaction object.
- Commit or roll back the transaction using the Commit or Rollback method of the transaction object.
- Close the database connection.

What is difference between Dataset.Clone and Dataset.Copy?

Clone: It only copies structure, does not copy data.

Copy: Copies both structure and data.

Can you explain the difference between an ADO.NET Dataset and an ADO Record set?

There two main basic differences between record set and dataset:

- With dataset you can retrieve data from two databases like oracle and sql server and merge them in one dataset, with record set this is not possible
- All representation of Dataset is using XML while record set uses COM.
- Record set cannot be transmitted on HTTP while Dataset can be.

Explain in detail the fundamental of connection pooling?

When a connection is opened first time, a connection pool is created and is based on the exact match of the connection string given to create the connection object. Connection pooling only works if the connection string is the same. If the connection string is different, then a new connection will be opened, and connection pooling will not be used.

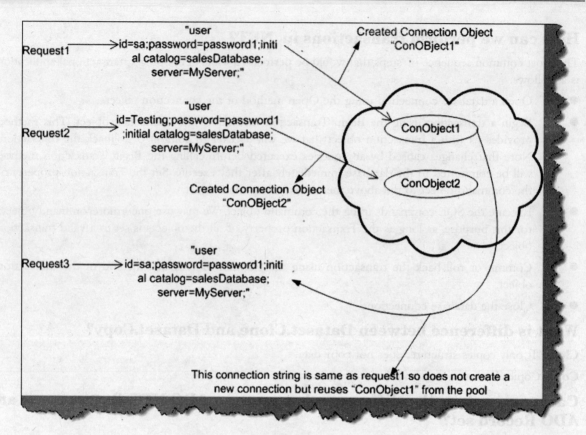

Figure 4.4: Connection pooling in action

Let us try to explain the same pictorially. In the above figure, you can see there are three requests "Request1", "Request2", and "Request3". "Request1" and "Request3" have same connection string so no new connection object is created for "Request3" as the connection string is same. They share the same object "ConObject1". However, new object "ConObject2" is created for "Request2" as the connection string is different.

> **Note:** *The difference between the connection string is that one has "User id=sa" and other has "User id=Testing".*

What is Maximum Pool Size in ADO.NET Connection String?

Maximum pool size decides the maximum number of connection objects to be pooled. Ifthe maximum pool size is reached and there is no usable connection available the requestis queued until connections are released back in to pool. So it's always a good habit tocall the close or dispose method of the connection as soon as you have finishedwork with the connection object.

How to enable and disable connection pooling?

For .NET it is enabled by default but if you want to just make yourself double sure, set Pooling=true inthe connection string. To disable connection pooling set Pooling=false in connectionstring if it is an ADO.NET Connection.

If it is an OLEDBConnection object set OLEDB Services=-4 in the connection string.

What are the major differences between classic ADO and ADO.NET?

Following are some major differences between both :

- In ADO we have recordset and in ADO.NET we have dataset.

- In recordset we can only have one table. If we want to accommodate more than one tables we need to do inner join and fill the recordset. Dataset can have multiple tables.

- All data persist in XML as compared to classic ADO where data persisted in Binary format also.

5
ASP.NET

What are the different events which fire ASP.NET page life cycle?

Following is the sequence in which the events occur:

- Init
- Load
- Validate
- Event
- Render

Note: *Remember the word SILVER: SI (Init) L (Load) V (Validate)E (Event) R (Render).*

Page_init event only occurs when first time the page is started, but Page Load occurs in subsequent request of the page.

What are Httphandlers and HttpModules?

Handlers and modules helps you inject pre-processing logic before the ASP.NET request reaches the website.

One of the scenaries where you would like use them is, before request reaches on the server you would like to check if the user has authenticated or not.

What is the difference between Httphandlers and HttpModules?

Httphandlers is an extension based processor. In other words the pre-processing logic is invoked depending on file extensions.

Httpmodule is an event based processor. In other words ASP.NET emits lot of event like BeginRequest, AuthenticateRequest etc, we can write login functionality in those events using Httpmodule.

How do we write a Httphandler ?

- Create a class and implement "IHttpHandler".

```
public class clsHttpHandler: IHttpHandler
{

    public bool IsReusable
```

```
        {
            get { return true; }
        }

    public void ProcessRequest(HttpContext context)
    {
            // Put implementation here.
    }
}
```

- Define implementation for "processrequest" method.
- Register the class in web.config with file extension in httphandler tag.

```
<httpHandlers>
<add verb="*" path="*.gif" type="clsHttpHandler"/>
</httpHandlers>
```

How do we write an HttpModule?

- Create a class and implement IHttpModule interface.
- Attach events with your methods and put implementation in those events as shown in the below code snippet.

```
public class clsHttpModule: IHttpModule
{

    public void Init(HttpApplication context)
    {
            this.httpApp = context;
            httpApp.Context.Response.Clear();
            httpApp.AuthenticateRequest += new
            EventHandler(OnAuthentication);
            httpApp.AuthorizeRequest += new EventHandler(OnAuthorization);
            httpApp.BeginRequest += new EventHandler(OnBeginrequest);
            httpApp.EndRequest += new EventHandler(OnEndRequest);
            httpApp.ResolveRequestCache += new EventH

    }
    void OnUpdateRequestCache(object sender, EventArgs a)
    {
            //Implementation
    }
    void OnReleaseRequestState(object sender, EventArgs a)
    {
            //Implementation
    }
```

```
      void OnPostRequestHandlerExecute(object sender, EventArgs a)
      {
            //Implementation
      }
      void OnPreRequestHandlerExecute(object sender, EventArgs a)
      {
            //Implementation
      }
      void OnAcquireRequestState(object sender, EventArgs a)
      {
            //Implementation
      }
      void OnResolveRequestCache(object sender, EventArgs a)
      {
            //Implementation
      }
      void OnAuthorization(object sender, EventArgs a)
      {
            //Implementation
      }
      void OnAuthentication(object sender, EventArgs a)
      {

            //Implementation
      }
      void OnBeginrequest(object sender, EventArgs a)
      {

            //Implementation
      }
      void OnEndRequest(object sender, EventArgs a)
      {
            //Implementation

      }

}
```

- Register the class in web.config in httpmodule tag as shown in the below code snippet.

```
<httpModules>
<add name="clsHttpModule" type="clsHttpModule"/>
</httpModules>
```

Can you explain how ASP.NET application life cycle works?

> **Note:** *When any one asks for page life the SILVER answer is appropriate, but when interviewer is asking for application life cycle, two more things come in to picture handlers and modules.*

Below is how ASP.NET events fire.

- First the HttpModule events like BeginRequest, AuthenticateRequest fires.
- Then the HttpHandlers fires if the file extension match of the request page name.
- Finally Page events fire i.e. init, load, validate, event and render.

In which event are the controls fully loaded?

Page load event guarantees that all controls are fully loaded. Controls are also accessed in Page_Init events but you will see that view state is not fully loaded during this event.

How can we identify that the Page is Post Back?

Page object has an "IsPostBack" property, which can be checked to know the page is posted back.

What is the use of @ Register directives?

@Register directive informs the compiler of any custom server control added to the page.

What is the use of Smart Navigation property?

It's a feature provided by ASP.NET to prevent flickering and redrawing when the page is posted back.

What is AppSetting Section in "Web.Config" file?

Web.config file defines configuration for a web project. Using "AppSetting" section, we can define user-defined values. Example below is a "Connection String" section, which will be used throughout the project for database connection.

```
<Configuration>
<appSettings>
<add key="ConnectionString" value="server=xyz;pwd=www;database=testing" /
>
</appSettings>
```

Where is View State information stored?

In HTML Hidden Fields.

How can we create custom controls in ASP.NET?

User controls are created using .ASCX in ASP.NET. After .ASCX file is created you need to two things in order that the ASCX can be used in project:.

- Register the ASCX control in page using the <percentage@ Register directive.Example

> *<%@ Register tag prefix="Accounting" Tag name="footer" Src="Footer.ascx" %>*

- Now to use the above accounting footer in page you can use the below directive.

> *<Accounting: footer runat="server" />*

How many types of validation controls are provided by ASP.NET?

There are six main types of validation controls:

RequiredFieldValidator

It checks whether the control have any value. It is used when you want the control should not be empty.

RangeValidator

It checks if the value in validated control is in that specific range. Example TxtCustomerCode should not be more than eight lengths.

CompareValidator

It checks that the value in controls should match some specific value. Example Textbox TxtPie should be equal to 3.14.

RegularExpressionValidator

When we want the control, value should match with a specific regular expression.

CustomValidator

It is used to define User Defined validation.

Validation Summary

It displays summary of all current validation errors on an ASP.NET page.

How can we force all the validation control to run?

Page.Validate

How can we check if all the validation control are valid and proper?

Using the Page.IsValid () property you can check whether all the validation are done.

If client side validation is enabled, will server side code still run ?

When client side validation is enabled server emit's JavaScript code for the custom validators. However, note that does not mean that server side checks on custom validators do not execute. It does this redundant check two times, as some of the validators do not support client side scripting.

Which JavaScript file is referenced for validating the validators at the client side?

WebUIValidation.js JavaScript file installed at "aspnet_client" root IIS directory is used to validate the validation controls at the client side

How to disable client side script in validators?

Set 'EnableClientScript' to false.

How can I show the entire validation error message in a message box on the client side?

In validation summary set "ShowMessageBox" to true.

If a validation is very complex what will you do ?

Best is to go for CustomValidators. Below is a sample code for a custom validator, which checks that a textbox should not have zero value

```
<asp:CustomValidator id="CustomValidator1" runat="server"
ErrorMessage="Number not divisible by Zero"
ControlToValidate="txtNumber"
OnServerValidate="ServerValidate"
ClientValidationFunction="CheckZero" /><br>
Input:
<asp:TextBox id="txtNumber" runat="server" />
<script language="javascript">
<!-function CheckZero(source, args) {
        int val = parseInt(args.Value, 10);
        if (value==0) {
            args.
            IsValid = false;
        }
}
// ->
</script>
```

Can you explain "AutoPostBack"?

If we want the control to automatically post back in case of any event, we will need to check this attribute as true. For example on a Combo Box change if we need to send the event immediately to the server side then we need to mark "AutoPostBack" attribute to true.

How can you enable automatic paging in Data Grid?

Following are the points to be done in order to enable paging in Data grid:

●   Set the "Allow Paging" to true.

●   In PageIndexChanged event set the current page index clicked.

What is the use of "GLOBAL.ASAX" file?

It allows to execute ASP.NET application level events and setting application-level variables.

What is the difference between "Web.config" and "Machine.Config"?

"Web.config" files apply settings to each web application, while "Machine.config" file apply settings to all ASP.NET applications.

What is a SESSION and APPLICATION object?

Session object store information between HTTP requests for a particular user, while application object are global across users.

What is the difference between 'Server.Transfer' and 'response.Redirect'?

Following are the major differences between them:

'Response.Redirect' sends message to the browser saying it to move to some different page, while 'Server.Transfer' does not send any message to the browser but rather redirects the user directly from the server itself. So in 'server.transfer' there is no round trip while 'response.redirect' has a round trip and hence puts a load on server.

Using 'Server.Transfer' you cannot redirect to a different from the server itself. Example if your server is www.yahoo.com you cannot use 'server.Transfer' to move to www.microsoft.com but yes, you can move to www.yahoo.com/travels, i.e. within websites. Cross server redirect is possible only by using Response. Redirect.

With 'server.transfer' you can preserve your information. It has a parameter called as "preserveForm". Therefore, the existing query string etc. will be able in the calling page.

If you are navigating within the same website use "Server. Transfer" or else go for "response. Redirect ()"

What is the difference between Authentication and authorization?

This can be a tricky question. These two concepts seem altogether similar but there is wide range of difference.

Authentication is verifying the identity of a user and authorization is process where we check does this identity have access rights to the system. Authorization is the process of allowing an authenticated user access to resources.

What is impersonation in ASP.NET?

By default, ASP.NET executes in the security context of a restricted user account on the local machine. Sometimes you need to access network resources such as a file on a shared drive, which requires additional permissions. One way to overcome this restriction is to use impersonation. With impersonation, ASP.NET can execute the request using the identity of the client who is making the request, or ASP.NET can impersonate a specific account you can specify the account in web.config.

What are the various ways of authentication techniques in ASP.NET?

There are 3 major ways of doing authentication and authorization:

- Windows: In this mode the users are stored in windows local user groups.

- Forms: In this mode we create a login screen and use the forms authentication class to do validations. It's a ticket based authentication.

- Passport: In this mode the users are validated from Microsoft sites like hotmail, devhood, MSN etc, ticket is generated and that ticket can be used to do authentication and authorization in your web application.

Can you explain Forms authentication in detail?

In old ASP if you are said to create a login page and do authentication you have to do hell lot of custom coding. Now in ASP.NET that has been made easy by introducing Forms authentication. So let us see in detail what form authentication is.

Forms authentication uses a ticket cookie to see that user is authenticated or not. That means when user is authenticated first time a cookie is set to tell that this user is authenticated. If the cookies expire then Forms authentication mechanism sends the user to the login page.

Following are the steps, which defines steps for Forms authentication:

● Configure Web.config file with forms authentication tag. As shown below in the config file you can see we have give the cookie name and loginurl page.

```
<configuration>
<system.web>
<!- Other settings omitted. ->
<authentication mode="Forms">
<forms name="logincookies"
loginUrl="login.aspx"
protection="All"
timeout="30"
path="/" />
</authentication>
</system.web>
</configuration>
```

● Remove anonymous access to the IIS web application, following are changes done to web.config file.

```
<configuration>
<system.web>
<!- Other settings omitted. ->
<authorization>
<deny users="?" />
</authorization>
</system.web>
</configuration>
```

● Create the login page, which will accept user information. You will have create your login page that is the Login.aspx, which will actually take the user data.

● Finally a small coding in the login button.

Let us assume that the login page has two textboxes 'txtName' and 'txtpassword'.

Also, import System.Web.Security and put the following code in login button of the page.

```
If Page.IsValid Then
If FormsAuthentication.Authenticate(txtName.Text, txtPassword.Text) Then
FormsAuthentication.RedirectFromLoginPage(txtName.Text, False)
Else
lblStatus.Text = "Error not proper user"
End If
End If
```

How do I sign out in forms authentication?

FormsAuthentication.Signout()

If cookies are disabled how will forms authentication work?

It will pass data through query strings.

How do we implement windows authentication?

- Create users in your local windows user group.
- In web.config file set the authentication mode to windows.
- In web.config file set <deny users="?"/>.

Once you do the above three steps your asp.net pages will authenticated and authorized from the users stored in windows local user group.

How can we do single sign on in ASP.NET?

For single signon we need to use forms authentication and put the same machine key in the web.config files of all web applications who will participate in single sign on.

Can you explain membership and role providers in ASP.Net 2.0?

A membership and role provider helps to automate your authentication and authorization code. When we want to implement user authentication and authorization in any project following are the routine task:

- Creation of user and roles tables.
- Code level implementation for maintaining those tables.
- User interface for 'userid' and 'password'.

All the above tasks are automated using membership and roles.

In order to implement membership and roles run aspnet_regsql.exe from 'C:\WINDOWS\Microsoft.NET\Framework\v2.0.50727' folder.

This will create necessary readymade tables like users, roles etc. You can then use the readymade API of membership and roles to create user and roles as shown in the code snippet.

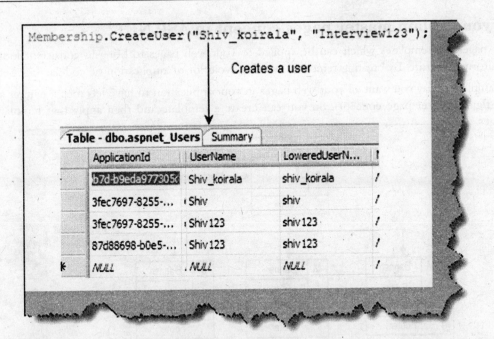

Figure 5.1: Membership API

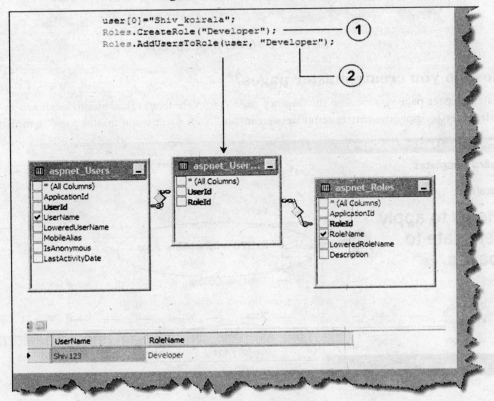

Figure 5.2: Roles API

Can you explain master pages concept in ASP.NET?

Master pages are templates which can be applied to your web pages to bring in consistent look and feel and uniform structure. By creating templates we also avoid lot of duplication of code across web pages.

For example let's say you want all your web pages in your application to have left menu, banner and footer (Refer figure Master page concept). So you can create a template and then apply that template to your webpages.

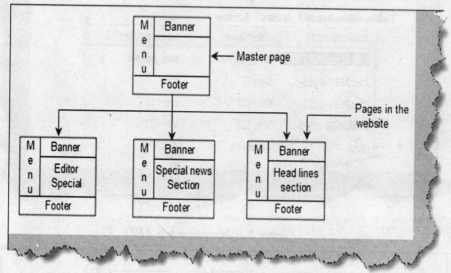

Figure 5.3: Master page concept

So how do you create master pages?

To create a master page you can use the "master page" template from visual studio as shown in the below figure. In order to apply the master template we can use "Web form using master page" template.

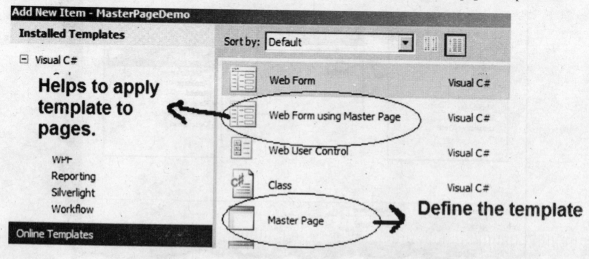

Figure 5.4: create master pages

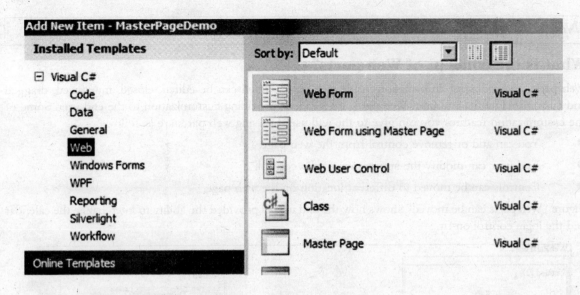

Figure 5.4: create master pages

In the master page you can define place holder using "ContentPlaceHolder" control. This is the place where your ASP.NET pages will be plug in their data.

```
<body>
This is the common template
<asp:ContentPlaceHolder ID="ContentPlaceHolder1" runat="server">
</asp:ContentPlaceHolder>
</body>
```

Once the master page template is created with the necessary place holders. You can then later in the web pages use the "MasterPageFile" to refer the template and you can use the content place holder to plug data.

For instance you can see the below code snippet of a page which uses master pages. You can also see how the "ContentPlaceHolder1" is used to place a simple text data "Company was established in 1990".

```
<%@ Page Title="" Language="C#" MasterPageFile="~/WebSiteTemplate.Master"
AutoEventWireup="true" CodeBehind="Aboutus.aspx.cs" Inherits="MasterPageDemo.
Aboutus" %>

<asp:Content ID="Content1" ContentPlaceHolderID="ContentPlaceHolder1"
runat="server">
<p>
     Company was established in 1990</p>
</asp:Content>
```

What is the concept of Web parts?

Web part is a window of information inside web pages which can be edited, closed, minimized, dragged and customized by the end user. Web parts are all about providing customization to the end user. Some of the customization features you can give to the end user by using web parts are as follows:

● You can add or remove control from the web page.

● End user can modify the appearance of the control.

● Controls can be moved to different location on the web page.

Figure "Web parts can be moved" shows how the end user is provided the ability to interchange the calendar and the login control on fly.

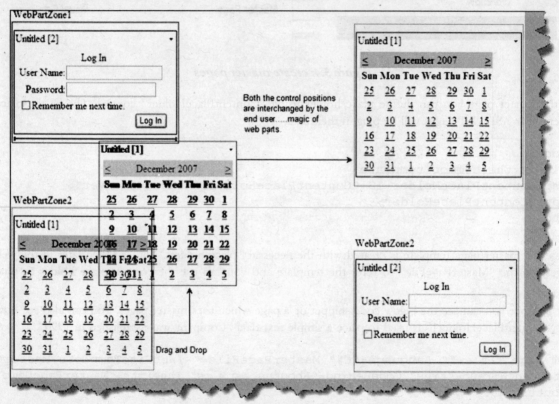

Figure 5.5: Web parts can be moved

Figure 'Edit information using web parts' shows one more magic of web parts. End user can edit appearance information of the web part which has a calendar control inside.

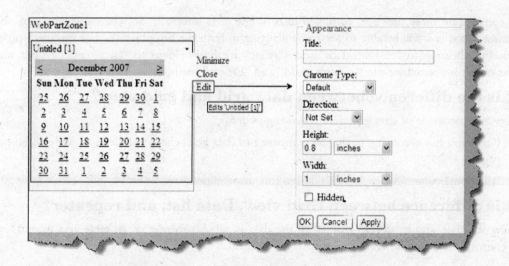

Figure 5.6: Edit information using web parts

The above customization either can be set at a personal level or for all users.

What are partial classes in ASP.NET ?

A partial class allows a single class to be divided in to two separate physical files. During compile time these files get compiled in to single class. For instance you can see in the below figure we have the customer class divided in to two different files "customer1.cs" and "customer2.cs".

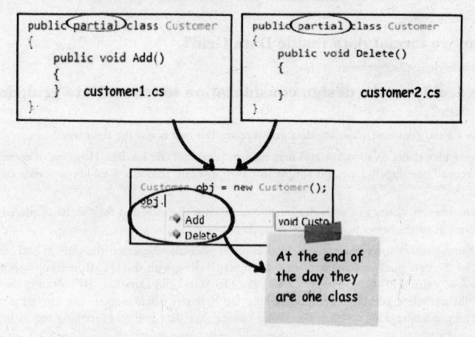

Figure 5.7: Partial classes

During compilation these files gets compiled in to single class internally. So when you create an object of the customer class you will be able to see methods lying in both the physical files. For instance you can see "Add" method belongs to "customer1.cs" and "Delete" method belongs to "customer2.cs", but when the customer object is created we can see both "Add" and "Delete" methods.

What is the difference between data grid and grid view?

Grid view is a successor of data grid with following benefits:

- Grid view has automatic paging as compared to data grid where you need to write some code for paging.
- Additional column types and rich design time capabilities.

What is difference between Grid view, Data list, and repeater?

Grid view and data grid by default display all the data in tabular format i.e. in table and rows. Developer has no control to change the table data display of datagrid.

Data list also displays data in a table but gives some flexibility in terms of displaying data row wise and column wise using the repeat direction property.\

Repeater control is highly customizable. It does not display data in table by default. So you can customize from scratch the way you want to display data.

From performance point of view, how do they rate?

Repeater is fastest followed by Datalist / Gridview and finally data grid.

What is the method to customize columns in Data Grid?

Use the template column.

How can we format data inside Data Grid?

Use the DataFormatString property.

How to decide on the design consideration to take a Data grid, data list, or repeater?

Many make a blind choice of choosing data grid directly, but that is not the right way.

Data grid provides ability to allow the end-user to sort, page, and edit its data. However, it comes at a cost of speed. Second, the display format is simple that is in row and columns. Real life scenarios can be more demanding that

With its templates, the Data List provides more control over the look and feel of the displayed data than the Data Grid. It offers better performance than data grid

Repeater control allows for complete and total control. With the Repeater, the only HTML emitted are the values of the data binding statements in the templates along with the HTML markup specified in the templates—no "extra" HTML is emitted, as with the Data Grid and Data List. By requiring the developer to specify the complete generated HTML markup, the Repeater often requires the longest development time. However, repeater does not provide editing features like data grid so everything has to be coded by programmer. However, the Repeater does boast the best performance of the three data Web controls. Repeater is fastest followed by Datalist and finally data grid.

What are major events in GLOBAL.ASAX file?

The Global. Sax file, which is derived from the Http Application class, maintains a pool of Http Application objects, and assigns them to applications as needed. The Global. Sax file contains the following events:

Application_Init: Fired when an application initializes or is first called. It is invoked for all Http Application object instances.

Application Error: Fired when an unhandled exception is encountered within the application.

Application Start: Fired when the first instance of the Http Application class is created. It allows you to create objects that are accessible by all Http Application instances.

Application End: Fired when the last instance of an Http Application class is destroyed. It is fired only once during an application's lifetime.

Session Start: Fired when a new user visits the application Web site.

Session End: Fired when a user's session times out, ends, or they leave the application Web site.

How can we kill a user session?

Session.abandon

How do you upload a file in ASP.NET?

By using System.Web.HttpPostedFile class.

How do I send email message from ASP.NET?

ASP.NET provides two namespace SystemWEB.mailmessage class and System.Web.Mail.Smtpmail class. Just a small homework create an Asp.NET project and send an email at shiv_koirala@yahoo.com. Do not Spam ;-) .

What are different IIS isolation levels?

IIS has three level of isolation:

LOW (IIS process): In this main IIS, process, and ASP.NET application run in same process. So if any one crashes the other is also affected. Example let us say (well this is not possible) I have hosted yahoo, hotmail .amazon and goggle on a single PC. So all application and the IIS process runs on the same process. In case any website crashes, it affects every one.

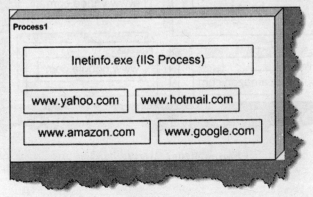

Figure 5.8: LOW (IIS process)

Medium (Pooled): In Medium pooled scenario, the IIS, and web application run in different process. Therefore, in this case there are two processes process1 and process2. In process1, the IIS process is running and in process2, we have all Web application running.

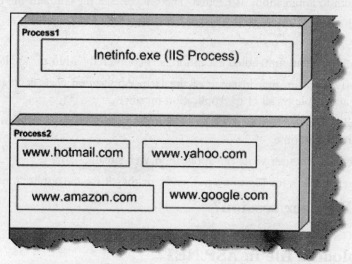

Figure 5.9: Medium (Pooled)

High (Isolated): In high isolated scenario every process is running is their own process. In below figure there are five processes and every one handling individual application. This consumes heavy memory but has highest reliability.

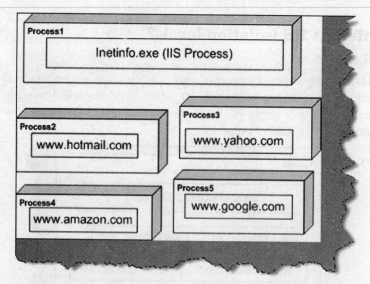

Figure 5.10: High (Isolated)

ASP used STA threading model, what is the threading model used for ASP.NET.

ASP.NET uses MTA threading model.

What is the use of <%@ page aspcompat=true %> attribute?

This attribute works like a compatibility option. As mentioned before ASP works in STA model and ASP.NET works in MTA model, but what if your ASP.NET application is using a VB COM component. In order that VB COM runs properly in ASP.NET threading model, we have to set attribute. After defining the ASPCOMPAT directive attribute ASP.NET pages runs in STA model thus building the compatibility between ASP.NET and old COM components that does not support MTA model.

Explain the differences between Server-side and Client-side code?

Server side code is executed at the server side on IIS in ASP.NET framework, while client side code is executed on the browser.

How to use a checkbox in a data grid?

Following are the steps to be done:

● In ASPX page you have to add Item template tag in data grid.

```
<ItemTemplate>
<asp:CheckBox  id="CheckBox1"  runat="server"  AutoPostBack="True"
OnCheckedChanged="Check_Clicked"></asp:CheckBox>
</ItemTemplate>
```

If you look at the Item template, we have "OnCheckChanged" event. This "OnCheckChanged" event has "Check Clicked" subroutine is actually in behind code. Note this method, which is in behind code, should either be "protected" or "public"

Following below is the subroutine, which defines the method

```
Protected Sub Check Clicked (By Val sender As Object, By Val e As EventArgs)
'Do something
End Sub
```

What is the difference between "Web farms" and "Web garden"?

"Web farms" are used to have some redundancy to minimize failures and to meet heavy load demands.

It consists of two or more web server of the same configuration and they stream the same kind of contents. When any request comes there is switching / routing logic, which decides which web server from the farm, handles the request. For instance, we have two servers "Server1" and "Server2" which have the same configuration and content. Therefore, there is a special switch, which stands in between these two servers and the users and routes the request accordingly.

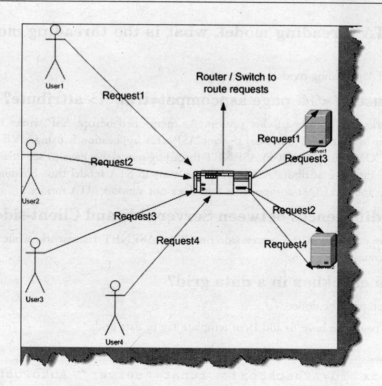

Figure 5.11: Webfarm

Above figure explains in detail how web farm work. You can see there is a router in between which takes a request and sees which one of the server is least loaded and forwards the request to that server. Therefore, for request1 it route is server1, for request2 it routes server2, for request3 it routes to server3 and final request4 is routed to server4. So you can see because we have web farm at place server1 and server2 are loaded with two request each rather than one server loading to full. One more advantage of using this kind of architecture is if one of the servers goes down we can still run with the other server thus having 24x7 uptime.

The routing logic can be a number of different options:

● **Round robin:** Each node gets a request sent to it "in turn". Therefore, server1 gets a request, then server2 again, then server1, then server2 again. As shown in the above figure.

● **Least Active:** Whichever node show to have the lowest number of current connects gets new connects sent to it. This is good to help keep the load balanced between the server nodes.

● **Fastest Reply:** Whichever node replies faster is the one that gets new requests. This is also a good option - especially if there are nodes that might not be "equal" in performance. If one performs better than the other, then send more requests there rather than which is moving slowly?

Before we try to understand what a web garden is let's try to understand how IIS handles processes. All requests to IIS are routed to "aspnet_wp.exe" for IIS 5.0 and "w3wp.exe" for IIS 6.0. In normal case i.e. with out web garden, we have one worker process instance ("aspnet_wp.exe" / "w3wp.exe") across all requests. This one instance of worker process uses the CPU processor as directed by the operating system.

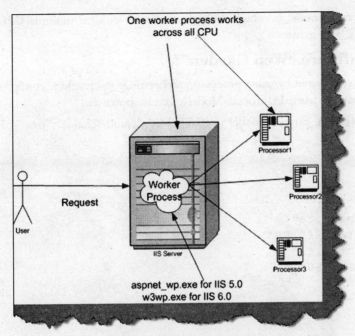

Figure 5.12: Web garden

However, when we enable web garden for a web server it creates different instances of the worker process and each of these worker process runs on different CPU. You can see in the below diagram we have different worker process instances created which run on different CPU's.

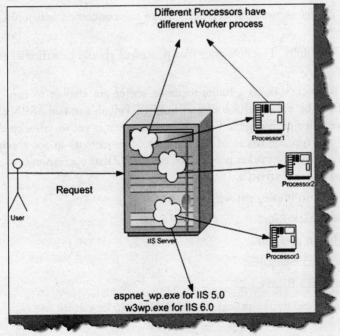

Figure 5.13: Worker process

In short, we can define a model in which multiple processes run on multiple CPUs in a single server machine are termed as Web garden.

How do we configure "Web Garden"?

"Web garden" can be configured by using process model settings in "machine.config" or "Web.config" file. The configuration section is named <process Model> and is shown in

The following example. The process model is enabled by default (enable="true"). Below is the snippet from config file.

```
<process Model
enable="true"
timeout="infinite"
idle Timeout="infinite"
shutdown Timeout="0:00:05"
requestLimit="infinite"
requestQueueLimit="5000"
memoryLimit="80"
webGarden="false"
cpuMask="12"
userName=""
password=""
logLevel="errors"
clientConnectedCheck="0:00:05"
/>
```

From the above process model section for web garden, we are concerned with only two attributes "web garden" and "cpuMask".

WebGarden: Controls CPU affinity. True indicates that processes should be affinities to the corresponding CPU. The default is False.

CpuMask: Specifies which processors on a multiprocessor server are eligible to run ASP.NET processes. The cpuMask value specifies a bit pattern that indicates the CPUs eligible to run ASP.NET threads. ASP.NET launches one worker process for each eligible CPU. If web Garden is set to false, cpuMask is ignored and only one worker process will run regardless of the number of processors in the machine. If web Garden is set to true, ASP.NET launches one worker process for each CPU that corresponds to a set bit in cpuMask. The default value of cpuMask is 0xffffffff.

Below are detail steps of how to implement web garden

- Click Start and then click Run.
- Type calc.exe and then click OK.
- Go to View menu, click Scientific.
- Go to View menu, click Binary.
- Use zero and one to specify the processors ASP.NET can or cannot use.

Use one for the processor that you want to use for ASP.NET. Use 0 for the processor that you do not want to use for ASP.NET. For example, if you want to use the first two processors for ASP.NET of a four-processor computer, type 1100.

- On the View menu, click Decimal. Note the decimal number.

- Open the Web.config or machine.config file in a text editor such as Notepad. The Web.config file is located in the folder where the application is saved.

- In the Web.config file, add the process Model configuration element under the System. Web element. Before adding <process Model> to Web.config file, the user has to make sure that the allow Definition attribute in the <process Model> section of the Web.config file is set to everywhere.

- Add and then set the web Garden attribute of the process Model element to True.

- Add and then set the cpuMask attribute of the process Model element to the result that is determined in your calculation.

Do not preface the number with zerox because the result of the calculation is a decimal number. The following example demonstrates the process Model element that is configured to enable only the first two processors of a four-processor computer.

```
<processModel
enable="true"
webGarden="true"
cpuMask="12" />
Save the Web.config file. The ASP.NET application automatically restarts
and uses only the specified processors.
```

What's the difference between trace and debug in ASP.NET?

Debug and trace enables you to monitor application for errors and exception with out VS.NET IDE. In **Debug** mode compiler inserts some debugging code inside the executable. As the debugging code is the part of the executable they run on the same thread where the code runs and they do not given you the exact efficiency of the code (as they run on the same thread). So for every full executable DLL you will see a debug file also as shown in figure 'Debug Mode'.

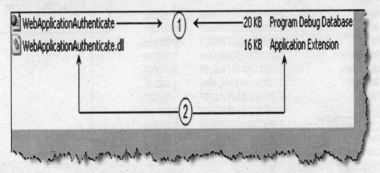

Figure 5.14: PDB files

Trace works in both debug as well as release mode. The main advantage of using trace over debug is to do performance analysis which can not be done by debug. Trace runs on a different thread thus it does not impact the main code thread.

> **Note:** *There is also a fundamental difference in thinking when we want to use trace and when want to debug. Tracing is a process about getting information regarding program's execution. On the other hand debugging is about finding errors in the code.*

How do you enable tracing in on an ASP.NET page?

To enable tracing on an ASP.NET page we need to put the 'trace' attribute to true on the page attribute as shown in figure 'Tracing in Action' (Its numbered as 1 in the figure). In the behind code we can use the trace object to put tracing like one we have shown on the page load numbered as (4). We have used the 'trace.write' to display our tracing. You can also see the trace data which is circled. 2 and 3 show the actual data. You can see how trace shows in details the tracing information for a page with events and time period for execution. If you make the 'trace' as false you will only see the actual display i.e. 'This is the actual data'. So you can enable and disable trace with out actually compiling and uploading new DLL's on production environment.

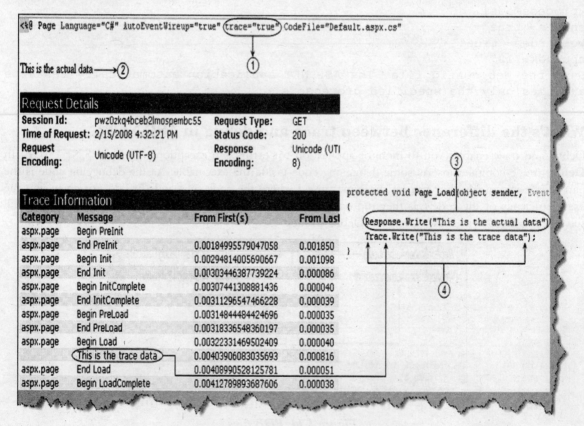

Figure 5.15: Tracing in action

The above sample enables tracing only at page level. To enable tracing on application level we need to modify the 'web.config' file and put the 'trace' tag with 'enabled=true'.

> *<trace enabled="true" requestLimit="10" pageOutput="false" localOnly="true" />*

Which namespace is needed to implement debug and trace ?

Debug and trace class belongs to 'System.Diagnostic' namespace.

Can you explain the concept of trace listener?

'Tracelistener' are objects that get tracing information from the trace class and they output the data to some medium. For instance you can see from the figure 'TraceListener' how it listens to the trace object and outputs the same to UI, File or a windows event log. There are three different types of 'tracelistener' first is the 'defaulttracelistener' (this outputs the data to UI), second is 'textwritertracelistener' (this outputs to a file) and the final one is 'Eventlogtracelistener' which outputs the same to a windows event log.

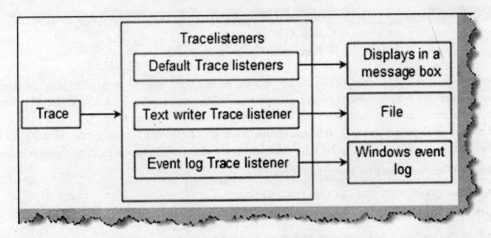

Figure 5.16: Trace listeners

Below is a code snippet for 'textwritertracelistener' and 'eventlogtracelistener'. Using 'textwritertracelistener' we have forwarded the trace's to 'ErrorLog.txt' file and in the second snippet we have used the 'Eventlogtracelistener' to forward the trace's to windows event log.

```
FileStream objStream = new FileStream("C:\\ErrorLog.txt",FileMode.OpenOrCreate) ;
TextWriterTraceListener objTraceListener = new TextWriterTraceListener(objStream) ;
Trace.Listeners.Add(objTraceListener) ;
Trace.WriteLine("This is text listener message") ;
```
→ textwritertracelistener

```
EventLogTraceListener objListener = new EventLogTraceListener() ;
EventLog objLog = new EventLog("MyEventLog") ;
objListener.EventLog = objLog ;
```
→ eventlogtracelistener

Figure 5.17: Tracelistener in action

What are trace switches?

Trace switches helps us to control and govern the tracing behavior of a project. There are two types of trace switches 'BooleanSwitch' and 'TraceSwitch'.**BooleanSwitch**, as the name says, is a kind of on/off switch which can be either enabled (true) or disabled (false).

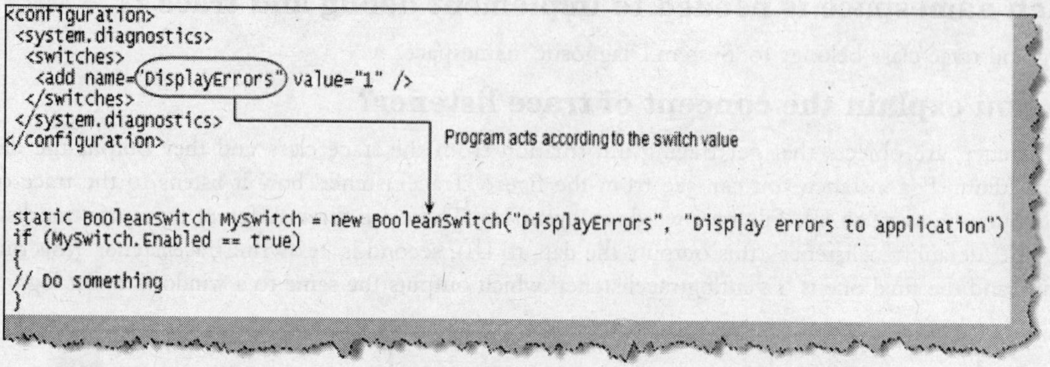

```
<configuration>
 <system.diagnostics>
  <switches>
   <add name="DisplayErrors" value="1" />
  </switches>
 </system.diagnostics>
</configuration>
                                            Program acts according to the switch value

static BooleanSwitch MySwitch = new BooleanSwitch("DisplayErrors", "Display errors to application")
if (MySwitch.Enabled == true)
{
// Do something
}
```

Figure 5.18: Trace switches

'**TraceSwitch**' on the other hand offers more options rather than simple true/false like 'BooleanSwitch'. Tracing is enabled for a TraceSwitch object using the Level property. When we set the Level property of a switch to a particular level, it includes all levels from the indicated level down. For example, if you set a TraceSwitch's Level property to TraceLevel.Info, then all the lower levels, from TraceLevel.Error to TraceLevel.Warning, will be taken in to account. Below are the various levels in 'TraceSwitch' object.

Off → Outputs no messages to Trace Listeners

Error → Outputs only error messages to Trace Listeners

Warning → Outputs error and warning messages to Trace Listeners

Info → Outputs informational, warning and error messages to Trace Listeners

Verbose → Outputs all messages to Trace Listeners

```
TraceSwitch objSwitch = new TraceSwitch("TraceWarningandError", "Error in
trace") ;
objSwitch.Level = TraceLevel.Warning ;
```

What is an application object?

Application object is used when we want data to be shared across users globally in an ASP.NET application.

What is the use of cache object?

It also does the same thing as the application object i.e. sharing and caching global data across ASP.NET pages in a web application.

What is the difference between Cache object and application object?

The main difference between the Cache and Application objects is that the Cache object provides features, such as dependencies and expiration policies.

How can get access to cache object?

The Cache object is defined in the 'System.Web.Caching' namespace. You can get a reference to the Cache object by using the Cache property of the HttpContext class in the 'System.Web' namespace or by using the Cache property of the Page object.

What are dependencies in cache and types of dependencies?

When you add an item to the cache, you can define dependency relationships that can force that item to be removed from the cache under specific activities of dependencies.Example if the cache object is dependent on file and when the file data changes you want the cache object to be update. Following are the supported dependency:

● **File dependency:** Allows you to invalidate a specific cache item when a disk based file or files change.

● **Time-based expiration:** Allows you to invalidate a specific cache item depending on predefined time.

● **Key dependency:** Allows you to invalidate a specific cache item depending when another cached item changes.

Can you show a simple code showing file dependency in cache?

```
PartialClass Default_aspx

PublicSub displayAnnouncement()
Dim announcement AsString
If Cache("announcement") IsNothingThen
Dim file AsNew _
System.IO.StreamReader _
(Server.MapPath("announcement.txt"))
announcement = file.ReadToEnd
file.Close()
Dim depends AsNew _
System.Web.Caching.CacheDependency _
(Server.MapPath("announcement.txt"))
Cache.Insert("announcement", announcement, depends)
EndIf
Response.Write(CType(Cache("announcement"), String))
EndSub

PrivateSub Page_Init(ByVal sender AsObject, ByVal e As
System.EventArgs) HandlesMe.Init
displayAnnouncement()
EndSub
End Class
```

Above given method displayAnnouncement() displays banner text from Announcement.txt file which is lying in application path of the web directory. Above method, first checks whether the Cache object is nothing, if the cache object is nothing then it moves further to load the cache data from the file. Whenever the file data changes the cache object is removed and set to nothing.

What is Cache Callback in Cache?

Cache object is dependent on its dependencies example file based, time based etc...Cache items remove the object when cache dependencies change.ASP.NET provides capability to execute a callback method when that item is removed from cache.

What is scavenging?

When server running your ASP.NET application runs low on memory resources, items are removed from cache depending on cache item priority. Cache item priority is set when you add item to cache. By setting the cache item priority controls, the items scavenging are removed according to priority.

What are different types of caching using cache object of ASP.NET?

You can use two types of output caching to cache information that is to be transmitted to and displayed in a Web browser:

- **Page Output Caching**

  Page output caching adds the response of page to cache object. Later when page is requested page is displayed from cache rather than creating the page object and displaying it. Page output caching is good if the site is fairly static.

- **Page Fragment Caching**

  If parts of the page are changing, you can wrap the static sections as user controls and cache the user controls using page fragment caching.

How can you cache different version of same page using ASP.NET cache object?

Output cache functionality is achieved by using "OutputCache" attribute on ASP.NET page header. Below is the syntax

```
<%@    OutputCache    Duration="20"    Location="Server"    VaryByParam="state"
VaryByCustom="minorversion" VaryByHeader="Accept-Language"%>
```

- **VaryByParam:** Caches different version depending on input parameters send through HTTP POST/GET.

- **VaryByHeader:** Caches different version depending on the contents of the page header.

- **VaryByCustom:** Lets you customize the way the cache handles page variations by declaring the attribute and overriding the GetVaryByCustomString handler.

- **VaryByControl:** Caches different versions of a user control based on the value of properties of ASP objects in the control.

How will implement Page Fragment Caching?

Page fragment caching involves the caching of a fragment of the page, rather than the entire page. When portions of the page are need to be dynamically created for each user request this is best method as compared to page caching. You can wrap Web Forms user control and cache the control so that these portions of the page do not need to be recreated each time.

Can you compare ASP.NET sessions with classic ASP?

ASP.NET session caches per user session state. It basically uses "HttpSessionState" class.

Following are the limitations in classic ASP sessions:

- ASP session state is dependent on IIS process very heavily. So if IIS restarts ASP session variables are also recycled. ASP.NET session can be independent of the hosting environment thus ASP.NET session can be maintained even if IIS reboots.

- ASP session state has no inherent solution to work with Web Farms. ASP.NET session can be stored in state server and SQL SERVER which can support multiple server.

- ASP session only functions when browser supports cookies. ASP.NET session can be used with browser side cookies or independent of it.

Which are the various modes of storing ASP.NET session?

- **InProc:** In this mode Session, state is stored in the memory space of the Aspnet_wp.exe process. This is the default setting. If the IIS reboots or web application restarts then session state is lost.

- **StateServer:** In this mode Session state is serialized and stored in a separate process (Aspnet_state.exe); therefore, the state can be stored on a separate computer(a state server).

- **SQL SERVER:** In this mode Session, state is serialized and stored in a SQL Server database.

Session state can be specified in <sessionState> element of application configuration file. Using State Server and SQL SERVER session state can be shared across web farms but note this comes at speed cost as ASP.NET needs to serialize and deserialize data over network repeatedly.

Do session use cookies?

Yes, session use cookies. The session id value is stored in the browser client temp directory. This id is used to get the session data from the server in every post back.

Is Session_End event supported in all session modes?

Session_End event occurs only in "Inproc mode". "State Server" and "SQL SERVER" do not have Session_End event.

Where do you specify session state mode in ASP.NET?

```
<sessionState mode="SQLServer"
stateConnectionString="tcpip=192.168.1.1:42424"
sqlConnectionString="data source=192.168.1.1; Integrated
Security=SSPI"
cookieless="false"
timeout="20"
/>
```

Above is sample session state mode specified for SQL SERVER.

What are the other ways you can maintain state?

Other than session variables, you can use the following technique to store state:

- Hidden fields
- View state
- Hidden frames
- Cookies
- Query strings

What are benefits and Limitation of using Hidden fields?

Following are the benefits of using Hidden fields:

- They are simple to implement.
- As data is cached on client side, they work with Web Farms.
- All browsers support hidden field.
- No server resources are required.

Following are limitations of Hidden field:

- They can be tampered creating a security hole.
- Page performance decreases if you store large data, as the data are stored in pages itself.
- Hidden fields do not support rich structures as HTML hidden fields are only single valued. Then you have to work around with delimiters etc to handle complex structures.

Below is how you will actually implement hidden field in a project

```
<input        id="HiddenValue"        type="hidden"        value="Initial        Value"
runat="server"NAME="HiddenValue">
```

What is ViewState?

Viewstate is a built-in structure for automatically retaining values between multiple requests for the same page. Viewstate is internally maintained as a hidden field on the page but is hashed, providing greater security than developer-implemented hidden fields do.

How do we ensure viewstate is not tampered?

View state is a simple HTML hidden field. So it's possible very much possible that some one can tamper this hidden field easily. To ensure that viewstate is not tampered we can set the "EnableViewStateMac" attribute to true. This attribute is found in the "page" directive in ASPX page.Below is a simple code snippet which shows how to use the same.

```
<%@ Page EnableViewStateMac="true" %>
```

Does the performance for viewstate vary according to User controls?

Performance of viewstate varies depending on the type of server control to which it is applied. Label, TextBox, CheckBox, RadioButton, and HyperLink are server controls that perform well with ViewState. DropDownList, ListBox, DataGrid, and DataList suffer from poor performance because of their size and the large amounts of data making roundtrips to the server.

What are benefits and Limitation of using Viewstate for state management?

Following are the benefits of using Viewstate:

- No server resources are required because state is in a structure in the page code.

- Simplicity.

- States are retained automatically.

- The values in view state are hashed, compressed, and encoded, thus representing a higher state of security than hidden fields.

- View state is good for caching data in Web frame configurations because the data is cached on the client.

Following are limitation of using Viewstate:

- Page loading and posting performance decreases when large values are stored because view state is stored in the page.

- Although view state stores data in a hashed format, it can still be tampered because it is stored in a hidden field on the page. The information in the hidden field can also be seen if the page output source is viewed directly, creating a potential security risk.

Below is sample of storing values in view state.

```
this.ViewState["EnterTime"] = DateTime.Now.ToString();
```

How can you use Hidden frames to cache client data ?

This technique is implemented by creating a Hidden frame in page which will contain your data to be cached.

```
<FRAMESET cols="100%,*,*">
<FRAMESET rows="100%">
<FRAME src="data_of_frame1.html"></FRAMESET>
<FRAME src="data_of_hidden_frame.html">
<FRAME src="data_of_hidden_frame.html" frameborder="0" noresize
scrolling="yes">
</FRAMESET>
```

Above is a sample of hidden frames where the first frame "data_of_frame1.html" is visible and the remaining frames are hidden by giving whole col section to first frame. 100 % is allocated to first frame and remaining frames thus remain hidden.

What are benefits and limitations of using Hidden frames?

Following are the benefits of using hidden frames:

- You can cache more than one data field.
- The ability to cache and access data items stored in different hidden forms.
- The ability to access JScript® variable values stored in different frames if they come from the same site.

The limitations of using hidden frames are:

- Hidden frames are not supported on all browsers.
- Hidden frames data can be tampered thus creating security hole.

What are benefits and limitations of using Cookies?

Following are benefits of using cookies for state management:

- No server resources are required as they are stored in client.
- They are light weight and simple to use

Following are limitation of using cookies:

- Most browsers place a 4096-byte limit on the size of a cookie, although support for 8192-byte cookies is becoming more common in the new browser and client-device versions available today.
- Some users disable their browser or client device's ability to receive cookies, thereby limiting the use of cookies.
- Cookies can be tampered and thus creating a security hole.
- Cookies can expire thus leading to inconsistency.

Below is sample code of implementing cookies

```
Request.Cookies.Add(New HttpCookie("name", "user1"))
```

What is Query String and what are benefits and limitations of using Query Strings?

A query string is information sent to the server appended to the end of a page URL.

Following are the benefits of using query string for state management:

- No server resources are required. The query string containing in the HTTP requests for a specific URL.
- All browsers support query strings.

Following are limitations of query string:

- Query string data is directly visible to user thus leading to security problems.-
- Most browsers and client devices impose a 255-character limit on URL length.

Below is a sample "Login" query string passed in URL http://www.querystring.com/login.asp?login=testing.

This query string data can then be requested later by using Request.QueryString("login").

What is Absolute and Sliding expiration?

Absolute Expiration allows you to specify the duration of the cache, starting from the time the cache is activated. The following example shows that the cache has a cache dependency specified, as well as an expiration time of one minute.

> *Cache.Insert("announcement", announcement, depends, _*
>
> *DateTime.Now.AddMinutes(1), Nothing)*

Sliding Expiration specifies that the cache will expire if a request is not made within a specified duration. Sliding expiration policy is useful whenever you have a large number of items that need to be cached, because this policy enables you to keep only the most frequently accessed items in memory. For example, the following code specifies that the cache will have a sliding duration of one minute. If a request is made 59 seconds after the cache is accessed, the validity of the cache would be reset to another minute:

```
Cache.Insert("announcement", announcement, depends, _
DateTime.MaxValue, _
TimeSpan.FromMinutes(1))
```

What is cross page posting?

> **Note:** *This is a feature in ASP.NET 2.0*

By default, button controls in ASP.NET pages post back to the same page that contains the button, where you can write an event handler for the post. In most cases this is the desired behavior, but occasionaly you will also want to be able to post to another page in your application. The Server.Transfer method can be used to move between pages, however the URL does not change. Instead, the cross page-posting feature in ASP.NET 2.0 allows you to fire a normal post back to a different page in the application. In the target page, you can then access the values of server controls in the source page that initiated the post back.

To use cross page posting, you can set the PostBackUrl property of a Button, LinkButton or ImageButton control, which specifies the target page. In the target page, you can then access the PreviousPage property to retrieve values from the source page. By default, the PreviousPage property is of type Page, so you must access controls using the FindControl method. You can also enable strongly-typed access to the source page by setting the @PreviousPageType directive in the target page to the virtual path or Type name of the source page.

Here is a systematic guide for implementing the cross-page post back using controls that implement the IButtonControl interface.

- Create a Web Form and insert a Button control on it using the VS .NET designer.
- Set the button's PostBackUrl property to the Web Form you want to post back. For instance in this case it is "nextpage.aspx"

> *<asp:Button ID="Button1" runat="server"*
>
> *PostBackUrl="~/nextpage.aspx" Text="Post to nextpage" />*

When the PostBackUrl property of the IButtonControl is set, the ASP.NET framework binds the corresponding HTML element to new JavaScript function named WebForm_DoPostBackWithOptions. The corresponding HTML rendered by the ASP.NET 2.0 will look like this:

```
<input type="submit" name="Button1" value="Post to Page 2"
onclick="javascript:WebForm_DoPostBackWithOptions(new
WebForm_PostBackOptions("Button1", ",false","Page2.aspx", false, false))"
id="Button1" />
```

How do we access viewstate value of the current page in the next page ?

View state is page specific; it contains information about controls embedded on the particular page. ASP.NET 2.0 resolves this by embedding a hidden input field name, __POSTBACK. This field is embedded only when there is an IButtonControl on the page and its PostBackUrl property is set to a non-null value. This field contains the view state information of the poster page. To access the view state of the poster page, you can use the new PreviousPage property of the page:

> Page poster = this.PreviousPage;

Then you can find any control from the previous page and read its state:

> Label posterLabel = poster.findControl("myLabel");
> string lbl = posterLabel.Text;

This cross-page post back feature also solves the problem of posting a Form to multiple pages, because each control, in theory, can point to different post back URL.

Can we post and access view state in another ASP.NET page?

You cannot access view state in other pages directly. You can use the previous page property of post back if you want to access.

What is SQL Cache Dependency in ASP.NET 2.0?

SQL Cache dependency helps to cache tables in ASP.NET application in memory. So rather than making SQL server trips we can fetch the data from the cached object from ASP.NET.

How do we enable SQL Cache Dependency in ASP.NET 2.0?

Below are the broader steps to enable a SQL Cache Dependency:
- Enable notifications for the database.
- Enable notifications for individual tables.
- Enable ASP.NET polling using "web.config" file.
- Finally use the Cache dependency object in your ASP.NET code

Enable notifications for the database.

Before you can use SQL Server cache invalidation, you need to enable notifications for the database. This task is performed with the aspnet_regsql.exe command-line utility, which is located in the c:\[WinDir]\Microsoft.NET\Framework\[Version] directory.

```
aspnet_regsql -ed -E -d Northwind

-ed: command-line switch
-E: Use trusted connection
-S: Specify server name it other than the current computer you are working
on
-d: Database Name
```

So now, let us try to understand what happens in the database because of "aspnet_regsql.exe". After we execute the "aspnet_regsql -ed -E -d Northwind" command you will see one new table and four new stored procedures created.

Figure 5.19: SQL Cache table created for notification

Essentially, when a change takes place, a record is written in this table. The SQL Server polling queries this table for changes.

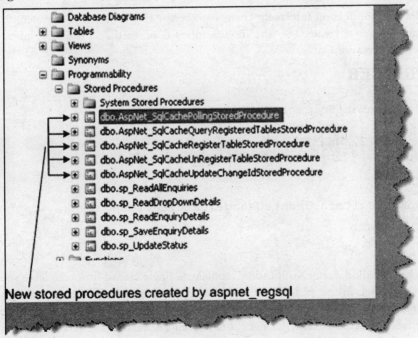

Figure 5.20: Stored procedures

Just to make brief run of what the stored procedures do.

"AspNet_SqlCacheRegisterTableStoredProcedure": This stored procedure sets a table to support notifications. This process works by adding a notification trigger to the table, which will fire when any row is inserted, deleted, or updated.

"AspNet_SqlCacheUnRegisterTableStoredProcedure": This stored procedure takes a registered table and removes the notification trigger so that notifications won't be generated.

"AspNet_SqlCacheUpdateChangeIdStoredProcedure": The notification trigger calls this stored procedure to update the AspNet_SqlCacheTablesForChangeNotification table, thereby indicating that the table has changed.

AspNet_SqlCacheQueryRegisteredTablesStoredProcedure: This extracts just the table names from the AspNet_SqlCacheTablesForChangeNotification table. It is used to get a quick look at all the registered tables.

AspNet_SqlCachePollingStoredProcedure: This will get the list of changes from the AspNet_SqlCacheTablesForChangeNotification table. It is used to perform polling.

Enabling notification for individual tables

Once the necessary stored procedure and tables are created then we have to notify saying which table needs to be enabled for notifications.

That can be achieved by two ways:

- aspnet_regsql -et -E -d Northwind -t Products
- Exec spNet_SqlCacheRegisterTableStoredProcedure 'TableName'

Registering tables for notification internally creates triggerfor the tables. For instance, for a "products" table the following trigger is created. So any modifications done to the "Products" table will update the "AspNet_SqlCacheNotification' table.

CREATE TRIGGER

```
dbo.[Products_AspNet_SqlCacheNotification_Trigger] ON
[Products]
FOR INSERT, UPDATE, DELETE
AS
BEGIN
SET NOCOUNT ON
EXEC dbo.AspNet_SqlCacheUpdateChangeIdStoredProcedure
N'Products'
END
```

"AspNet_SqlCacheTablesForChangeNotification" contains a single record for every table you're monitoring. When you make a change in the table (such as inserting, deleting or updating a record), the change Id column is incremented by 1.ASP.NET queries this table repeatedly keeps track of the most recent changed values for every table. When this value changes in a subsequent read, ASP.NET knows that the table has changed.

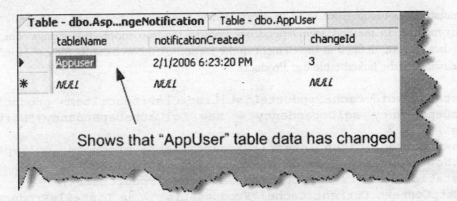

Figure 5.21: Notification tables

Enable ASP.NET polling using "web.config" file

Now that all our database side is configured in order to get the SQL Cache working in the ASP.NET side we need to do some configuration in the web.config file.

We need to set two attributes in the "web.config" file:

● Set "Enabled" attribute to true to set the caching on.

● Set the poll time attribute to the number of milliseconds between each poll

Below is the snapshot of the web.config file.

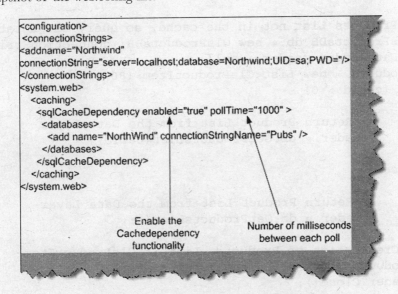

Figure 5.22: Cache dependency

Finally use the Cache dependency object in your ASP.NET code

Now comes the final step to use our cache dependency with programmatic data caching, a data source control, and output caching.

For programmatic data caching, we need to create a new SqlCacheDependency and supply that to the Cache.Insert() method. In the SqlCacheDependency constructor, you supply two strings. The first is the name of the database you defined in the element in the section of the web.config file e.g: Northwind. The second is the name of the linked table e.g: Products.

```
private static void CacheProductsList(List<ClsProductItem> products)
{SqlCacheDependency sqlDependency = new SqlCacheDependency("Northwind",
"Products");
HttpContext.Current.Cache.Insert("ProductsList", products, sqlDependency,
DateTime.Now.AddDays(1), Cache.NoSlidingExpiration);}
private static List<ClsProductItem> GetCachedProductList()
{return HttpContext.Current.Cache["ProductsList"] as List<ClsProductItem>;}
```

ClsProductItem is business class, and here we are trying to cache a list of ClsProductItem instead of DataSet or DataTable.

The following method is used by an ObjectDataSource Control to retrieve List of Products

```
public static List<ClsProductItem> GetProductsList(int catId, string sortBy)
{
     //Try to Get Products List from the Cache
     List<ClsProductItem> products = GetCachedProductList();
     if (products == null)
     {
          //Products List not in the cache, so query the Database layer
          ClsProductsDB db = new ClsProductsDB(_connectionString);
          DbDataReader reader = null;
          products = new List<ClsProductItem>(80);
          if (catId > 0)
          {
               //Return Product List from the Data Layer
               reader = db.GetProductsList(catId);
          }
          else
          {
               //Return Product List from the Data Layer
               reader = db.GetProductsList();
          }
          //Create List of Products -List if ClsProductItem-
          products = BuildProductsList(reader);
          reader.Close();

          //Add entry to products list in the Cache
          CacheProductsList(products);

     }
     products.Sort(new ClsProductItemComparer(sortBy));
```

```
    if (sortBy.Contains("DESC")) products.Reverse();
    return products;

}
```

To perform the same trick with output caching, you simply need to set the SqlDependency property with the database dependency name and the table name, separated by a colon:

<%@ *OutputCache Duration="600" SqlDependency="Northwind:Products" VaryByParam="none"* %>

The same technique works with the SqlDataSource and ObjectDataSource controls:

<asp:SqlDataSource EnableCaching="True" SqlCacheDependency="Northwind:Products" ... />

Note: *ObjectDataSource doesn't support built in caching for Custom types such as the one in our example. It only supports this feature for DataSets and DataTables.*

Just to make a sample check run the SQL Server profiler and see that does the SQL actually hit the database after the first run.

What is Post Cache substitution?

Post cache substitution is used when we want to cache the whole page but we also need some dynamic region inside that cached page. Some examples like QuoteoftheDay, RandomPhotos, and AdRotator etc. are examples where we can implement Post Cache Substitution.

Post-cache substitution can be achieved by two means:

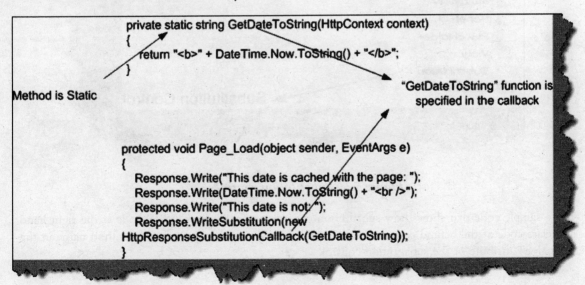

Figure 5.23: "Writesubstitution" in action

- Call the new Response.WriteSubstitution method, passing it a reference to the desired substitution method callback.

- Add a <asp:Substitution> control to the page at the desired location, and set its methodName attribute to the name of the callback method.

You can see we have a static function here "GetDateToString()". We pass the response substitution callback to the "WriteSubstitution" method. So now, when ASP.NET page framework retrieves the cached page, it automatically triggers your callback method to get the dynamic content. It then inserts your content into the cached HTML of the page. Even if your page has not been cached yet (for example, it's being rendered for the first time), ASP.NET still calls your callback in the same way to get the dynamic content. So you create a method that generates some dynamic content, and by doing so you guarantee that your method is always called, and it's content is never cached.

Ok the below example was by using "WriteSubstitution" now let's try to see how we can do by using "<asp:substitution>" control. You can get the "<asp:substitution>" control from the editor toolbox.

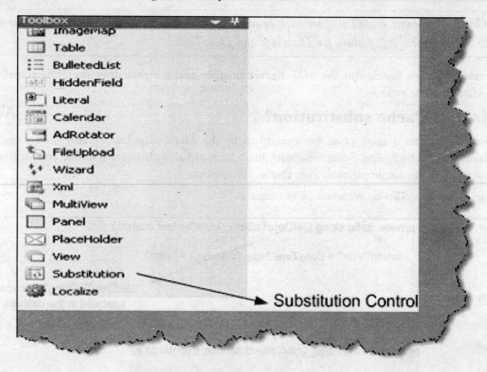

Figure 5.24: Substitution control

Below is a sample code that shows how substitution control works. We have ASPX code at the right hand side and class code at the behind code at the left hand side. We need to provide the method name in the "methodname" attribute of the substitution control.

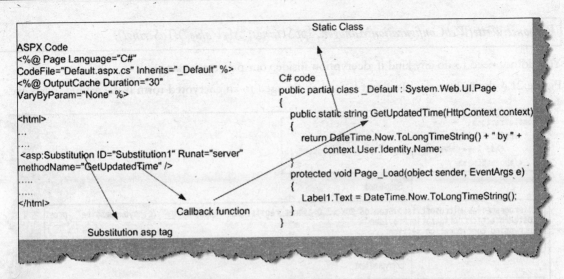

Figure 5.25: How Substitution control works

Why do we need methods to be static for Post Cache substitution?

ASP.NET should be able to call this method even when there is no instance of your page class available. When your page is served from the cache, the page object is not created. Therefore, ASP.NET skips the page life cycle when the page is coming from cache, which means it will not create any control objects or raise any control events. If your dynamic content depends on the values of other controls, you will need to use a different technique, because these control objects will not be available to your callback

How do we encrypt web.config files in ASP.NET?

Encryption can be done in ASP.NET using the "aspnet_regiis.exe" tool. There are two encryption options provided by ASP.NET:

Windows Data Protection API (DPAPI) Provider (DataProtectionConfigurationProvider) - this provider uses the built-in cryptography capabilities of Windows to encrypt and decrypt the configuration sections. By default this provider uses the machine's key.

RSA Protected Configuration Provider (RSAProtectedConfigurationProvider) - uses RSA public key encryption to encrypt/decrypt the configuration sections. With this provider you need to create key containers that hold the public and private keys used for encrypting and decrypting the configuration information.

While encrypting the config files we can choose what kind of provider we need for encryption. So let's understand step by step how we can actually encrypt the web.config file sections.

Step 1: Go to the command prompt of the framework.

Step 2: Run the aspnet_regiis.exe as shown in the figure. We have provided the section which we need to encrypt and the provider. If the command is successfully executed, you should get a succeeded message of encryption. You can see we have decrypted the appSettings section. We have also shown how the unencrypted config file looks after running aspnet_regiis.exe.

Step 3: Once the file is encrypted you can use the same in your program in a normal fashion. For instance the below defined appSetting key "MyValue" in figure "aspnet_regiis.exe in Action" can be displayed simply by:

> *Response.Write(WebConfigurationManager.AppSettings("MyValue").ToString())*

You do not need to do any kind if decryption inside your program again.

Figure 21.4 shows how the plain text is further changed to an encrypted form using aspnet_regiis.exe.

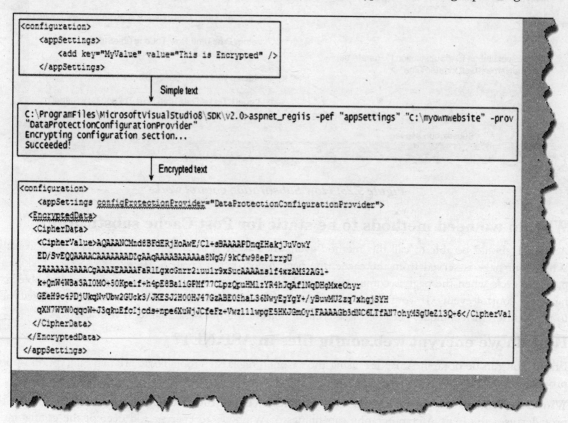

Figure 5.26: Encryption

Below is the aspnet_regiis in different forms for your referral.

```
- Generic form for encrypting the Web.config file for a particular
website...
aspnet_regiis.exe -pef section physical_directory -prov provider
 - or -
aspnet_regiis.exe -pe section -app virtual_directory -prov provider


- Concrete example of encrypting the Web.config file for a
particular website

aspnet_regiis.exe -pef "connectionStrings" "C:\Inetpub\wwwroot\MySite" -
prov "DataProtectionConfigurationProvider"
```

```
— or —
aspnet_regiis.exe -pe "connectionStrings" -app "/MyWebSite" -prov
"DataProtectionConfigurationProvider"
```

— Generic form for decrypting the Web.config file for a particular website...
```
aspnet_regiis.exe -pdf section physical_directory
 — or —
aspnet_regiis.exe -pd section -app virtual_directory
```

— Concrete example of decrypting the Web.config file for a particular website...
```
aspnet_regiis.exe -pdf "connectionStrings" "C:\Inetpub\wwwroot\MyWebSite"
 — or —
aspnet_regiis.exe -pd "connectionStrings" -app "/MyWebSite"
```

In .NET 1.X how was the encryption implemented for config files?

Encrypting in .NET 1.X was a bit different and cryptic as compared to ASP.NET 2.0. It is a three step procedure to implement encryption of config files:

Step 1: Use the aspnet_setreg.exe to make a registry entry using the following command. "-k" is the keyname in the registry and "-c" is the key value.

> *aspnet_setreg.exe-k:SOFTWARE\Your_Service\SessionState -*
> *c:myConnectionString="DSN=test;uid=test;pwd=test;"*

Step 2: We give the registry path with the key name "myConnectionString" in the value attribute.

```
<appSettings>
<add key="myConnectionString"
value="registry:HKLM\SOFTWARE\Your_Service\SessionState\ASPNET_SETREG,myConnectionString"
/>
```

Step 3: In the code we need to finally decrypt the connection string. For that we need to use Ncrypto DLL.

> **Note:** *We have provided the same in the CD zipped in "aspnetreg.zip" file. It has the aspnet_setreg.exe and also the Ncrypto DLL. You can use the DLL and practice the same on .NET 1.X*

In the code we need to decrypt back the value so that we can get original string in the process. Below code snippet "Decrypting the connectionstring" shows step by step how the decryption process happens. In the below code there are four important steps we need to understand.

Step 1: We need to take the path value using the split section. In step 1 we have taken out the path using the ":" and "," separator.

Step 2: Using the "OpenSubKey" function we open a connection to the path which we just obtained from parsing.

Step 3: We get the value in byte array.

Step 4: We decode the byte array back in to a string value using the "Unprotect" function.

```
using NCrypto.Security.Cryptography;
private string DecryptString()
{
string pConnectionString = ConfigurationSettings.AppSettings _
["myConnectionString"]
string smyConnectionString = null;
try
{
     registry:HKLM\SOFTWARE\Your_Service\SessionState\ASPNET_SETREG,myConnectionString

char[] cSeparators = {':', ','};
byte[] registryBytes;
//Split the value using : character
string[] regKeyPath = pConnectionString.Split(cSeparators[0]);    ──> Step 1
//Get the Registry Key path
regKeyPath = regKeyPath[1].Split(cSeparators[1]);
RegistryKey regKeyHive = Registry.LocalMachine;
RegistryKey regKey = regKeyHive.OpenSubKey(regKeyPath[0].Replace("HKLM\\", ""));  ──> Step 2
//get the encrypted value
registryBytes = (byte[])regKey.GetValue(regKeyPath[1]);    ──> Step 3
//Decrypt the value into Connection String
smyConnectionString = Encoding.Unicode.GetString( _
ProtectedData.Unprotect(registryBytes));    ──> Step 4
smyConnectionString = smyConnectionString.Replace( _
regKeyPath[1] + "=", "");
}
catch(Exception e)
{

}
return smyConnectionString;
}
```

Figure 5.27: 1.1 encryption

Note: *This is on the marked improvements in ASP.NET 2.0 we do not need to write a decrypt function. In short we just do the encryption using aspnet_regiis.exe and then call then just read the config value.*

How do you send an email using ASP.NET ?

We need to import the 'System.Web.Mail' namespace and use SMTP (Simple mail transfer protocol) component for the same. Below is the code snippet for the same.

```
// create the mail message
MailMessage objEmail = new MailMessage();
objEmail.To = "shiv_koirala@yahoo.com";
objEmail.From = "shiv_koirala@yahoo.com";
objEmail.Cc = "shiv_koirala@yahoo.com";
objEmail.Subject= "Test Email";
```

```
objEmail.Body= "Hi This is test email";
// finally send the email
SmtpMail.Send(objEmail);
```

How did you do deployment and setup in ASP.NET ?

Below are the steps to prepare deployment and setup in ASP.NET.

Step 1 → Click on File → New project → Setup and Deployment → Web setup project.

Step 2 → Right click on the 'Web Application Folder' as shown in figure 'IIS Web application properties' and click 'Properties Window'. You will be popped with all necessary properties needed to set the IIS web application property. To understand how the mapping works in the same figure we have shown the IIS website dialog box mapped to the properties of 'Web application folder' property in the setup.

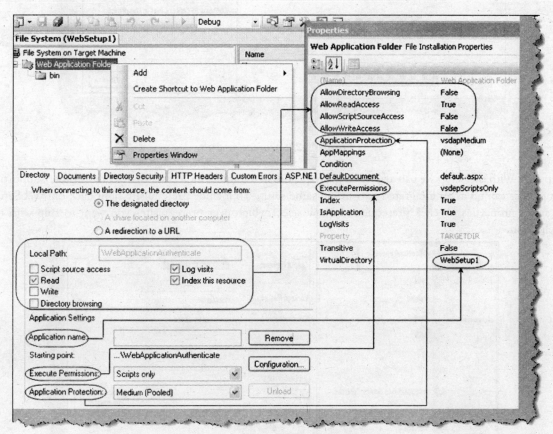

Figure 5.28: IIS web application properties

Step 3 → We now need to specify the application whose setup needs to be prepared. So click on file → add existing project → selection the solution and add it to the IDE. Now we need to add the output binary files to the setup. So go to the setup project → click add → project output → select content files and click ok.

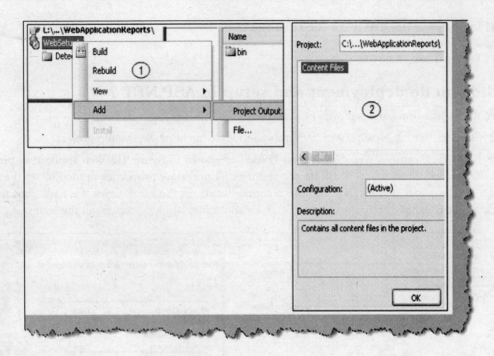

Figure 5.29: project output

Step 4 → With the setup we can also need prerequisites like framework, crystal setup or any other supporting setup. This can go as an integrated part in the same setup. To include prerequisite right click on 'WebSetup' → select properties → click prerequisites. Now select which ever prerequisites you want to ship with the application.

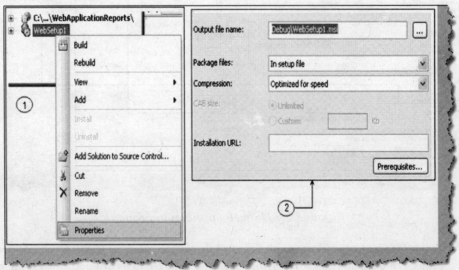

Figure 5.30: Prerequisites in Websetup

Once done compile the setup and you should see the setup is created.

6
MVC (Model View Controller)

Note: *In case you are new to MVC, see 4 videos Learn MVC step by step videos given in DVD.*

What is MVC?

MVC is an architectural pattern which separates the representation and the user interaction. It's divided in to three broader sections, "Model", "View" and "Controller". Below is how each one of them handles the task.

- The "View" is responsible for look and feel.
- "Model" represents the real world object and provides data to the "View".
- The "Controller" is responsible to take the end user request and load the appropriate "Model" and "View".

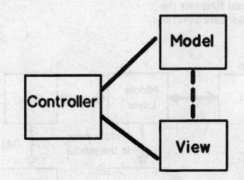

Figure 6.1: MVC (Model view controller)

Can you explain the complete flow of MVC?

Below are the steps how control flows in MVC (Model, view and controller) architecture:

- All end user requests are first sent to the controller.
- The controller depending on the request decides which model to load. The controller loads the model and attaches the model with the appropriate view.
- The final view is then attached with the model data and sent as a response to the end user on the browser.

Is MVC suitable for both windows and web application?

MVC architecture is suited for web application than windows. For window application MVP i.e. "Model view presenter" is more applicable.IfyouareusingWPFandSLMVVMismoresuitableduetobindings.

What are the benefits of using MVC?

There are two big benefits of MVC:

- Separation of concerns is achieved as we are moving the code behind to a separate class file. By moving the binding code to a separate class file we can reuse the code to a great extent.

- Automated UI testing is possible because now the behind code (UI interaction code) has moved to a simple.NET class. This gives us opportunity to write unit tests and automate manual testing.

Is MVC different from a 3 layered architecture?

MVC is an evolution of a 3 layered traditional architecture. Many components of 3 layered architecture are part of MVC. So below is how the mapping goes.

Functionality	3 layered / tiered architecture	Model view controller architecture
Look and Feel	User interface.	View.
UI logic	User interface.	Controller
Business logic /validations	Middle layer	Model.
Request is first sent to	User interface	Controller.
Accessing data	Data access layer.	Data access layer.

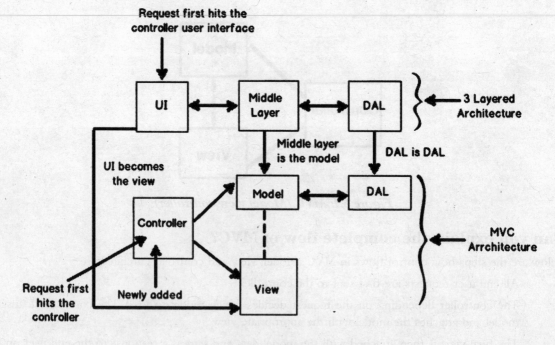

Figure 6.2: 3 layered architecture

What is the latest version of MVC?

When this note was written, four versions where released of MVC. MVC 1, MVC 2, MVC 3 and MVC 4. So the latest is MVC 4.

What is the difference between each version of MVC?

Below is a detail table of differences. But during interview it's difficult to talk about all of them due to time limitation. So I have highlighted important differences which you can run through before the interviewer.

MVC 2	MVC 3	MVC 4
Client-Side Validation	**Razor**	**ASP.NET Web API**
Templated Helpers	Readymade project	Refreshed and modernized
Areas	templates	default project templates
Asynchronous Controllers	**HTML 5 enabled templates**	New mobile project
Html.ValidationSummary Helper Method	**Support for Multiple View**	template
DefaultValueAttribute in Action-Method	**Engines**	**Many new features to**
Parameters	**JavaScript and Ajax**	**support mobile apps**
Binding Binary Data with Model Binders	Model Validation	Enhanced support for
DataAnnotations Attributes	Improvements	asynchronous methods
Model-Validator Providers		
New RequireHttpsAttribute Action Filter		
Templated Helpers		
Display Model-Level Errors		

What are routing in MVC?

Routing helps you to define a URL structure and map the URL with the controller.

For instance let's say we want that when any user types "http://localhost/View/ViewCustomer/", it goes to the "Customer" Controller and invokes "DisplayCustomer" action. This is defined by adding an entry in to the "routes" collection using the "maproute" function. Below is the under lined code which shows how the URL structure and mapping with controller and action is defined.

```
routes.MapRoute(
      "View", // Route name
      "View/ViewCustomer/{id}", // URL with parameters
      new { controller = "Customer", action = "DisplayCustomer", id
= UrlParameter.Optional }); // Parameter defaults
```

Where is the route mapping code written?

The route mapping code is written in the "global.asax" file.

Can we map multiple URL's to the same action?

Yes, you can, you just need to make two entries with different key names and specify the same controller and action.

How can we navigate from one view to other view using hyperlink?

By using "ActionLink" method as shown in the below code. The below code will create a simple URL which help to navigate to the "Home" controller and invoke the "GotoHome" action.

```
<%= Html.ActionLink("Home","Gotohome") %>
```

How can we restrict MVC actions to be invoked only by GET or POST?

We can decorate the MVC action by "HttpGet" or "HttpPost" attribute to restrict the type of HTTP calls. For instance you can see in the below code snippet the "DisplayCustomer" action can only be invoked by "HttpGet". If we try to make Http post on "DisplayCustomer" it will throw an error.

```
[HttpGet]
public ViewResult DisplayCustomer(int id)
{
Customer objCustomer = Customers[id];

return View("DisplayCustomer",objCustomer);
}
```

How can we maintain session in MVC?

Sessions can be maintained in MVC by 3 ways tempdata, viewdata and viewbag.

What is the difference between tempdata, viewdata and viewbag?

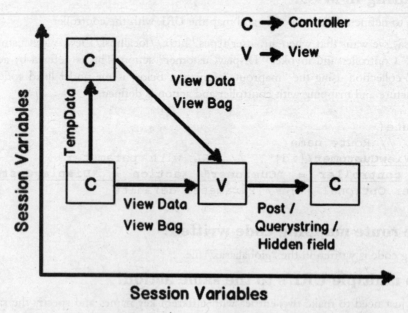

Figure 6.3: difference between tempdata, viewdata and viewbag

Temp data: Helps to maintain data when you move from one controller to other controller or from one action to other action. In other words when you redirect,"tempdata" helps to maintain data between those redirects. It internally uses session variables.

View data: Helps to maintain data when you move from controller to view.

View Bag: It's a dynamic wrapper around view data. When you use "Viewbag" type casting is not required. It uses the dynamic keyword internally.

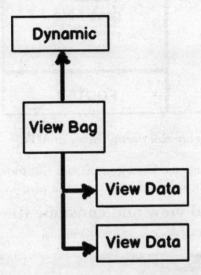

Figure 6.4:dynamic keyword

Session variables: By using session variables we can maintain data from any entity to any entity.

Hidden fields and HTML controls: Helps to maintain data from UI to controller only. So you can send data from HTML controls or hidden fields to the controller using POST or GET HTTP methods.

Below is a summary table which shows different mechanism of persistence.

Maintains data between	ViewData/ViewBag	TempData	Hidden fields	Session
Controller to Controller	No	Yes	No	Yes
Controller to View	Yes	No	No	Yes
View to Controller	No	No	Yes	Yes

What are partial views in MVC?

Partial view is a reusable view (like a user control) which can be embedded inside other view. For example let's say all your pages of your site have a standard structure with left menu, header and footer as shown in the image below.

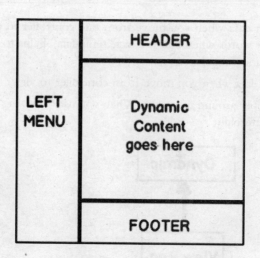

Figure 6.5: partial views in MVC

For every page you would like to reuse the left menu, header and footer controls. So you can go and create partial views for each of these items and then you call that partial view in the main view.

How did you create partial view and consume the same?

When you add a view to your project you need to check the "Create partial view" check box.

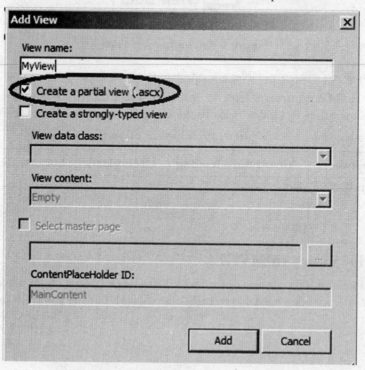

Figure6.6:createpartialview

Once the partial view is created you can then call the partial view in the main view using "Html.RenderPartial" method as shown in the below code snippet.

```
<body>
<div>
<% Html.RenderPartial("MyView"); %>
</div>
</body>
```

How can we do validations in MVC?

One of the easy ways of doing validation in MVC is by using data annotations. Data annotations are nothing but attributes which you can be applied on the model properties. For example in the below code snippet we have a simple "customer" class with a property "customercode".

This"CustomerCode" property is tagged with a "Required" data annotation attribute. In other words if this model is not provided customer code it will not accept the same.

```
public class Customer
{
     [Required(ErrorMessage="Customer code is required")]
     public string CustomerCode
     {
          set;
          get;
     }
}
```

In order to display the validation error message we need to use "ValidateMessageFor" method which belongs to the "Html" helper class.

```
<% using (Html.BeginForm("PostCustomer", "Home", FormMethod.Post))
{ %>
<%=Html.TextBoxFor(m => m.CustomerCode)%>
<%=Html.ValidationMessageFor(m => m.CustomerCode)%>
<input type="submit" value="Submit customer data" />
<%}%>
```

Later in the controller we can check if the model is proper or not by using "ModelState.IsValid" property and accordingly we can take actions.

```
public ActionResult PostCustomer(Customer obj)
{
     if (ModelState.IsValid)
     {
          obj.Save();
          return View("Thanks");
```

```
        }
        else
        {
                return View("Customer");
        }
}
```

Below is a simple view of how the error message is displayed on the view.

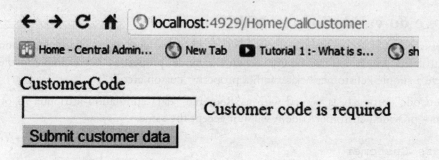

Figure 6.7: validations in MVC

Can we display all errors in one go?

Yes we can, use "ValidationSummary" method from HTML helper class.

```
<%= Html.ValidationSummary() %>
```

What are the other data annotation attributes for validation in MVC?

If you want to check string length, you can use "StringLength".

```
[StringLength(160)]
public string FirstName { get; set; }
```

In case you want to use regular expression, you can use "RegularExpression" attribute.

```
[RegularExpression(@"[A-Za-z0-9._%+-]+@[A-Za-z0-9.-]+\.[A-Za-z]{2,4}")]
public string Email { get; set; }
```

If you want to check whether the numbers are in range, you can use the "Range" attribute.

```
[Range(10,25)]
public int Age { get; set; }
```

Some time you would like to compare value of one field with other field, we can use the "Compare" attribute.

```
public string Password { get; set; }
[Compare("Password")]
public string ConfirmPass { get; set; }
```

In case you want to get a particular error message, you can use the "Errors" collection.

> *var ErrMessage = ModelState["Email"].Errors[0].ErrorMessage;*

If you have created the model object yourself you can explicitly call "TryUpdateModel" in your controller to check if the object is valid or not.

> *TryUpdateModel(NewCustomer);*

In case you want add errors in the controller you can use "AddModelError" function.

> *ModelState.AddModelError("FirstName", "This is my server-side error.");*

How can we enable data annotation validation on client side?

It's a two-step process first reference the necessary jquery files.

```
<script src="<%= Url.Content("~/Scripts/jquery-1.5.1.js") %>" type="text/
javascript"></script>
<script src="<%= Url.Content("~/Scripts/jquery.validate.js") %>" type="text/
javascript"></script>
<script src="<%= Url.Content("~/Scripts/jquery.validate.unobtrusive.js")
%>" type="text/javascript"></script>
```

Second step is to call "EnableClientValidation" method.

> *<% Html.EnableClientValidation(); %>*

What is razor in MVC?

It's a light weight view engine. Till MVC we had only one view type i.e.ASPX, Razor was introduced in MVC 3.

Why razor when we already had ASPX?

Razor is clean, lightweight and syntaxes are easy as compared to ASPX. For example in ASPX to display simple time we need to write.

> *<%=DateTime.Now%>*

In Razor it's just one line of code.

> *@DateTime.Now*

So which is a better fit Razor or ASPX?

As per Microsoft razor is more preferred because it's light weight and has simple syntaxes.

How can you do authentication and authorization in MVC?

You can use windows or forms authentication for MVC.

How to implement windows authentication for MVC?

For windows authentication you need to go and modify the "web.config" file and set authentication mode to windows.

```
<authentication mode="Windows"/>
<authorization>
      <deny users="?"/>
</authorization>
```

Then in the controller or on the action you can use the "Authorize" attribute which specifies which users have access to these controllers and actions. Below is the code snippet for the same. Now only the users specified in the controller and action can access the same.

```
[Authorize(Users= @"WIN-3LI600MWLQN\Administrator")]
public class StartController: Controller
{
    //
    // GET: /Start/
    [Authorize(Users = @"WIN-3LI600MWLQN\Administrator")]
    public ActionResult Index()
    {
        return View("MyView");
    }
}
```

How do you implement forms authentication in MVC?

Forms authentication is implemented the same way as we do in ASP.NET. So the first step is to set authentication mode equal to forms. The "loginUrl" points to a controller here rather than page.

```
<authentication mode="Forms">
<forms loginUrl="~/Home/Login" timeout="2880"/>
</authentication>
```

We also need to create a controller where we will check the user is proper or not. If the user is proper we will set the cookie value.

```
public ActionResult Login()
{
      if ((Request.Form["txtUserName"] == "Shiv") &&
      (Request.Form["txtPassword"] == "Shiv@123"))
      {
            FormsAuthentication.SetAuthCookie("Shiv",true);
            return View("About");
      }
      else
      {
            return View("Index");
      }

}
```

All the other actions need to be attributed with "Authorize" attribute so that any unauthorized user if he makes a call to these controllers it will redirect to the controller (in this case the controller is "Login") which will do authentication.

```
[Authorize]
PublicActionResult Default()
{
      return View();
}

[Authorize]
publicActionResult About()
{
      return View();
}
```

How to implement Ajax in MVC?

You can implement Ajax in two ways in MVC:

- Ajax libraries
- Jquery

Below is a simple sample of how to implement Ajax by using "Ajax" helper library. In the below code you can see we have a simple form which is created by using "Ajax.BeginForm" syntax. This form calls a controller action called as "getCustomer". So now the submit action click will be an asynchronous ajax call.

```
<script language="javascript">
function OnSuccess(data1)
{
      // Do something here
```

```
}
</script>
<div>
<%
var AjaxOpt = new AjaxOptions{OnSuccess="OnSuccess"};
%>
<% using (Ajax.BeginForm("getCustomer","MyAjax",AjaxOpt)) { %>
<input id="txtCustomerCode" type="text" /><br />
<input id="txtCustomerName" type="text" /><br />
<input id="Submit2" type="submit" value="submit"/></div>
<%} %>
```

In case you want to make ajax calls on hyperlink clicks you can use "Ajax.ActionLink" function as shown in the below code.

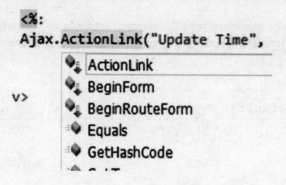

Figure 6.8: implement Ajax in MVC

So if you want to create Ajax asynchronous hyperlink by name "GetDate" which calls the "GetDate" function on the controller, below is the code for the same. Once the controller responds this data is displayed in the HTML DIV tag by name "DateDiv".

```
<span id="DateDiv" />
<%:
Ajax.ActionLink("Get Date","GetDate",
new AjaxOptions {UpdateTargetId = "DateDiv" })
%>
```

Below is the controller code. You can see how "GetDate" function has a pause of 10 seconds.

```
public class Default1Controller: Controller
{
        public string GetDate()
        {
                Thread.Sleep(10000);
```

```
                    return DateTime.Now.ToString();
        }
}
```

The second way of making Ajax call in MVC is by using Jquery. In the below code you can see we are making an ajax POST call to a URL "/MyAjax/getCustomer". This is done by using "$.post". All this logic is put in to a function called as "GetData" and you can make a call to the "GetData" function on a button or a hyper link click event as you want.

```
function GetData()
{
        var url = "/MyAjax/getCustomer";
        $.post(url, function (data)
        {

            $("#txtCustomerCode").val(data.CustomerCode);
            $("#txtCustomerName").val(data.CustomerName);
        }
        )
}
```

What kind of events can be tracked in AJAX ?

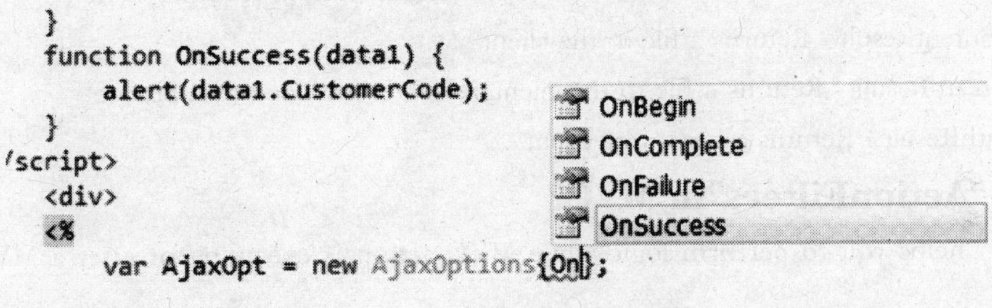

```
        }
        function OnSuccess(data1) {
            alert(data1.CustomerCode);
        }
    /script>
        <div>
        <%
            var AjaxOpt = new AjaxOptions{On};
```

OnBegin
OnComplete
OnFailure
OnSuccess

Figure 6.9: tracked in AJAX

What is the difference between "ActionResult" and "ViewResult"?

"ActionResult" is anabstract class while "ViewResult" derives from "ActionResult" class. "ActionResult" has several derived classes like "ViewResult","JsonResult", "FileStreamResult" and so on.

"ActionResult" can be used to exploit polymorphism and dynamism. So if you are returning different types of view dynamically "ActionResult" is the best thing. For example in the below code snippet you can see we have a simple action called as "DynamicView". Depending on the flag ("IsHtmlView") it will either return "ViewResult" or "JsonResult".

```
public ActionResult DynamicView()
{
        if (IsHtmlView)
```

```
            return View(); // returns simple ViewResult
    else
            return Json(); // returns JsonResult view
}
```

What are the different types of results in MVC?

> **Note:** *It's difficult to remember all the 12 types. But some important ones you can remember for the interview are "ActionResult", "ViewResult" and "JsonResult". Below is a detailed list for your interest.*

There 12 kinds of results in MVC, at the top is "ActionResult"class which is a base class that canhave 11subtypes'sas listed below:

1.   ViewResult - Renders a specified view to the response stream

2.   PartialViewResult - Renders a specified partial view to the response stream

3.   EmptyResult - An empty response is returned

4.   RedirectResult - Performs an HTTP redirection to a specified URL

5.   RedirectToRouteResult - Performs an HTTP redirection to a URL that is determined by the routing engine, based on given route data

6.   JsonResult - Serializes a given ViewData object to JSON format

7.   JavaScriptResult - Returns a piece of JavaScript code that can be executed on the client

8.   ContentResult - Writes content to the response stream without requiring a view

9.   FileContentResult - Returns a file to the client

10.   FileStreamResult - Returns a file to the client, which is provided by a Stream

11.   FilePathResult - Returns a file to the client

What are "ActionFilters"in MVC?

"ActionFilters" helps you to perform logic while MVC action is executing or after a MVC action has executed.

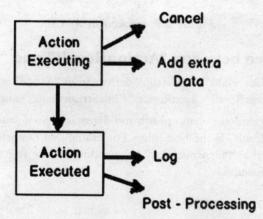

Figure 6.10: "ActionFilters"in MVC

Action filters are useful in the following scenarios:

1. Implement post-processinglogic beforethe action happens.

2. Cancel a current execution.

3. Inspect the returned value.

4. Provide extra data to the action.

You can create action filters by two ways:

● Inline action filter.

● Creating an "ActionFilter" attribute.

To create a inline action attribute we need to implement "IActionFilter" interface. The "IActionFilter" interface has two methods "OnActionExecuted" and "OnActionExecuting". We can implement pre-processing logic or cancellation logic in these methods.

```
public class Default1Controller: Controller, IActionFilter
{
        public ActionResult Index(Customer obj)
        {
                return View(obj);
        }
        void IActionFilter.OnActionExecuted(ActionExecutedContext
        filterContext)
        {
                Trace.WriteLine("Action Executed");
        }
        void IActionFilter.OnActionExecuting(ActionExecutingContext
        filterContext)
        {
                Trace.WriteLine("Action is executing");
        }
}
```

The problem with inline action attribute is that it cannot be reused across controllers. So we can convert the inline action filter to an action filter attribute. To create an action filter attribute we need to inherit from "ActionFilterAttribute" and implement "IActionFilter" interface as shown in the below code.

```
public class MyActionAttribute: ActionFilterAttribute, IActionFilter
{
        void IActionFilter.OnActionExecuted(ActionExecutedContext
        filterContext)
        {
                Trace.WriteLine("Action Executed");
        }

        void IActionFilter.OnActionExecuting(ActionExecutingContext
        filterContext)
```

```
{
      Trace.WriteLine("Action executing");
}
}
```

Later we can decorate the controllers on which we want the action attribute to execute. You can see in the below code I have decorated the "Default1Controller" with "MyActionAttribute" class which was created in the previous code.

```
[MyActionAttribute]
public class Default1Controller: Controller
{
      public ActionResult Index(Customer obj)
      {
            return View(obj);
      }
}
```

Can we create our custom view engine using MVC?

Yes, we can create our own custom view engine in MVC. To create our own custom view engine we need to follow 3 steps:

Let' say we want to create a custom view engine where in the user can type a command like "<DateTime>" and it should display the current date and time.

Step 1: We need to create a class which implements "IView" interface. In this class we should write the logic of how the view will be rendered in the "render" function. Below is a simple code snippet for the same.

```
public class MyCustomView: IView
{

      private string _FolderPath; // Define where our views are stored

      public string FolderPath
      {
            get { return _FolderPath; }
            set { _FolderPath = value; }
      }

      public void Render(ViewContext viewContext, System.IO.TextWriter
      writer)
      {
            // Parsing logic <dateTime>
            // read the view file
            string strFileData = File.ReadAllText(_FolderPath);
```

```
                // we need to and replace <datetime> datetime.now value
                string strFinal = strFileData.Replace("<DateTime>",
                DateTime.Now.ToString());
                // this replaced data has to sent for display
                writer.Write(strFinal);


        }

 }
```

Step 2: We need to create a class which inherits from "VirtualPathProviderViewEngine" and in this class we need to provide the folder path and the extension of the view name. For instance for razor the extension is "cshtml", for aspx the view extension is ".aspx", so in the same way for our custom view we need to provide an extension. Below is how the code looks like. You can see the "ViewLocationFormats" is set to the "Views" folder and the extension is ".myview".

```
public class MyViewEngineProvider: VirtualPathProviderViewEngine
{
        // We will create the object of Mycustome view
        public MyViewEngineProvider() // constructor
        {
                // Define the location of the View file
                this.ViewLocationFormats = new string[] { "~/Views/{1}/
                {0}.myview", "~/Views/Shared/{0}.myview" }; //location and
                extension of our views
        }

        protected override IView CreateView(ControllerContext
        controllerContext, string viewPath, string masterPath)
        {
                var physicalpath =
                controllerContext.HttpContext.Server.MapPath(viewPath);
                MyCustomView obj = new MyCustomView(); // Custom view engine
                class
                obj.FolderPath = physicalpath; // set the path where the views
                will be stored
                return obj; // returned this view paresing logic so that it
                can be registered in the view engine collection
        }
        protected override IView CreatePartialView(ControllerContext
        controllerContext, string partialPath)
        {
                var physicalpath =
                controllerContext.HttpContext.Server.MapPath(partialPath);
                MyCustomView obj = new MyCustomView(); // Custom view engine
                class
```

```
          obj.FolderPath = physicalpath; // set the path where the views
          will be stored
          return obj; // returned this view paresing logic so that it
          can be registered in the view engine collection
     }
}
```

Step 3: We need to register the view in the custom view collection. The best place to register the custom view engine in the "ViewEngines" collection is the "global.asax" file. Below is the code snippet for the same.

```
protected void Application_Start()
{
     // Step3: register this object in the view engine collection
     ViewEngines.Engines.Add(new MyViewEngineProvider());
     …..
}
```

Below is a simple output of the custom view written using the commands defined at the top.

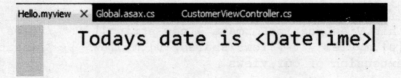

Figure6.11:customviewengineusingMVC

If you invoke this view you should see the following output.

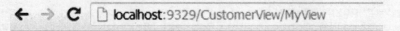

Todays date is 1/17/2013 10:23:39 AM

Figure 6.12: output

How to send result back in JSON format in MVC?

In MVC we have "JsonResult" class by which we can return back data in JSON format. Below is a simple sample code which returns back "Customer" object in JSON format using "JsonResult".

```
public JsonResult getCustomer()
{
     Customer obj = new Customer();
     obj.CustomerCode = "1001";
     obj.CustomerName = "Shiv";
```

```
        return Json(obj,JsonRequestBehavior.AllowGet);
}
```

Below is the JSON output of the above code if you invoke the action via the browser.

← → C 🗋 localhost:1402/Myajax/getCustomer

{"CustomerCode":"1001","CustomerName":"Shiv"}

Figure 6.13: JSON format in MVC

What is "WebAPI"?

HTTP is the most used protocol.For past many years browser was the most preferred client by which we can consume data exposed over HTTP. But as years passed by client variety started spreading out. We had demand to consume data on HTTP from clients like mobile,javascripts,windows application etc.

For satisfying the broad range of client "REST" was the proposed approach. You can read more about "REST" from WCF chapter.

"WebAPI" is the technology by which you can expose data over HTTP following REST principles.

But WCF SOAP also does the same thing, so how does "WebAPI" differ?

	SOAP	WEB API
Size	Heavy weight because of complicated WSDL structure.	Light weight, only the necessary information is transferred.
Protocol	Independent ofprotocols.	Only for HTTP protocol
Formats	To parse SOAP message, the client needs to understand WSDL format. Writing custom code for parsing WSDL is a heavy duty task. If your client is smart enough to create proxy objects like how we have in .NET (add reference) then SOAP is easier to consume and call.	Output of "WebAPI" are simple string message, JSON, Simple XML format etc. So writing parsing logic for the same in very easy.
Principles	SOAP follows WS-* specification.	WEB API follows REST principles. (Please refer about REST in WCF chapter).

With WCF also you can implement REST, So why "WebAPI"?

WCF was brought in to implement SOA, never the intention was to implement REST."WebAPI'" is built from scratch and the only goal is to create HTTP services using REST. Due to the one point focus for creating "REST" service "WebAPI" is more preferred.

How to implement "WebAPI" in MVC?

Below are the steps to implement "webAPI":

Step1: Create the project using the "WebAPI" template.

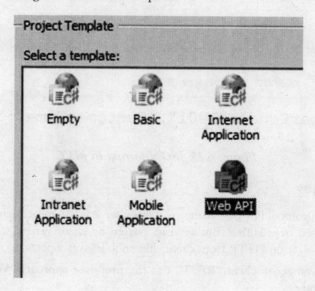

Figure 6.14: implement "WebAPI" in MVC

Step 2: Once you have created the project you will notice that the controller now inherits from "ApiController" and you can now implement "post","get","put" and "delete" methods of HTTP protocol.

```
public class ValuesController: ApiController
{
     // GET api/values
     public IEnumerable<string> Get()
     {
          return new string[] { "value1", "value2" };
     }

     // GET api/values/5
     public string Get(int id)
     {
          return "value";
     }

     // POST api/values
     public void Post([FromBody]string value)
     {
     }

     // PUT api/values/5
     public void Put(int id, [FromBody]string value)
     {
```

```
    }

    // DELETE api/values/5
    public void Delete(int id)
    {
    }
}
```

Step 3: If you make a HTTP GET call you should get the below results.

```
← → C  🗋 localhost:50465/Api/Values

This XML file does not appear to have

▼<ArrayOfstring xmlns:i="http:/
 xmlns="http://schemas.microsof
    <string>value1</string>
    <string>value2</string>
 </ArrayOfstring>
```

Figure 6.15: HTTP

7

SQL SERVER

What is normalization?

Note: *A regular .NET programmer working on projects often stumbles in this question, which is but obvious. Bad part is sometimes interviewer can take this as a very basic question to be answered and it can be a turning point for the interview. So let's cram it.*

It is set of rules that have been established to aid in the design of tables that are meant to be connected through relationships. This set of rules is known as Normalization.

Benefits of normalizing your database will include:

- Avoiding repetitive entries
- Reducing required storage space
- Preventing the need to restructure existing tables to accommodate new data.
- Increased speed and flexibility of queries, sorts, and summaries.

Note: *During interview candidates are expected to answer minimum three normal forms.*

Following are the three normal forms:

First Normal Form

For a table to be in first normal form, data must be broken up into the smallest units possible. In addition to breaking data up into the smallest meaningful values, tables in first normal form should not contain repetitions groups of fields.

Customer id	Customer Name	City1	City2	Unit Price	Qty	Total
3243244	Shivprasad koirala	xyz	PQR	1	12	12$
3043244	Sanjana koirala	xcv	123	10	1	10$

Figure 7.1: First Normal Form

For in the above example city1 and city2 are repeating. In order that this table to be in First normal form you have to modify the table structure as follows. Also not that the Customer Name is now broken down to first name and last name (First normal form data should be broken down to smallest unit).

Customer id	First Name	Last Name	City	Unit Price	Qty	Total
3243244	Shivprasad	Koirala	xyz	1	12	12$
3243244	Shivprasad	koirala	PQR	1	12	12$
3043244	Sanjana	koirala	xcv	2	20	40$
3043244	sanjana	Koirala	123	2	20	40$

Figure 7.2: Modified First Normal Form

Second Normal form

The second normal form states that each field in a multiple field primary key table must be directly related to the entire primary key. Or in other words, each non-key field should be a fact about all the fields in the primary key.

In the above table of customer, city is not linked to any primary field.

Customer id	First Name	Last Name	City	Unit Price	Qty	Total
3243244	Shivprasad	Koirala	xyz	1	12	12$
3243244	Shivprasad	koirala	PQR	1	12	12$
3043244	Sanjana	koirala	xcv	2	20	40$
3043244	sanjana	Koirala	123	2	20	40$

City id	City
1	xyz
2	PQR
3	xcv
4	123

Figure 7.3: Second Normal Form

That takes our database to a second normal form.

Third normal form

A non-key field should not depend on other Non-key field. The field "Total" is dependent on "Unit price" and "qty".

Customer id	First Name	Last Name	City	Unit Price	Qty
3243244	Shivprasad	Koirala	xyz	1	12
3243244	Shivprasad	koirala	PQR	1	12
3043244	Sanjana	koirala	xcv	2	20
3043244	sanjana	Koirala	123	2	20

Figure 7.4: Third Normal Form

So now the "Total" field is removed and is multiplication of Unit price * Qty.

Note: *Fourth and Fifth normal form is left as a home work to users.*

What is denormalization?

Denormalization is the process of putting one fact in numerous places (its vice-versa of normalization).Only one valid reason exists for denormalizing a relational design - to enhance performance or if we are doing data warehousing and data mining. The sacrifice to performance is that you increase redundancy in database.

What are the different types of joins? What is the difference between them ?

INNER JOIN

Inner join shows matches only when they exist in both tables. Example, in the below SQL there are two tables Customers and Orders and the inner join in made on Customers Customerid and Orders Customerid.So this SQL will only give you result with customers who have orders. If the customer does not have order, it will not display that record.

```
SELECT Customers.*, Orders.* FROM Customers INNER JOIN Orders ON Customers.CustomerID
=Orders.CustomerID
```

LEFT OUTER JOIN

Left join will display all records in left table of the SQL statement. In SQL below customers with or without orders will be displayed. Order data for customers without orders appears as NULL values. For example, you want to determine the amount ordered by each customer and you need to see who has not ordered anything as well. You can also see the LEFT OUTER JOIN as a mirror image of the RIGHT OUTER JOIN (Is covered in the next section) if you switch the side of each table.

> *SELECT Customers.*, Orders.* FROM Customers LEFT OUTER JOIN Orders ON Customers.CustomerID =Orders.CustomerID*

RIGHT OUTER JOIN

Right join will display all records in right table of the SQL statement. In SQL below all orders with or without matching customer records will be displayed. Customer data for orders without customers appears as NULL values. For example, you want to determine if there are any orders in the data with undefined CustomerID values (say, after a conversion or something like it). You can also see the RIGHT OUTER JOIN as a mirror image of the LEFT OUTER JOIN if you switch the side of each table.

> *SELECT Customers.*, Orders.* FROM Customers RIGHT OUTER JOIN Orders ON Customers.CustomerID =Orders.CustomerID*

What is a candidate key?

A table may have more than one combination of columns that could uniquely identify the rows in a table; each combination is a candidate key. During database design you can pick up one of the candidate keys to be the primary key. For example, in the supplier table supplierid and suppliername can be candidate key but you will only pick up supplierid as the primary key.

What are indexes and what is the difference between clustered and nonclustered?

Indexes in SQL Server are similar to the indexes in books. They help SQL Server retrieve the data quickly.

There are clustered and nonclustered indexes. A clustered index is a special type of index that reorders the way in which records in the table are physically stored. Therefore, table can have only one clustered index. The leaf nodes of a clustered index contain the data pages.

A nonclustered index is a special type of index in which the logical order of the index does not match the physical stored order of the rows on disk. The leaf node of a nonclustered index does not consist of the data pages. Instead, the leaf nodes contain index rows.

How can you increase SQL performance?

Following are tips which will increase your SQl performance:

- Every index increases the time takes to perform INSERTS, UPDATES, and DELETES, so the number of indexes should not be too much. Try to use maximum 4-5 indexes on one table, not more. If you have read-only table, then the number of indexes may be increased.

- Keep your indexes as narrow as possible. This reduces the size of the index and reduces the number of reads required to read the index.

- Try to create indexes on columns that have integer values rather than character values.

- If you create a composite (multi-column) index, the orders of the columns in the key are very important. Try to order the columns in the key as to enhance selectivity, with the most selective columns to the leftmost of the key.

- If you want to join several tables, try to create surrogate integer keys for this purpose and create indexes on their columns.

- Create surrogate integer primary key (identity for example) if your table will not have many insert operations.

- Clustered indexes are more preferable than nonclustered, if you need to select by a range of values or you need to sort results set with GROUP BY or ORDER BY.

- If your application will be performing the same query over and over on the same table, consider creating a covering index on the table.

- You can use the SQL Server Profiler Create Trace Wizard with "Identify Scans of Large Tables" trace to determine which tables in your database may need indexes. This trace will show which tables are being scanned by queries instead of using an index.

What is DTS?

DTS is used to import data and while importing it helps us to transform and modify data. The name itself is self explanatory DTS (Data transformation Services).

What is fill factor ?

The 'fill factor' option specifies how full SQL Server will make each index page. When there is no free space to insert new row on the index page, SQL Server will create new index page and transfer some rows from the previous page to the new one. This operation is called page splits. You can reduce the number of page splits by setting the appropriate fill factor option to reserve free space on each index page. The fill factor is a value from 1 through 100 that specifies the percentage of the index page to be left empty. The default value for fill factor is 0. It is treated similarly to a fill factor value of 100, the difference in that SQL Server leaves some space within the upper level of the index tree for FILLFACTOR = 0. The fill factor percentage is used only at the time when the index is created. If the table contains read-only data (or data that very rarely changed), you can set the 'fill factor' option to 100. When the table's data is modified very often, you can decrease the fill factor to 70% or whatever you think is best.

What is RAID and how does it work?

Redundant Array of Independent Disks (RAID) is a term used to describe the technique of improving data availability through the use of arrays of disks and various data-striping methodologies. Disk arrays are groups of disk drives that work together to achieve higher data-transfer and I/O rates than those provided by single large drives. An array is a set of multiple disk drives plus a specialized controller (an array controller) that keeps track of how data is distributed across the drives. Data for a particular file is written in segments to the different drives in the array rather than being written to a single drive.

For speed and reliability, it is better to have more disks. When these disks are arranged in certain patterns and are use a specific controller, they are called a Redundant Array of Inexpensive Disks (RAID) set. There are several numbers associated with RAID, but the most common are 1, 5 and 10.

RAID 1 works by duplicating the same writes on two hard drives. Let us assume you have two 20-Gigabyte drives. In RAID 1, data is written at the same time to both the drives. RAID1 is optimized for fast writes.

RAID 5 works by writing parts of data across all drives in the set (it requires at least three drives). If a drive failed, the entire set would be worthless. To combat this problem, one of the drives stores a "parity" bit. Think of a math problem, such as $3 + 7 = 10$. You can think of the drives as storing one of the numbers, and the 10 is the parity part. By removing any one of the numbers, you can get it back by referring to the other two, like this: 3 + X = 10. Of course, losing more than one could be evil. RAID 5 is optimized for reads.

RAID 10 is a bit of a combination of both types. It does not store a parity bit, so it is faster, but it duplicates the data on two drives to be safe. You need at least four drives for RAID 10. This type of RAID is probably the best compromise for a database server.

> **Note:** *It's difficult to cover complete aspect of RAID in this book. It's better to take some decent SQL SERVER book for in detail knowledge, but yes from interview aspect you can probably escape with this answer.*

What is the difference between DELETE and TRUNCATE TABLE?

Following are difference between them:

- DELETE table can have criteria while TRUNCATE cannot.
- TRUNCATE table does not invoke trigger.
- DELETE TABLE syntax logs the deletes thus make the delete operation slow. TRUNCATE table does not log any information but it logs information about deallocation of data page of the table so TRUNCATE table is faster as compared to delete table.

> **Note:** *Thanks to all the readers for pointing out my mistake for the above question in my first edition. I had mentioned that TRUNCATE table can not be rolled back while delete can be.*

If locking is not implemented, what issues can occur?

Following are the problems that occur if you do not implement locking properly in SQL SERVER.

Lost Updates

Lost updates occur if you let two transactions modify the same data at the same time, and the transaction that completes first is lost. You need to watch out for lost updates with the READ UNCOMMITTED isolation level. This isolation level disregards any type of locks, so two simultaneous data modifications are not aware of each other. Suppose that a customer has due of 2000$ to be paid. He pays 1000$ and again buys a product of 500$. Lets say that these two transactions are now been entered from two different counters of the company. Now both the counter user starts making entry at the same time 10:00 AM. Actually speaking at 10:01 AM the customer should have 2000-1000+500 = 1500$ pending to be paid. But as said in lost updates the first transaction is not considered and the second transaction overrides it. So the final pending is 2000$+500$ = 2500$.....I hope the company does not loose the customer.

Non-Repeatable Read

Non-repeatable reads occur if a transaction is able to read the same row multiple times and gets a different value each time. Again, this problem is most likely to occur with the READ UNCOMMITTED isolation level. Because you let two transactions modify data at the same time, you can get some unexpected results. For instance, a customer wants to book flight, so the travel agent checks for the flights availability. Travel agent finds a seat and goes ahead to book the seat. While the travel agent is booking the seat, some other travel agent books the seat. When this travel agent goes to update the record, he gets error saying that "Seat is already booked". In short, the travel agent gets different status at different times for the seat.

Dirty Reads

Dirty reads are a special case of non-repeatable read. This happens if you run a report while transactions are modifying the data that you are reporting on. For example, there is a customer invoice report, which runs on 1:00 AM in afternoon and after that all invoices are sent to the respective customer for payments. Let us say one of the customer has 1000$ to be paid. Customer pays 1000$ at 1:00 AM and at the same time report is run. Actually, customer has no money pending but is still issued an invoice.

Phantom Reads

Phantom reads occur due to a transaction being able to read a row on the first read, but not being able to modify the same row due to another transaction deleting rows from the same table. Lets say you edit a record in the mean time somebody comes and deletes the record, you then go for updating the record which does not exist...Panicked.

Interestingly, the phantom reads can occur even with the default isolation level supported by SQL Server: READ COMMITTED. The only isolation level that does not allow phantoms is SERIALIZABLE, which ensures that each transaction is completely isolated from others. In other words, no one can acquire any type of locks on the affected row while it is being modified.

What are different transaction levels in SQL SERVER?

Transaction Isolation level decides how is one process isolated from other process. Using transaction levels, you can implement locking in SQL SERVER.

There are four transaction levels in SQL SERVER:

READ COMMITTED

The shared lock is held for the duration of the transaction, meaning that no other transactions can change the data at the same time. Other transactions can insert and modify data in the same table, however, as long as it is not locked by the first transaction.

READ UNCOMMITTED

No shared locks and no exclusive locks are honored. This is the least restrictive isolation level resulting in the best concurrency but the least data integrity.

REPEATABLE READ

This setting disallows dirty and non-repeatable reads. However, even though the locks are held on read data, new rows can still be inserted in the table, and will subsequently be interpreted by the transaction.

SERIALIZABLE

This is the most restrictive setting holding shared locks on the range of data. This setting does not allow the insertion of new rows in the range that is locked; therefore, no phantoms are allowed.

Following is the syntax for setting transaction level in SQL SERVER.

SET TRANSACTION ISOLATION LEVEL SERIALIZABLE

What are the different locks in SQL SERVER?

Depending on the transaction level, six types of lock can be acquired on data:

Intent

The intent lock shows the future intention of SQL Server's lock manager to acquire locks on a specific unit of data for a particular transaction. SQL Server uses intent locks to queue exclusive locks, thereby ensuring that these locks will be placed on the data elements in the order the transactions were initiated. Intent locks come in three flavors: intent shared (IS), intent exclusive (IX), and shared with intent exclusive (SIX).

IS locks indicate that the transaction will read some (but not all) resources in the table or page by placing shared locks.

IX locks indicate that the transaction will modify some (but not all) resources in the table or page by placing exclusive locks.

SIX locks indicates that the transaction will read all resources, and modify some (but not all) of them. This will be accomplished by placing the shared locks on the resources read and exclusive locks on the rows modified. Only one SIX lock is allowed per resource at one time; therefore, SIX locks prevent other connections from modifying any data in the resource (page or table), although they do allow reading the data in the same resource.

Shared

Shared locks (S) allow transactions to read data with SELECT statements. Other connections are allowed to read the data at the same time; however, no transactions are allowed to modify data until the shared locks are released.

Update

Update locks (U) are acquired just prior to modifying the data. If a transaction modifies a row, then the update lock is escalated to an exclusive lock; otherwise, it is converted to a shared lock. Only one transaction can acquire update locks to a resource at one time. Using update locks prevents multiple connections from having a shared lock that want to eventually modify a resource using an exclusive lock. Shared locks are compatible with other shared locks, but are not compatible with Update locks.

Exclusive

Exclusive locks (X) completely lock the resource from any type of access including reads. They are issued when data is being modified through INSERT, UPDATE and DELETE statements.

Schema

Schema modification locks (Sch-M) are acquired when data definition language statements, such as CREATE TABLE, CREATE INDEX, ALTER TABLE, and so on are being executed. Schema stability locks (Sch-S) are acquired when store procedures are being compiled.

Bulk Update

Bulk update locks (BU) are used when performing a bulk-copy of data into a table with TABLOCK hint. These locks improve performance while bulk copying data into a table; however, they reduce concurrency by effectively disabling any other connections to read or modify data in the table.

Can we suggest locking hints to SQL SERVER?

We can give locking hints that helps you over ride default decision made by SQL Server. For instance, you can specify the ROWLOCK hint with your UPDATE statement to convince SQL Server to lock each row affected by that data modification. Whether it is prudent to do so is another story; what will happen if your UPDATE affects 95% of rows in the affected table? If the table contains 1000 rows, then SQL Server will have to acquire 950 individual locks, which is likely to cost a lot more in terms of memory than acquiring a single table lock. So think twice before you bombard your code with ROWLOCKS.

What is LOCK escalation?

Lock escalation is the process of converting of low-level locks (like rowlocks, page locks) into higher-level locks (like table locks). Every lock is a memory structure too many locks would mean, more memory being occupied by locks. To prevent this from happening, SQL Server escalates the many fine-grain locks to fewer coarse-grain locks. Lock escalation threshold was definable in SQL Server 6.5, but from SQL Server 7.0 onwards SQL Server dynamically manages it.

What are the different ways of moving data between databases in SQL Server?

There are lots of options available; you have to choose your option depending upon your requirements. Some of the options you have are BACKUP/RESTORE, detaching and attaching databases, replication, DTS, BCP, logshipping, INSERT...SELECT, SELECT...INTO, creating INSERT scripts to generate data.

What is the difference between a HAVING CLAUSE and a WHERE CLAUSE?

You can use Having Clause with the GROUP BY function in a query and WHERE Clause is applied to each row before, they are part of the GROUP BY function in a query.

What is the difference between UNION and UNION ALL SQL syntax?

UNION SQL syntax is used to select information from two tables. But it selects only distinct records from both the table, while UNION ALL selects all records from both the tables.

> **Note:** Selected records should have same datatype or else the syntax will not work.

How can you raise custom errors from stored procedure?

The RAISERROR statement is used to produce an ad hoc error message or to retrieve a custom message that is stored in the sysmessages table. You can use this statement with the error handling code presented in the previous section to implement custom error messages in your applications. The syntax of the statement is shown here.

```
RAISERROR ({msg_id |msg_str }{,severity,state }
     [,argument [,,...n ] ] ))
     [ WITH option [,,...n ] ]
```

A description of the components of the statement follows.

msg_id: The ID for an error message, which is stored in the error column in sysmessages.

msg_str:A custom message that is not contained in sysmessages.

Severity: The severity level associated with the error. The valid values are 0–25. Severity levels 0–18 can be used by any user, but 19–25 are only available to members of the fixed-server role sysadmin. When levels 19–25 are used, the WITH LOG option is required.

State A value that indicates the invocation state of the error. The valid values are 0–127. This value is not used by SQL Server.

Argument . . .

One or more variables that are used to customize the message. For example, you could pass the current process ID (@@SPID) so it could be displayed in the message.

WITH option, . . .

The three values that can be used with this optional argument are described here.

LOG: Forces the error to log in the SQL Server error log and the NT application log.

NOWAIT: Sends the message immediately to the client.

SETERROR: Sets @@ERROR to the unique ID for the message or 50,000.

The number of options available for the statement makes it seem complicated, but it is actually easy to use. The following shows how to create an ad hoc message with a severity of 10 and a state of 1.

RAISERROR ('An error occurred updating the Nonfatal table',10,1)

—Results—

An error occurred updating the Nonfatal table

The statement does not have to be used in conjunction with any other code, but for our purposes, it will be used with the error handling code presented earlier. The following alters the ps_NonFatal_INSERT procedure to use RAISERROR.

```
USE tempdb
go
ALTER PROCEDURE ps_NonFatal_INSERT

@Column2 int =NULL
AS
DECLARE @ErrorMsgID int

INSERT NonFatal VALUES (@Column2)
SET @ErrorMsgID =@@ERROR
IF @ErrorMsgID <>0
BEGIN
      RAISERROR ('An error occured updating the NonFatal table',10,1)
END
```

When an error-producing call is made to the procedure, the custom message is passed to the client.

What is ACID fundamental?

A transaction is a sequence of operations performed as a single logical unit of work. A logical unit of work must exhibit four properties, called the ACID (Atomicity, Consistency, Isolation, and Durability) properties, to qualify as a transaction:

Atomicity

● A transaction must be an atomic unit of work; either all of its data modifications are performed or none of them is performed.

Consistency

● When completed, a transaction must leave all data in a consistent state. In a relational database, all rules must be applied to the transaction's modifications to maintain all data integrity.

Isolation

● Modifications made by concurrent transactions must be isolated from the modifications made by any other concurrent transactions. A transaction either see data in the state it was before another concurrent transaction modified it, or it sees the data after the second transaction has completed, but it does not see an intermediate state. This is referred to as serializability because it results in the ability to reload the starting data and replay a series of transactions to end up with the data in the same state it was in after the original transactions were performed.

Durability

● After a transaction has completed, its effects are permanently in place in the system. The modifications persist even in the event of a system failure.

What is DBCC?

DBCC (Database Consistency Checker Commands) is used to check logical and physical consistency of database structure.DBCC statements can fix and detect problems. These statements are grouped in to four categories:

● Maintenance commands like DBCC DBREINDEX, DBCC DBREPAR etc,they are mainly used for maintenance tasks in SQL SERVER.

● Miscellaneous commands like DBCC ROWLOCK, DBCC TRACEO etc,   they are mainly used for enabling row-level locking or removing DLL from   memory.

● Status Commands like DBCC OPENTRAN, DBCC SHOWCONTIG etc,   they are mainly used for checking status of the database.

● Validation Commands like DBCC CHECKALLOC, DBCCCHECKCATALOGetc, they perform validation operations on database.

> **Note:** *Check MSDN for list of all DBCC commands, it is very much possible specially during DBA interviews they can ask in depth individual commands.*

Below is a sample screen in which DBCC SHOWCONTIG command is run. DBCC SHOWCONTIG is used to display fragmentation information for the data and indexes of the specified table.In the sample screen "Customer" table is checked for fragmentation

Fragmentation information.If "Scan density" is 100 then everything is contigious.The above image has scan density of 95.36% which is decent percentage. So such type of useful information can be collected by DBCC command and database performance and maintenance can be improved.

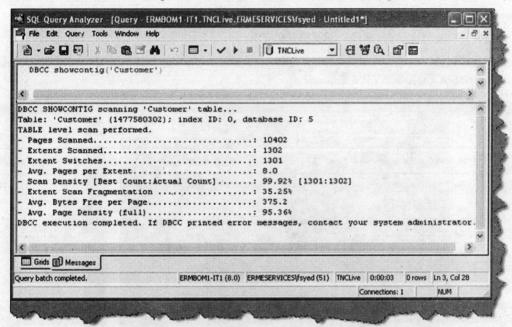

Figure 7.5: DBCC SHOWCONTIG command

What is the purpose of Replication?

Replication is way of keeping data synchronized in multiple databases. SQL server replication has two important aspects publisher and subscriber.

Publisher

Database server that makes data available for replication is known as Publisher.

Subscriber

Database Servers that get data from the publishers is called as Subscribers.

What are the different types of replication supported by SQL SERVER?

There are three types of replication supported by SQL SERVER:

Snapshot Replication.

Snapshot Replication takes snapshot of one database and moves it to the other database. After initial load data can be refreshed periodically. The only disadvantage of this type of replication is that all data has to be copied each time the table is refreshed.

Transactional Replication

In transactional replication, data is copied first time as in snapshot replication, but later only the transactions are synchronized rather than replicating the whole database. You can either specify to run continuously or on periodic basis.

Merge Replication.

Merge replication combines data from multiple sources into a single central database. Again as usual, the initial load is like snapshot but later it allows change of data both on subscriber and publisher, later when they come on-line it detects and combines them and updates accordingly.

What is BCP utility in SQL SERVER?

BCP (Bulk Copy Program) is a command line utility by which you can import and export large amounts of data in and out of SQL SERVER database.

Below is a sample which shows BCP in action.

Figure 7.6: BCP in action

What are the different types of triggers in SQL SERVER?

There are two types of triggers:

INSTEAD OF triggers

INSTEAD OF triggers fire in place of the triggering action. For example, if an INSTEAD OF UPDATE trigger exists on the Sales table and an UPDATE statement is executed against the Salestable, the UPDATE statement will not change a row in the sales table. Instead, the UPDATE statement causes the INSTEAD OF UPDATE trigger to be executed.

AFTER triggers

AFTER triggers execute following the SQL action, such as an insert, update, or delete. This is the traditional trigger which existed in SQL SERVER.

INSTEAD OF triggers are executed automatically before the Primary Key and the Foreign Key constraints are checked, whereas the traditional AFTER triggers is executed after these constraints are checked.

Unlike AFTER triggers, INSTEAD OF triggers can be created on views.

If we have multiple AFTER Triggers, can we specify sequence ?

If a table has multiple AFTER triggers, then you can specify which trigger should be executed first and which trigger should be executed last using the stored procedure sp_settriggerorder.

What is SQL injection?

It is a Form of attack on a database-driven Web site in which the attacker executes unauthorized SQL commands by taking advantage of insecure code on a system connected to the Internet, bypassing the firewall. SQL injection attacks are used to steal information from a database from which the data would normally not be available and/or to gain access to an organization's host computers through the computer that is hosting the database.

SQL injection attacks typically are easy to avoid by ensuring that a system has strong input validation.

As name suggest we inject SQL which can be relatively dangerous for the database. Example this is a simple SQL

```
SELECT email, passwd, login_id, full_name
FROM members
WHERE email = 'x'
```

Now somebody does not put "x" as the input but puts "x ; DROP TABLE members;". So the actual SQL which will execute is:

```
SELECT email, passwd, login_id, full_name
FROM members
WHERE email = 'x'; DROP TABLE members;
```

Think what will happen to your database.

What is the difference between Stored Procedure and User Defined Function?

Following are some major differences between a stored procedure and user defined functions:

- The main purpose of UDF was to increase reuse in stored procedure. So you can call UDF from a stored procedure and not vice versa.

- You cannot change any data using UDF while you can do everything with a stored procedure.

- UDF does not return output parameters while SP's return output parameters.

> **Note:** *SQL Server product is equivalently important from interview point of view. I have dedicated a complete book "SQL Server Interview questions" to crack SQL Server. If you are interested in buying the book mail bpb@bol.net.in / bpb@vsnl.com or call the nearest BPB book stall for my book. For shop phone numbers you can either see the back or front page of the book.*

8

Remoting, Web services and WCF

What is the Web services, remoting and WCF?

When you want to communicate with remote application you will use one of them.

So when both the applications are of .NET technologies remoting is used or else you will use web services or WCF.

What is an application domain?

Application domain is a logical isolation inside a process. This logical isolation has its own memory and own boundary. Any process which runs inside this logical isolation if crashed will not affect other processes running in other application domain.

Application domain helps to isolate process for better application stability.

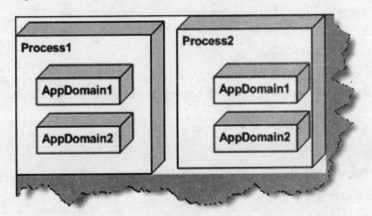

Figure 8.1: Application Domain

What is .NET Remoting?

.NET remoting helpsto make remote object calls, which exist in different Application Domains or different machine or different geographical boundary.

When client wants to make method call on the remote object it uses proxy for it. These method calls are called as "Messages". Messages are serialized using "formatter" class and sent to client "channel". Client

Channel communicates with Server Channel. Server Channel uses as formatter to deserialize the message and sends to the remote object.

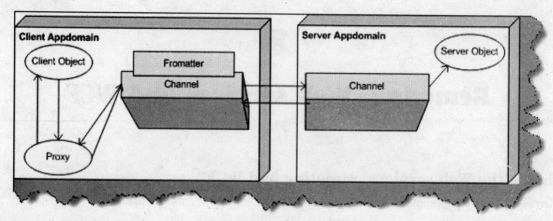

Figure 8.2: .NET Remoting

Which class does the remote object has to inherit?

All remote objects should inherit from System.MarshalbyRefObject.

What are two different types of remote object creation mode in .NET remoting?

There are two different ways in which object can be created using Remoting:

- SAO (Server Activated Objects) also called as Well-Known call mode.
- CAO (Client Activated Objects)

SAO has two modes "Single Call" and "Singleton". With Single Call object, the object is created with every method call thus making the object stateless. With Singleton, the object is created only once and the object is shared with all clients.

CAO are stateful as compared to SAO. In CAO, the creation request is sent from client side. Client holds a proxy to the server object created on server.

What are the basic steps to implement remoting?

Enabling remoting is a four step process:

- Create the interface which will act a proxy between server and client.

```
public interface MyInterface
{
        string SayHello(string strName);
}
```

- Implement the interface and inherit the class from 'MarshalByRefObject'.

```
public class ClsHello: MarshalByRefObject, MyInterface
{
    public string SayHello(string strName)
    {
        return "Hello from Remoting " + strName;
    }
}
```

- Create the server and host the object on a specific channel and formatter. In the below code snippet we have hosted 'clsHello' on Http channel and binary formatter.

```
static void Main(string[] args)
{
    HttpChannel objHttpChannel = new HttpChannel(1234);
    Console.WriteLine("Channel initialized");
    ChannelServices.RegisterChannel(objHttpChannel,false);
    Console.WriteLine("Channel Registered");
    RemotingConfiguration.RegisterWellKnownServiceType(typeof
    (ClsHello),"MySite",WellKnownObjectMode.Singleton);

    Console.WriteLine("Remoting Service Activated");
    Console.ReadLine();

}
```

- Create a client who can call the object via a interface and start making method calls.

```
static void Main(string[] args)
{
    HttpChannel objChannel = new HttpChannel();
    ChannelServices.RegisterChannel(objChannel,false);
    MyInterface iobj = (MyInterface)
    Activator.GetObject(typeof(MyInterface), "http://localhost:1234/
    MySite");
    Console.WriteLine(iobj.SayHello("Shiv"));
    Console.ReadLine();
}
```

What are drawbacks of remoting and how can we overcome the same?

The biggest drawback of remoting is that at both the ends i.e. client and server it should be .NET. In other words clients which are not .Net like java cannot call the server methods and functions.

It can overcome by using web services.

What is a Web Service?

Web Services are business logic components, which provide functionality via the Internet using standard protocols such as HTTP.

Web Services uses Simple Object Access Protocol (SOAP) in order to expose the business functionality.

SOAP defines a standardized format in XML, which can be exchanged between two entities over standard protocols such as HTTP. SOAP is platform independent so the consumer of a Web Service is therefore completely shielded from any implementation details about the platform exposing the Web Service. For the consumer it is simply a black box of send and receives XML over HTTP. So any web service hosted on windows can also be consumed by UNIX and LINUX platform.

What's the difference between web services and remoting?

Remoting works only when both the ends i.e. server and client are in .NET technologies. Web services are useful when the client is not .NET like java etc.

What is UDDI ?

Full form of UDDI is Universal Description, Discovery, and Integration. It's a directory which helps to publish and discover web services.

What is DISCO?

It is a Microsoft technology for publishing /discoveringweb service. DISCO can define a document format along with an interrogation algorithm, making it possible to discover the Web Services exposed on a server. DISCO makes it possible to discover the capabilities of each Web Service (via documentation) and how to interact with it. To publish a deployed Web Service using DISCO, you simply need to create a .disco file and place it in the root along with the other service-related configuration.

What is WSDL?

Web Service Description Language (WSDL)is a W3C specification which defines XML grammar for describing Web Services.XML grammar describes details such as:

- Where we can find the Web Service (its URI)?
- What are the methods and properties that service supports?
- Data type support.
- Supported protocols

In short, it is a bible of what the web service can do. Clients can consume this WSDL and build proxy objects that clients use to communicate with the Web Services. Full WSDL specification is available at http://www.w3.org/TR/wsdl.

What are the steps to create a web service and consume it?

- Create a new project by selecting the template "ASP.NET web service application".
- Expose the function which needs to be consumed by clients using 'WebMethod' attribute.

```
[WebMethod]
public string HelloWorld()
```

```
{
        return "Hello World";
}
```

- Create a client like windows application, right click on the client and add web reference. This creates a simple proxy at the client side.
- Create the object of the proxy and invoke the function and methods of the web service.

How do we secure a web service?

Web services follows the same ASP.NET authentication methodologies i.e. windows, forms and passport.

In the web service web.config file you can specify the authentication methodology and provide the credentials from the client using the below code snippet.

```
ServiceReference1.Service1SoapClient obj = new
ServiceReference1.Service1SoapClient();
obj.ClientCredentials.UserName.UserName = "shiv";
obj.ClientCredentials.UserName.Password = "shiv@123";
```

Does web service have state?

You can use session variables to maintain state in web service.

What is SOA?

SOA is an architectural style for building business applications using loosely coupled services which communicate using standard messages like XML.

What are WS-* specification?

In order to standardize SOA Microsoft, IBM, SUN and many other big companies came together and laid down specification called as WS-* which will bring SOA to a common platform.

Some of the below specifications are defined below:

- **Messaging (WS-Addressing)**: SOAP is the fundamental protocol for web services. WS Addressing defines some extra additions to SOAP headers, which makes SOAP free from underlying transport protocol. One of the good things about Message transmission is MTOM, also termed as Message Transmission Optimization Mechanism. They optimize transmission format for SOAP messages in XML-Binary formant using XML optimized packaging (XOP). Because the data will sent in binary and optimized format, it will give us huge performance gain.

- **Security (WS-Security, WS-Trust, and WS-Secure Conversation):** All the three WS- define authentication, security, data integrity and privacy features for a service.

- **Reliability (WS-Reliable Messaging):** This specification ensures end-to-end communication when we want SOAP messages to be traversed back and forth many times.

- **Transactions (WS-Coordination and WS-Atomic Transaction):** These two specifications enable transaction with SOAP messages.

- **Metadata (WS-Policy and WS-Metadata exchange):** WSDL is a implementation of WS-Metadata Exchange protocol. WS-Policy defines more dynamic features of a service, which cannot be expressed by WSDL.

How does Microsoft implement SOA and the above WS-* specifications?

By WCF, Windows communication foundation.

What is WCF?

WCF helps to implement SOA and WS-* specification. WCF is a combination of:
- NET remoting
- MSMQ
- Web services
- COM+.

What's the difference between WCF and Web services?

- WCF services can be hosted in multiple protocols like http, tcp etc. Web services can only be hosted on Http protocol.
- WCF has COM+ so you can call two different WCF services in a transaction, we can not call two different web services in one transaction.
- WCF integrates with MSMQ, for web services we will need to write code.

In simple words below equation shows the difference with simple equation.

$$WCF = Web\ services + Remoting + MSMQ + COM+$$
$$Web\ service = WCF - (Remoting + MSMQ + COM+)$$

What are end point, contract, address, and bindings?

When we want to host any WCF service we need to provide where to host it, how to host it and what to host.

- **Contract** (What)

  Contract is an agreement between two or more parties. It defines the protocol how client should communicate with your service. Technically, it describes parameters and return values for a method.
- **Address** (Where)

  An Address indicates where we can find this service. Address is a URL, which points to the location of the service.
- **Binding** (How)

  Bindings determine how this end can be accessed. It determines how communications is done. For instance, you expose your service, which can be accessed using SOAP over HTTP or BINARY over TCP. So for each of these communications medium two bindings will be created.
- **End point**: It's the combination of contract, address and binding.

In WCF web.config file we can specify end point, address, binding and contract as shown in the below code snippet.

> *<endpoint   address="http://www.questpond.com"   binding="wsHttpBinding"*
> *contract="WcfService3.IService1">*

> **Note:** *You can also remember end point by ABC where A stands for Address, B for bindings and C for Contract.*

What are the main components of WCF?

We need to define three main components in WCF:

- Service class.
- Hosting environment
- End point

What is a service contract, operation contract and Data Contract?

Other than address, binding and contract we also need to specify the service name, function / methods of the service and data types exposed by the service.

Service contract defines the service name, while operation contract defines functions / methods associated with the service. Below is a simple sample of service contract and operation contract.

```
[ServiceContract]
public interface InvoiceService
{
     [OperationContract]
     bool Pay(Invoice Obj);
}
```

Data Contract defines complex data types. Simple data types like int,boolean etc can be recognized but for custom class data types like customer, supplier etc we need to define them by using data contract. Below is a simple sample of a custom data type invoice class.

```
[DataContract]
public class Invoice
{
     string _InvNumber = true;
     DateTime _InvDate ;

     [DataMember]
     public stringInvNumber
     {
          get { return _ InvNumber; }
          set { _ InvNumber = value; }
```

```
        }

        [DataMember]
        public DateTimeInvDate
        {
               get { return _ InvDate; }
               set { _ InvDate = value; }
        }
}
```

What are the various ways of hosting a WCF service?

There are three major ways to host a WCF service:

●   **Self hosting:** In this we host the WCF service in his own app domain.

●   **II hosting:** In this the WCF service is hosted on IIS server.

●   **WAS:** You can also host WCF service on a special server software called as WAS (Windows activation server).

How do we host a WCF service in IIS?

In order to host a WCF service in IIS we need to create a .SVC file and the .SVC file will have the behind code of the WCF service.

By default when you create a WCF service the SVC file is created which the IIS reads to understand how to run the WCF service in IIS.

What are the advantages of hosting WCF Services in IIS as compared to self-hosting?

IIS hosting	Self hosting
As WCF service is hosted inside the shell of IIS we get all benefits of IIS like process recycling, automatic activation, security feature of IIS etc.	In self hosting we need to take care of all these things ourselves. That means lot of coding.
IIS only works for HTTP protocol.	We can use any protocol for self hosting.
In other words if its HTTP IIS is the best hoster, if its other protocols self hosting is the only option left.	

Automatic activation

IIS provides automatic activation that means the service is not necessary to be running in advance. When any message is received by the service it then launches and fulfills the request. But in case of self hosting the service should always be running.

Process recycling

If IIS finds that a service is not healthy that means if it has memory leaks etc, IIS recycles the process. Ok let us try to understand what is recycling in IIS process. For every browser instance, a worker process is spawned and the request is serviced. When the browser disconnects the worker, process stops and you loose all information. IIS also restarts the worker process. By default, the worker process is recycled at around 120 minutes. So why does IIS recycle. By restarting the worker process it ensures any bad code or memory leak do not cause issue to the whole system.

What are different bindings supported by WCF?

WCF includes predefined bindings. They cover most of bindings widely needed in day-to-day application.

BasicHttpBinding: It's simple SOAP over HTTP with not encryption.

WsHttpBinding: It is same like BasicHttpBinding but encrypted.

NetTcpBinding: This binding sends binary-encoded SOAP, including support for reliable message transfer, security, and transactions, directly over TCP.

NetNamedPipesBinding: This binding Sends binary-encoded SOAP over named pipes. This binding is only usable for WCF-to-WCF communication between processes on the same Windows-based machine.

> *Note: An interprocess control (IPC) protocol is used for exchanging information between two applications, possibly running on different computers in a network. The difference between Named pipes and TCP is that named pipes have good performance in terms of communication with in processes. But when it comes to communicate across network TCP holds the best choice. So if you are using WCF to communicate with process it's the best choice to use in terms for performance. Named pipes do not perform when the traffic is heavy as compared to TCPIP.*

NetMsmqBinding: This binding sends binary-encoded SOAP over MSMQ. This binding can only be used for WCF-to-WCF communication.

What is the difference between BasicHttpBinding and WsHttpBinding ?

BasichttpBinding is plain SOAP message while WshttpBiding is encrypted SOAP message.

> *WsHttpBingding = BasicHttpBinding + Encryption*

Can we overload WCF service methods and functions?

You can overload on the server side but at the client side they have to be referred by different names. You can see in the below code snippet add is an overloaded method but the client will identify them with different names i.e. 'AddIntegers' and 'AddDouble'.

```
[ServiceContract]
interface ICalculator
{
      [OperationContract(Name="AddIntegers")]
      int Add(int a,int b)

      [OperationContract(Name="AddDouble")]
      double Add(double a,double b)
}
```

What is a one-way operation?

Many times we have WCF service methods and function that have long running routine. We would like WCF client to make call to these function asynchronously. In other words the WCF client calls the functions and goes ahead doing their work and the WCF service completed his work at his own leisure.

This is achieved by marking IsOneWay=true on the operation contract as shown in the below code snippet.

When you mark Isoneway as true the function should not return anything. In one-way operation the WCF service does not intimate the client when done. It's like fire and forget.

```
[ServiceContract]
public interface IService1
{
        [OperationContract(IsOneWay=true)]
        void CallMe();
}
```

In the implementation we have made a sleep of 15 seconds.

```
public class Service1: IService1
{
        public void CallMe()
        {
                Thread.Sleep(15000);
        }
}
```

In one way contract we do not get call back, how can we solve the same?

By using duplex contract.

In duplex contracts when client initiates an operation the server service provides a reference call back URI back to the client. So the client initiates a call using the proxy class and when server finishes its work it notifies the client using the callback channel. This is called as duplex messaging in WCF. If you remember in the previous question, we had no way to know when the server finished its task.

How can we host a service on two different protocols on a single server?

You can host WCF service in two different bindings by providing two different end points as shown in the below code snippet.

```
<endpoint address="" binding="wsHttpBinding"
contract="WcfService3.IService1"/>
<endpoint address="" binding="BasicHttpBinding"
contract="WcfService3.IService1"/>
```

How can we integrate with WCF services with MSMQ?

By hosting your "NetMsMqBinding".

How can we do security in WCF services?

There are two ways of doing WCF security Transport security and message security.

Transport level security happens at the channel level. Transport level security is the easiest to implement as it happens at the communication level. WCF uses transport protocols like TCP, HTTP, MSMQ etc and every of these protocols have their own security mechanisms. One of the common implementation of transport level security is HTTPS. HTTPS is implemented over HTTP protocols with SSL providing the security mechanism. No coding change is required it's more of using the existing security mechanism provided by the protocol.

Message level security is implemented with message data itself. Due to this it is independent of the protocol. Some of the common ways of implementing message level security is by encrypting data using some standard encryption algorithm.

In what scenarios will you use message security and transport security?

	Transport	Message
Scenarios when we should be using one of them	When there are no intermediate systems in between this is the best methodology. If it's an intranet type of solution this is most recommended methodology.	When there are intermediate systems like one more WCF service through which message is routed then message security is the way to go.
Advantages	• Does not need any extra coding as protocol inherent security is used. • Performance is better as we can use hardware accelerators to enhance performance. • There is lot of interoperability support and communicating clients do not need to understand WS security as it's built in the protocol itself.	• Provides end to end security as it's not dependent on protocol. Any intermediate hop in network does not affect the application. • Supports wide set of security options as it is not dependent on protocol. We can also implement custom security.
Disadvantages	• As it's a protocol implemented security so it works only point to point. • As security is dependent on protocol it has limited security support and is bounded to the protocol security limitations.	• Needs application refactoring to implement security. • As every message is encrypted and signed there are performance issues. • Does not support interoperability with old ASMX webservices/

Where do we specify security option in WCF services?

There is a security tag in the web.config file where we can specify if we want to use transport security or message security. Below is a simple code snippet for the same.

```
<bindings>
<wsHttpBinding>
<binding name="TransportSecurity">
<security mode="Transport">
<transport clientCredentialType="None"/>
```

```
</security>
</binding>
</wsHttpBinding>
</bindings>
```

What are the different ways of doing WCF concurrency?

There are 3 ways of configuring WCF concurrency.

Single: A single request has access to the WCF service object at a given moment of time. So only one request will be processed at any given moment of time. The other requests have to wait until the request processed by the WCF service is not completed.

Multiple: In this scenario multiple requests can be handled by the WCF service object at any given moment of time. In other words request are processed at the same time by spawning multiple threads on the WCF server object.

So you have great a throughput here but you need to ensure concurrency issues related to WCF server objects.

Reentrant: A single request thread has access to the WCF service object, but the thread can exit the WCF service to call another WCF service or can also call WCF client through callback and reenter without deadlock.

WCF concurrency is configured by using concurrency mode attribute as shown in the below figure.

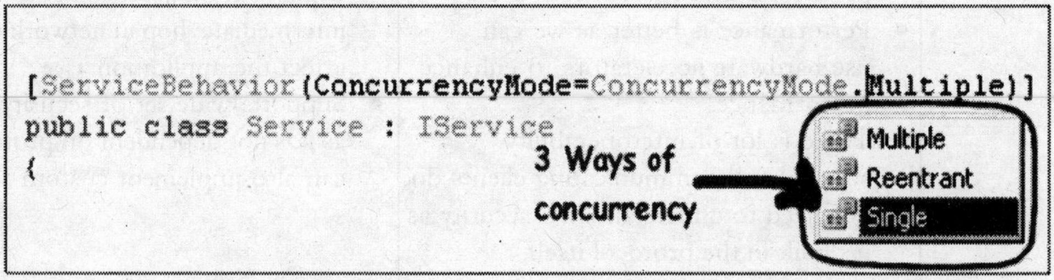

```
[ServiceBehavior(ConcurrencyMode=ConcurrencyMode.Multiple)]
public class Service : IService
{
```

3 Ways of concurrency → Multiple / Reentrant / Single

Figure 8.3: WCF concurrency configured

What are different ways of doing WCF instancing?

Per Call: New instance of WCF service are created for every call made by client.

Per session: One instance of WCF service is created for a session.

Single instance: Only one instance of WCF service is created for all clients.

To configure WCF instancing we need to use the InstanceContextmode attribute on the service as shown below.

```
[ServiceBehavior(InstanceContextMode = InstanceContextMode.Percall)]
public class Service: IService
{
}
```

What is REST?

REST stands for REpresentational State Transfer. REST is an architectural style where our services can communicate using simple HTTPGET, POST methods rather than using complicated SOAP format.

How can we make WCF rest enabled?

To enable a WCF service with REST principles we need to specify the binding as 'WebhttpBinding' in our end point.

> *<endpoint   address=""   binding="webHttpBinding"   contract="IService"*
> *behaviorConfiguration="WebBehavior1">*

We also neet to specify which HTTP method will invoke the function i.e. GET or POST by using the 'WebInvoke' attribute as shown in the below code snippet.

```
[OperationContract]
[WebInvoke(Method = "GET",ResponseFormat = WebMessageFormat.Xml,
     BodyStyle = WebMessageBodyStyle.Bare,
     UriTemplate = "GetData/{value}")]
     string GetData(string value
```

Can we call two WCF services in one transaction?

Yes we can call two WCF services in one transaction using the transaction flow attribute. So if you have 2 WCF services called in one transaction either both of the commit or none of the commit.

In order to enable transaction in WCF service we need to use the transaction flow attribute as shown in the below code snippet.

```
[ServiceContract]
     public interface IService1
     {
          [OperationContract]
          [TransactionFlow(TransactionFlowOption.Allowed)]
          void UpdateData();
     }
```

You also need to define transaction flow as true for wshttpbinding and this binding you need to specify in the end point.

```
<bindings>
     <wsHttpBinding>
          <binding name="TransactionalBind" transactionFlow="true"/>
     </wsHttpBinding>
</bindings>
```

> *<endpoint address="" binding="wsHttpBinding" bindingConfiguration="TransactionalBind" contract="WcfService1.IService1">*

Finally you can call both the WCF services in one transaction using the transaction scope object as shown in the below code snippet.

```
using (TransactionScope ts = new
TransactionScope(TransactionScopeOption.RequiresNew))
{
    try
    {
        ServiceReference1.Service1Client obj = new
        ServiceReference1.Service1Client();
        obj.UpdateData();
        ServiceReference2.Service1Client obj1 = new
        ServiceReference2.Service1Client();
        obj1.UpdateData();
        ts.Complete();
    }
    catch (Exception ex)
    {
        ts.Dispose();
    }
}
```

How can we enable debugging and tracing on WCF services?

WCF has readymade trace objects as shown in the below table.

Assembly Name	Description
System.ServiceModel	Logs the following: • Message process • Reading of configuration information • Transport-level action • Security requests
System.ServiceModel.MessageLogging	Generates tracing information for every message that flows through the system.
System.ServiceModel.IdentityModel	Generate trace data for authentication and authorization.
System.ServiceModel.Activation	Emits information regarding activation of the service.
System.Runtime.Serialization	Emits information when objects are serialized or deserialized. WCF always serializes and de-serializes information during request so it's a good event to see the content of the request.
System.IO.Log	Emits messages with respect to Common Log File System (CLFS).
CardSpace	Emits trace messages related to any CardSpace identity processing that occurs within WCF context.

We can then enable tracing using the <system.diagnostic> tag as shown in the below code snippet. Depending on your needs you can make an entry of the trace objects in the web.config file.

```
<system.diagnostics>
<sources>
<source name="System.ServiceModel"
 switchValue="Information, ActivityTracing">
<listeners>
<add name="log"
      type="System.Diagnostics.XmlWriterTraceListener"
      initializeData="c:\Traces.svclog" />
</listeners>
</source>
</sources>
</system.diagnostics>
```

Now if you run the WCF service you can see a XML file created as shown below.

```
#<E2ETraceEvent xmlns="http://schemas.microsoft.com/2004/06/E2ETraceEvent">
<System xmlns="http://schemas.microsoft.com/2004/06/windows/eventlog/system">
<EventID>0</EventID>
<Type>3</Type>
<SubType Name="Transfer">0</SubType>
<Level>255</Level>
<TimeCreated SystemTime="2009-04-30T03:21:09.5625000Z" />
<Source Name="System.ServiceModel" />
<Correlation  ActivityID="{00000000-0000-0000-0000-000000000000}"
RelatedActivityID="{d11829b7-d2db-46d5-a4ac-49a37a56376e}" />
<Execution ProcessName="WebDev.WebServer" ProcessID="2660" ThreadID="8"
/>
<Channel/>
<Computer>COMPAQ-JZP37MD0</Computer>
</System>
<ApplicationData></ApplicationData>
</E2ETraceEvent>
```

How are exceptions thrown in WCF?

If you want to inform the WCF client that there is error we need to throw a "FaultException" as shown in the below code snippet.

```
throw new FaultException(Error.Message.ToString());
```

> **Note:** *A cross question after this question can be, why can't we raise a normal .NET exception. In other words he will try to compare normal exception with fault exception. The next question answers the same in detail.*

What is the difference between WCF fault exceptions and .NET exceptions?

If you throw a normal .NET exception from a WCF service as shown in the below code snippet.

throw new Exception("Divide by zero");

Your WCF client will get a very generic error with a message as shown in the below figure. Now this kind of message can be very confusing as it does not pinpoint what exactly the error is.

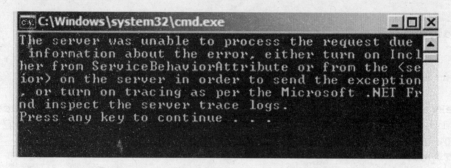

Figure 8.4: Generic error in WCF client

If you use a raise a fault exception as shown in the below code, your WCF clients will see the complete clear error rather than a generic error as shown previously.

throw new FaultException("Divide by zero");

Your WCF client will now see a better error description as shown below.

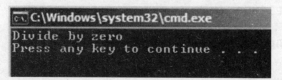

Figure 8.5: Better error using FaultException

9
WPF and Silverlight

What is WPF?

WPF(Windows Presentation foundation) is a graphical subsystem for displaying user interfaces, documents, images, movies etc. It uses XAML which is a XML descriptive language to represent UI elements.

What is the need of WPF when we had windowsforms?

- WPF uses directx internally while windows forms use GDI. In other words WPF uses hardware acceleration while windows form uses software acceleration.

- WPF elements are expressed using XAML file while windows are event based and they have their own format of expressing the elements.

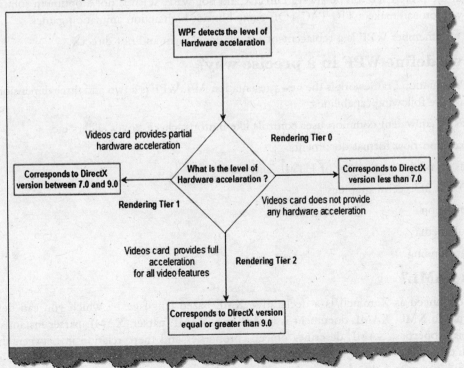

Figure 9.1: Working of Hardware Acceleration

- WPF XAML can be reused and migrated to web applications like WPF web and Silverlight, in windows we need to rewrite the whole thing from scratch to put the same to web.

How does hardware acceleration work with WPF?

Hardware acceleration is a process in which we use hardware to perform some functions rather than performing those functions using the software which is running in the CPU.

WPF exploits hardware acceleration in a two tier manner.

WPF API first detects the level of hardware acceleration using parameters like RAM of video card, per pixel value etc. Depending on that it either uses Tier 0, Tier 1 or Tier 2 rendering mode.

Tier 0: If the video card does not support hardware acceleration then WPF uses Tier 0 rendering mode. In other words it uses software acceleration. This corresponds to working of DirectX version less than 7.0.

Tier 1: If the video card supports partial hardware acceleration then WPF uses Tier 1 rendering mode. This corresponds to working of DirectX version between 7.0 and 9.0.

Tier 2: If the video card supports hardware acceleration then WPF uses Tier 2 rendering mode. This corresponds to working of DirectX version equal or greater than 9.0.

Does that mean WPF has replaced DirectX?

No, WPF does not replace DirectX. DirectX will still be still needed to make cutting edge games. The video performance of directX is still many times higher than WPF API. So when it comes to game development the preference will be always DirectX and not WPF. WPF is not a optimum solution to make games, oh yes you can make a TIC TAC TOE game but not high action animation games.

One point to remember WPF is a replacement for windows form and not directX.

So can we define WPF in a precise way?

Windows Presentation Framework is the new presentation API. WPF is a two and three dimensional graphics engine. It has the following capabilities:

- Has all equivalent common user controls like buttons, check boxes sliders etc.
- Fixed and flow format documents
- Has all of the capabilities of HTML and Flash
- 2D and 3D vector graphics
- Animation
- Multimedia
- Data binding

What is XAML?

XAML (pronounced as Zammel) is a declarative XML-based language by which you can define object and properties in XML. XAML document is loaded by a XAML parser. XAML parser instantiates objects and set their properties. XAML describes objects, properties and there relation in between them. Using XAML, you can create any kind of objects that means graphical or non-graphical. WPF parses the XAML document and instantiates the objects and creates the relation as defined by XAML.

So XAML is a XML document which defines objects and properties and WPF loads this document in actual memory.

So is XAML meant only for WPF ?

No,XAML is not meant only for WPF.XAML is a XML-based language and it had various variants.

WPF XAML is used to describe WPF content, such as WPF objects, controls and documents. In WPF XAML we also have XPS XAML which defines an XML representation of electronic documents.

Silverlight XAML is a subset of WPF XAML meant for Silverlight applications. Silverlight is a cross-platform browser plug-in which helps us to create rich web content with 2-dimensional graphics, animation, and audio and video.

WWF XAML helps us to describe Windows Workflow Foundation content. WWF engine then uses this XAML and invokes workflow accordingly.

Can you explain the overall architecture of WPF?

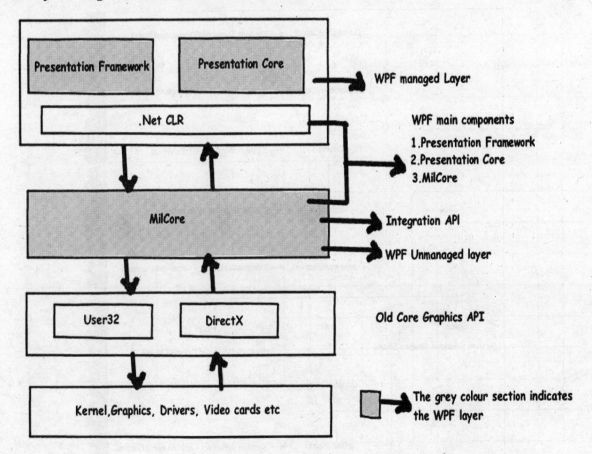

Figure 9.2: Architecture of WPF

Above figure shows the overall architecture of WPF. It has three major sections presentation core, presentation framework and milcore. In the same diagram we have shown how other section like direct and operating system interact with the system. So let's go section by section to understand how every section works.

User32: It decides which goes where on the screen.

DirectX: As said previously WPF uses directX internally. DirectX talks with drivers and renders the content.

Milcore: Mil stands for media integration library. This section is a unmanaged code because it acts like a bridge between WPF managed and DirectX / User32 unmanaged API.

Presentation core: This is a low level API exposed by WPF providing features for 2D, 3D, geometry etc.

Presentation framework: This section has high level features like application controls, layouts . Content etc which helps you to build up your application.

Which are the different namespaces and classes in WPF ?

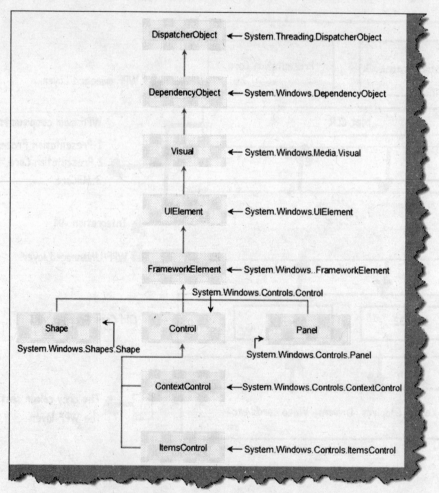

Figure 9.3: 10 important namespaces

There are ten important namespaces / classes in WPF.

System.Threading.DispatcherObject

All WPF objects derive from the DispatcherObject. WPF works on STA model i.e. Single Threading Apartment Model. The main duty of this object is to handle concurrency and threading. When any message like mouse clicks, button clicks etc are initiated they are sent to the DispatcherObject who verifies whether code is running on the correct thread. In the coming section we will look in to detail how WPF threading works.

System.Windows.DependencyObject

When WPF was designed property based architecture was considered. In other words rather than using methods, functions and events object behavior will interact using properties. For now we will only restrict ourselves to this definition. In the coming section we have dedicated question for the same.

System.Windows.Media.Visual

Visual class is a drawing object which abstracts drawing instructions, how drawing should be drawn like clipping, opacity and other functionalities. Visual class also acts like a bridge between unmanaged MilCore.dll and WPF managed classes. When any class derived from visual it can be displayed on windows. If you want to create your own customized user interface then you can program using visual objects.

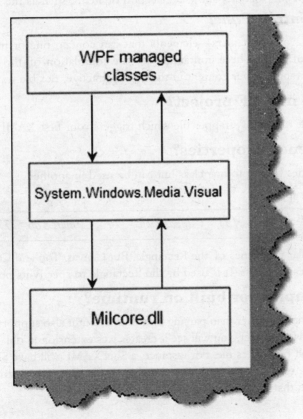

Figure 9.4: Visual Object

System.Windows.UIElement

UIElement handled three important aspects layout, input and events.

System.Windows.FrameworkElement

FrameWorkElement uses the foundation set by UIElement. It adds key properties like HorizontalAlignment, VerticalAlignment, margins etc.

System.Windows.Shapes.Shape

This class helps us to create basic shapes such as Rectangle, Polygon, Ellipse, Line, and Path.

System.Windows.Controls.Control

This class has controls like TextBox,Button,ListBox etc. It adds some extra properties like font,foreground and background colors.

System.Windows.Controls.ContentControl

It holds a single piece of content. This can start from a simple label and go down to a unit level of string in a layout panel using shapes.

System.Windows.Controls.ItemsControl

This is the base class for all controls that show a collection of items, such as the ListBox and TreeView.

System.Windows.Controls.Panel

This class is used for all layout containers—elements that can contain one or more children and arrange them as per specific layout rules. These containers are the foundation of the WPF layout system, and using them is the key to arranging your content in the most attractive, flexible way possible.

What is App.xaml in WPF project?

App.xaml is the start up file or a boot strapper file which triggers your first XAML page from your prohect.

What are dependency properties?

These dependency properties belong to one class but can be used in another.

Consider the below code snippet:

```
<Rectangle Height="72" Width="131" Canvas.Left="74" Canvas.Top="77" />
```

Height and Width are regular properties of the Rectangle. But Canvas. Top and Canvas. Left is dependency property as it belongs the canvas class. It is used by the Rectangle to specify its position within Canvas.

Are XAML file compiled or built on runtime?

XAML files are usually compiled rather than parsing on runtime. But it also supports parsing during runtime. When we build a XAML based project, you will see it creates g.cs extension in obi\Debug folder. Therefore, for every XAMl file you will find a g.cs file. For instance, a Shiv.XAML will have Shiv.g.cs file in obi\Debug folder. In short, in runtime you actually donot see the XAML file. But if you want to do runtime, parsing of XAML file it also allows that to be done.

Can you explain how we can separate code and XAML?

This is one of the most important features of WPF, separating the XAML from the code to be handled. So designers can independently work on the presentation of the application and developers can actually write the code logic independent of how the presentation is.

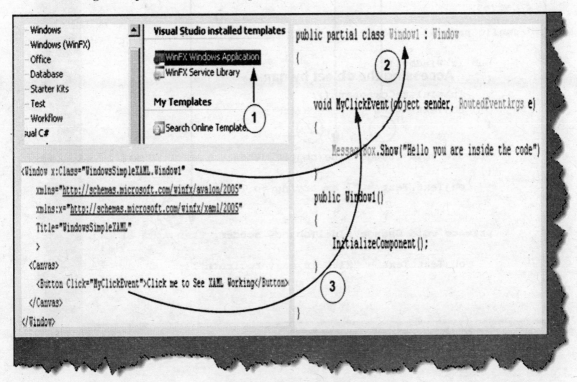

Figure 9.5: Code and XAML

Above is the code snippet, which shows a XAML file and the code completely detached from the XAML presentation. In order to associate a class with XAML file you need to specify the x: Class attribute. Any event specified on the XAML object can be connected by defining a method with sender and event values. You can see from the above code snippet we have linked the MyClickEvent to an event in the behind code.

How can we access XAML objects in behind code?

To access XAML objects in behind code you just need to define them with the same name as given in the XAML document. For instance in the below code snippet we named the object as objtext and the object is defined with the same name in the behind code.

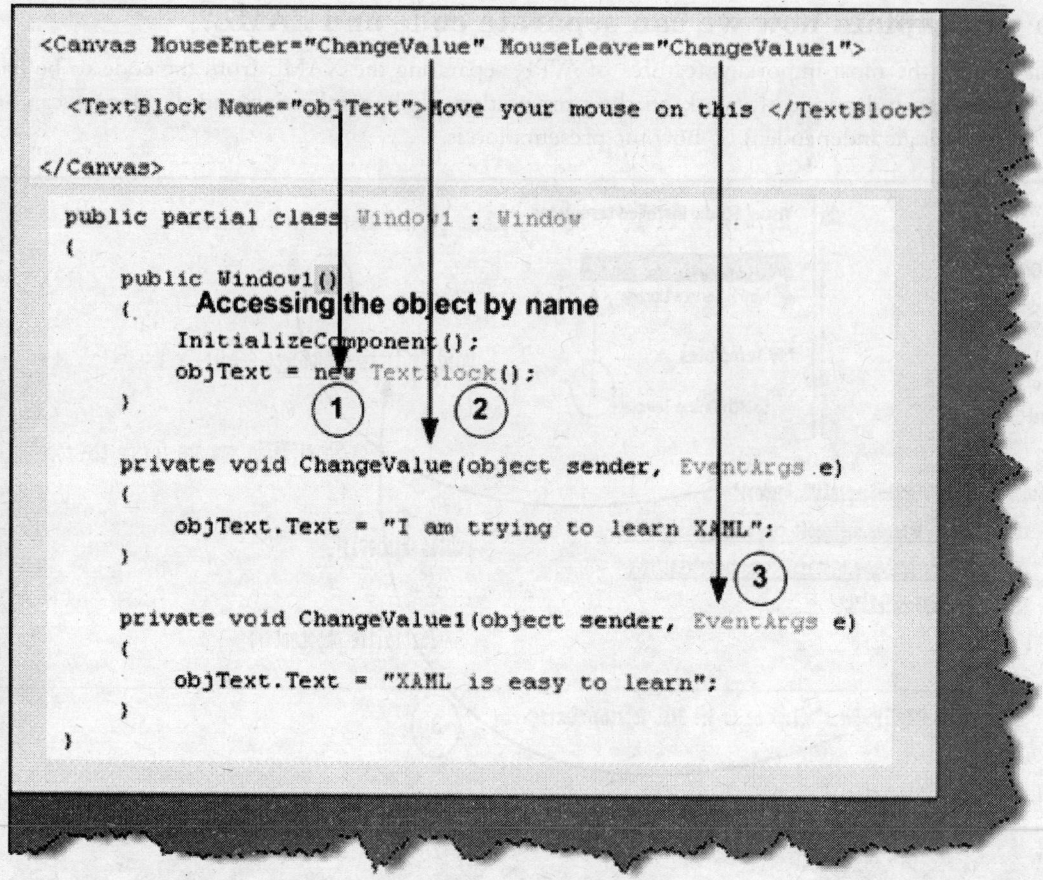

```
<Canvas MouseEnter="ChangeValue" MouseLeave="ChangeValue1">

  <TextBlock Name="objText">Move your mouse on this </TextBlock>

</Canvas>

public partial class Window1 : Window
{
    public Window1()
    {     Accessing the object by name
        InitializeComponent();
        objText = new TextBlock();
    }
              (1)      (2)

    private void ChangeValue(object sender, EventArgs e)
    {
        objText.Text = "I am trying to learn XAML";
    }
                                        (3)

    private void ChangeValue1(object sender, EventArgs e)
    {
        objText.Text = "XAML is easy to learn";
    }
}
```

Figure 9.6: XAML objects in behind code

What is SilverLight?

Silver light is 16. Windows Presentation Framework (Vista Series)a web browser plug-in by which we can enable animations, graphics and audio video. You can compare silver light with flash. We can view animations with flash and it's installed as a plug-in in the browser.

Can SilverLight run in other platforms other than window?

Yes, animations made in SilverLight can run in other platforms other than window. In whatever platform you want run you just need the SilverLight plug-in.

Come on, even WPF runs under browser why SilverLight ?

Yes there is something called as WPF browser application which can run WPF in browser. For WPF browser application you need .Net framework to be installed in the client location while for silver light you need only the plug-in. So in other words WPF browser applications are OS dependent while SilverLight is not. SilverLight plug-in can run in other OS other than windows while we all know .NET framework only runs in windows.

Can SilverLight run in other platforms other than window?

Yes, animations made in SilverLight can run in other platforms other than window. In whatever platform you want run you just need the SilverLight plug-in.

What is the relationship between Silver Light, WPF and XAML?

As explained previously XAML is a XML file which defines the UI elements. This XML file can be read by WPF framework or Silver light framework for rendering. Microsoft first developed WPF and they used XAML files to describe the UI elements to the WPF framework. Microsoft then extended WPF and made WPF/e which helped to render the UI in the browser. WPF/e was the code name for Silver Light. Later Microsoft launched Silver Light officially.

So the XAML just defines the XML structure to represent the UI elements. Both the frameworks i.e. WPF and Silverlight then reads the UI elements and renders the UI elements in the respective platform.

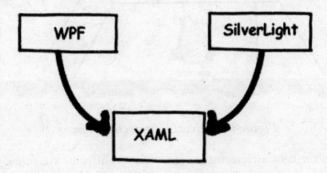

Figure 9.7: XAML

What is XAP file in Silverlight?

XAP file is a compressed file which downloads all the necessary DLL's, code at the browser client so that Silverlight application can run inside the browser.

Can you explain Sliver Light architecture?

Before we talk about silver light architecture let's discuss what is silver light is really made of technically. Silver light has borrowed lot of things from existing Microsoft technologies. We can think silver light plug-in as a combination of some technologies from core .NET framework, vector animations, media and JavaScript.

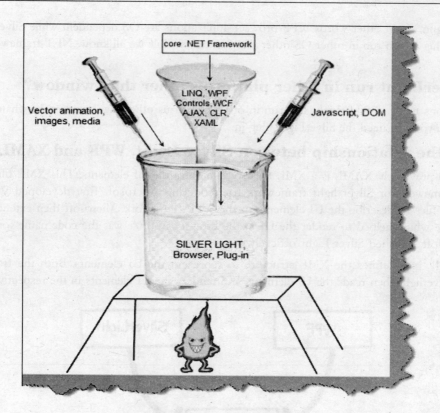

Figure 9.8: SilverLight Architecture

So we can visualize the silver light architecture as combination of some functionalities from core .NET framework, Ajax and some functionalities like animation, media etc provided by core silver light framework.

We can think silver light architecture as a combination of four important blocks:

- **Some .NET framework components:** Silver light uses some components from .NET framework. One of the main components is WPF. Many of the UI components (check box, buttons, text boxes etc), XAML parsing etc are taken from the core WPF system. It also has taken components like WCF to simplify data access. It also have CLR for memory management, safety checking and garbage collection. The base class libraries of Net are used for string manipulations, algorithms, expressions, collections and globalization.

- **Presentation core:** The core presentation framework has functionalities to display vector 2d animations, images, media, DRM and handle inputs like mouse and keyboard.

- **Other technologies:** Silver light interacts with other technologies like Ajax and javascript. So it also borrows some functionalities from there technologies.

- **Hosting:** Silver light animations finally run under the browser environment. So it has a the hosting functionality which helps to host the application the browser, expose a DOM by which JavaScript can manipulate the silver light components and it also has a installer functionality which helps to install silver light application and plug-in in the browser environment.

One of the things which you can notice from the architecture diagram is that the presentation core reads from the XAML file for rendering. The XAML is a component which is a part of the .NET framework and the rendering part is done by the presentation core.

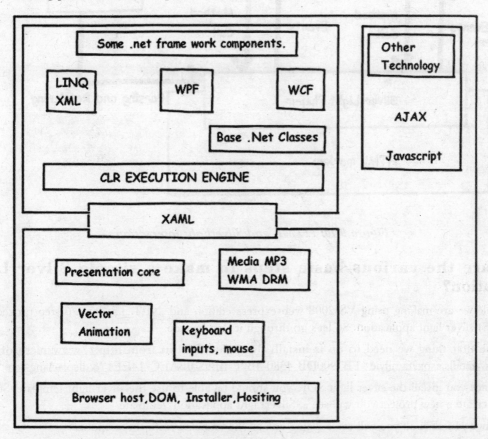

Figure 8.9: Silverlight interaction

The application is a typical HTML which runs under the browser. There are markups which instantiates the silver light plug-in. Now when user interacts with the silver light application it sends event to JavaScript system or the .NET system. This depends on which programming language you are using. The program code which is either in JavaScript of .NET can make calls to the silver light run-time and achieve the necessary functionalities. XAML will be read and parsed by the silver light runtime and then rendered accordingly to the browser.

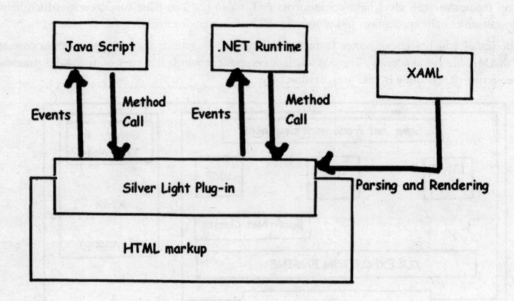

Figure 9.10: HTML and Silverlight interaction

What are the various basic steps to make a simple Silver Light application?

This sample we are making using VS 2008 web express edition and .NET 3.5. It's a 6 step procedure to run our first silver light application. So let's go through it step by step.

Step1: The first thing we need to do is install silverlight SDK kit from http://www.microsoft.com/downloads/details.aspx?familyid=FB7900DB-4380-4B0F-BB95-0BAEC714EE17&displaylang=en

Step 2: Once you install the silver light SDK you should be able to use the silver light template. So when you go to create a new project you will see a 'SilverLight application' template.

Step 3: Once you click ok you will see a dialog box as shown below with three options.

Add a ASP.NET web project to the solution to host silver light: This option is the default option, and it will create a new Web application project that is configured to host and run your Silverlight application. If you are creating a new silver light application then this is the option to go.

Automatically generate Test Page To Host Silverlight at build time: Thisoption will create a new page at run time every time you try to debug and test your application. If you want to only concentrate on your silver light application then this option is worth looking at.

Link This Silverlight Control Into An Existing Web Site: If you have a existing silver light application then this option helps to link the silver light application with the existing web application project. You will not see this option enabled to new projects, you need to have an existing web application.

For this example we have selected the first option. Once you click ok you should see the full IDE environment for silver light.

So let's run through some basic points regarding the IDE view what we see. You will see there are two projects one is your web application and the other is the silver light application. In the silver light application we two XAML files one is App.XAML and the other is Page.XAML.

App.XAML has the global level information.

Step 4: Now for simplicity sake we just use the TextBlock tag to display a text. You can see as we type in the Page.XAML its displayed in the viewer.

Step 5: Now we need to consume the silver light application in a ASPX page. So in the HTML / ASPX page we need to first refer the silver light name space using the 'Register' attribute.

```
<%@Register Assembly="System.Web.Silverlight" Namespace="System.Web.UI.SilverlightControls"
TagPrefix="asp" %>
```

We also need to refer the script manager from the silver light name space. The script manager control is functionality from AJAX. The main purpose of this control is to manage the download and referencing of JavaScript libraries.

```
<asp:ScriptManager ID="ScriptManager1" runat="server"></asp:ScriptManager>
```

Finally we need to refer the silver light application. You can see that in the source we have referred to the XAP file. XAP file is nothing but a compiled silver light application which is compressed and ZIP. It basically has all the files that's needed for the application in a compressed format. If you rename the file to ZIP extension you can open the same using WINZIP.

```
<asp:Silverlight ID="Xaml1" runat="server"
Source="~/ClientBin/MyFirstSilverLightApplication.xap"
MinimumVersion="2.0.31005.0" Width="100%" Height="100%" />
```

So your final ASPX / HTML code consuming the silver light application looks something as shown below.

```
<%@ Page Language="C#" AutoEventWireup="true" %>
<%@         Register         Assembly="System.Web.Silverlight"
Namespace="System.Web.UI.SilverlightControls"
 TagPrefix="asp" %>
<!DOCTYPE html PUBLIC "-//W3C//DTD XHTML 1.0 Transitional//EN" "http://
www.w3.org/TR/xhtml1/DTD/xhtml1-transitional.dtd">
<html xmlns="http://www.w3.org/1999/xhtml" style="height:100%;">
<head runat="server">
<title>MyFirstSilverLightApplication</title>
</head>
<body style="height:100%;margin:0;">
<form id="form1" runat="server" style="height:100%;">
<asp:ScriptManager ID="ScriptManager1" runat="server"></asp:ScriptManager>
<div style="height:100%;">
```

```
<asp:Silverlight ID="Xaml1" runat="server" Source="~/ClientBin/
MyFirstSilverLightApplication.xap"
     MinimumVersion="2.0.31005.0" Width="100%" Height="100%" />
</div>
</form>
</body>
</html>
```

Step 6: So finally set the web application as start up and also set this page as start up and run it. You should be pleased to see your first silver light application running.

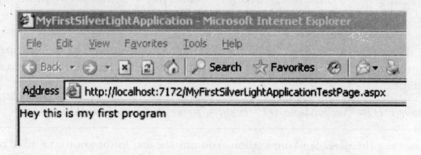

Figure 9.11: Running SilverLight Application

What are the different kinds of bindings in Silverlight?

There are three kind of bindings one way, two way and one time binding.

- **One way binding:** data flows from object to UI and not vice-versa.

- **Two way bindings:** data flows from object to UI and also vice-versa.

- In one time binding data flows from object to the UI only once. There is no tracking mechanism to update data on either side. One time binding has marked performance improvement as compared to the previous two bindings discussed. This binding is a good choice for reports where the data is loaded only once and viewed.

In order to specify bindings we need to use the binding path attribute on the UI elements as shown in the below code snippet.

```
<TextBox x:Name="txtEnterAge" Text="{Binding Path=Age, Mode=TwoWay}"
Height="30" Width="150" VerticalAlignment="Center"
HorizontalAlignment="Center"></TextBox>
```

How does Silverlight connect with databases?

If you remember the Silverlight architecture, it does not contain ADO.NET. In order to make insert, update and deletes via Silverlight, we need to call WCF services and WCF services in turn will do insert updates and deletes on SQL Server.

What are the 2 important points we noted when we call WCF service from Silverlight?

●   We can only WCF services asynchronously from Silverlight.

●   We need to create crossdomain and client access policy XML file where the WCF service is hosted.

What are the different ways of doing alignment in Silverlight and WPF?

There are three ways provided by Silverlight for layout management Canvas, Grid and Stack panel.

Canvas is the simplest methodology for layout management. It supports absolute positioning using 'X' and 'Y' coordinates. 'Canvas.Left' helps to specify the X co-ordinate while 'Canvas.Top' helps to provide the 'Y' coordinates.

Below is a simple code snippet which shows how rectangle objectsare positioned using 'Canvas' on co-ordinates (50,150).

```
<Canvas x:Name="MyCanvas">
<Rectangle Fill="Blue" Width="100"
                       Height="100"
                       Canvas.Left="50"
                       Canvas.Top="150"/>

</Canvas>
```

Grid layout helps you position your controls using rows and columns. It's very similar to table defined in HTML.

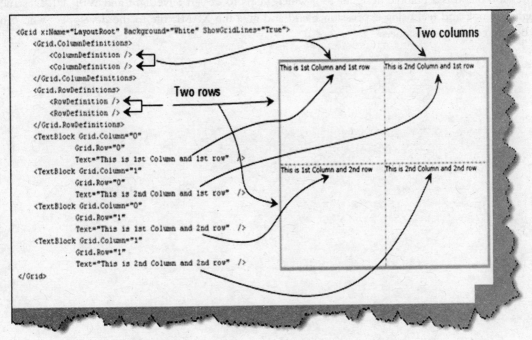

Figure 9.12: Grid layout to position controls

As the name so the behavior. Stack allows you to arrange your UI elements vertically or horizontally.

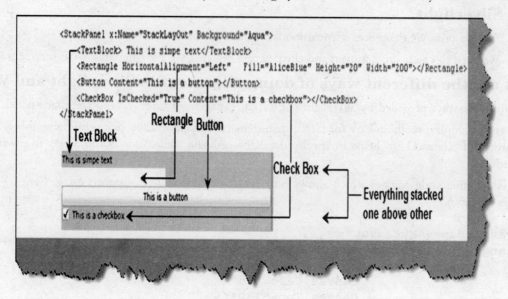

Figure 9.13: arranging UI elements

What is expression blend?

Expression blend is a graphic designer tool which helps to design Silverlight and WPF UI. Designers can design the look and feel using expression blend and give the XAML file to the developers who can write the behind code for the same.

10

LINQ and Entity framework

Define LINQ?

LINQ is a uniform programming model for any kind of data access. It is also an OR mapper which helps us to expedite our business object creation process.

LINQ enables you to query and manipulate data independently of data sources. Below figure 'LINQ' shows how .NET language stands over LINQ programming model and works in a uniformed manner over any kind of data source. It's like a query language which can query any data source and any transform. LINQ also provides full type safety and compile time checking.

LINQ can serve as a good entity for middle tier. So it will sit in between the UI and data access layer.

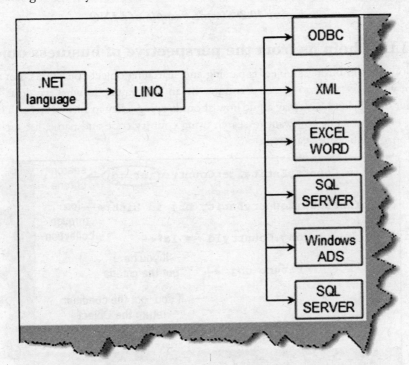

Figure 10.1: LINQ

Below is a simple sample of LINQ. We have a collection of data 'objcountries' to which LINQ will is making a query with country name 'India'. The collection 'objcountries' can be any data source dataset, datareader, XML etc. Below figure 'LINQ code snippet' shows how the 'ObjCountries' can be any can of data. We then query for the 'CountryCode' and loop through the same.

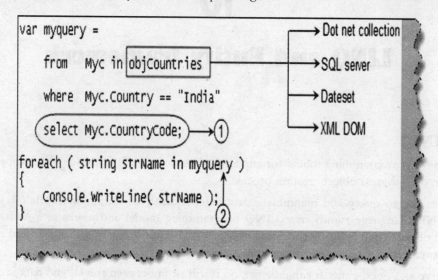

Figure 10.2: Simple Sample of LINQ

How does LINQ help us from the perspective of business objects?

One of the tedious jobs in business object is parsing and searching object collections. For instance consider the below figure where we want to search a country by an 'ID' value. So what we do is loop through the collection and get the object. Many may argue how about keeping a key in List or Array. The below example is just a sample. For instance if you want to search using country code and name, list / collection keys will not work with those multi-value searches.

```
public CountryEntity getCountry(int id)    search
{                                          criteria
    foreach (CountryEntity obj in List)    loop
    {                                      through
                                           collection
        if (obj.CountryId == id)
        {
                                   If you have
            return obj;            got the criteria
        }
    }                         If you got the condition
    return null;              return the Object
}
```

Figure 10.3: Search country by ID value

In other words using LINQ we can query business object collections and filter the collection in a single LINQ query.

Can you explain how a basic LINQ Query looks like?

Below is a simple LINQ query which selects all customer data from 'ObjCustomer' collection.

```
from clsCustomer obj in objCustomer select obj
```

How do we write a LINQ query to search with criteria?

We need to put the where clause before the 'select' keyword.

```
return from clsCustomer Obj in objCustomer where Obj.customerCode == "001" select Obj;
```

How can do a join using LINQ query?

Below is the LINQ code snippet for creating joins between object collections. In this case we are creating a join on customer and orders. If you remember the order collection was contained in the customer class.

```
return from clsCustomer ObjCust in objCustomer
from clsOrder ObjOrder in ObjCust.Orders
select ObjCust;
```

How can we do a group by using LINQ query?

Below is the code snippet which shows how group by query is written using LINQ. You can see we have created first a temp variable i.e. 'GroupTemp' and then we have used the 'Select' clause to return the same.

```
var GroupCustomers = from ObjCust in objCustomer
                     group ObjCust by ObjCust.City into GroupTemp
                     select new {GroupTemp.Key,GroupTemp};
```

What are entity classes in LINQ?

Entity classes are classes which map to table structure of your data source. Entity classes represent your business model. Class name of entity class map to table name using the 'Table' attribute while table column name map to properties of the class.

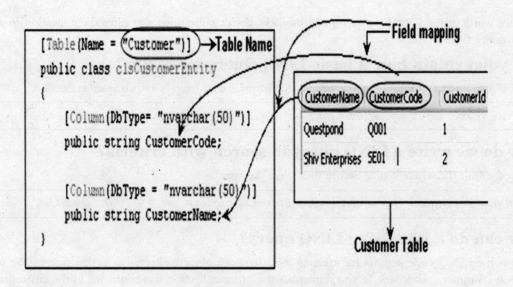

Figure 10.4: Entity class

How can we load the LINQ entity class?

The LINQ entity classes are loaded by using data context class.

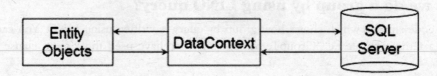

Figure 10.5: Load the LINQ

For instance below is a simple code snippet where the data context object load a entity class clscustomerentity.

```
DataContext objContext = new DataContext(strConnectionString);
Table<clsCustomerEntity> objTable =objContext.GetTable<clsCustomerEntity>();
```

How do we define 1 to many and many to 1 relationship in LINQ?

1 to many relationships are defined by using EntitySet and many to 1 is defined by using entity ref. Below is a simple code snippet which shows 'clsCustomer' having many 'clsAddresses' object.

```
[Table(Name = "Customer")]
public class clsCustomer
{
        private EntitySet<clsAddresses> _CustomerAddresses;
```

```
[Association(Storage = "_CustomerAddresses",ThisKey="CustomerId", OtherKey
= "CustomerId")]
public EntitySet<clsAddresses> Addresses
{
      set
      {
            _CustomerAddresses = value;
      }
      get
      {
            return _CustomerAddresses;
      }

      }
}
```

If we need to define one to one relationship we need to use the entityref attribute as shown in the below code snippet.

```
public class clsAddresses
{
      ....
      ....
      private EntityRef<clsPhone> _Phone;
      ....
      ....
}
```

How can we call a stored procedure using LINQ ?

We can use the function attribute as shown in the below code snippet with the stored procedure name.

```
[Function(Name = "usp_SelectCustomer", IsComposable = false)]
public ISingleResult<clsCustomerEntity> getCustomerAll()
{
  IExecuteResult objResult =
  this.ExecuteMethodCall(this,(MethodInfo)(MethodInfo.GetCurrentMethod()));
```

How can we insert, update and delete using LINQ?

Insert, update and delete operations in LINQ are done by using 'InsertOnSubmit', 'DeleteOnSubmit' and 'SubmitChanges'.

To add a new record using LINQ below is the code snippet.

```
DataContext objContext = new DataContext(strConnectionString);
clsCustomerEntity objCustomerData = new clsCustomerEntity();
```

```
objCustomerData.CustomerCode = txtCustomerCode.Text;
objCustomerData.CustomerName = txtCustomerName.Text;
objContext.GetTable<clsCustomerEntity>().InsertOnSubmit(objCustomerData);
objContext.SubmitChanges();
```

Below is the code for updating a record by LINQ.

```
clsCustomerEntity objCustomerData =
(clsCustomerEntity)MyQuery.First<clsCustomerEntity>();
objCustomerData.CustomerCode = txtCustomerCode.Text;
objCustomerData.CustomerName = txtCustomerName.Text;
objContext.SubmitChanges();
```

Below is the code for deleting record using LINQ.

```
objContext.GetTable<clsCustomerEntity>().DeleteOnSubmit(objCustomerData);
objContext.SubmitChanges();
```

What are DBML files in LINQ?

DBML stands for database markup language which is a XML file. In big projects we will have large number of tables, developing entity classes for those tables will be very difficult. DBML files helps to automate the creation of entity classes by simple drag and drop as shown in the below figure.

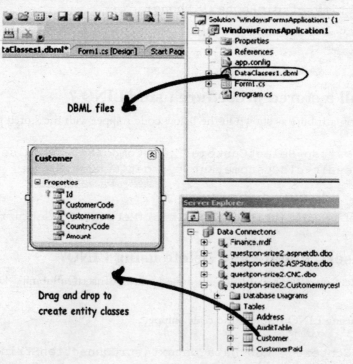

Figure 10.6: Entities

What is Entity framework?

ADO.NET entity is an ORM (object relational mapping) which abstracts data model by providing a simplified object model.

In other words the complete middle tier development is expedited using entity framework.

What's the difference between LINQ to SQL and Entity framework?

● LINQ to SQL is good for rapid development with SQL Server. EF is for enterprise scenarios and works with SQL server as well as other databases.

● LINQ maps directly to tables. One LINQ entity class maps to one table. EF has a conceptual model and that conceptual model map to storage model via mappings. So one EF class can map to multiple tables or one table can map to multiple classes.

● LINQ ismore targeted towards rapid development while EF is for enterprise level where the need is to develop loosely coupled framework.

What are CSDL, SSDL and MSL?

CSDL (Conceptual Schema definition language) is the conceptual abstraction which is exposed to the application.

SSDL (Storage schema definition language) defines the mapping with your RDBMS data structure.

MSL (Mapping Schema language) connects the CSDL and SSDL.

CSDL, SSDL and MSL are actually XML files.

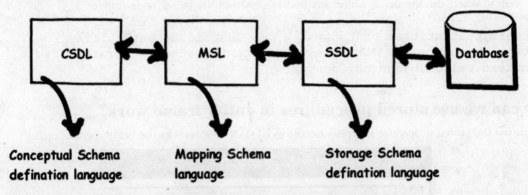

Figure 10.7: CSDL, MSL and SSDL

What is the work of EDMX file?

EDMX stands for Entity Data Model XML. It helps to create entity classes to interact with database.

How can we browse using entity framework classes?

In order to browse through records you can create the context class and inside the context class you can go and get the records. For instance in the below code snippet we have created a customer class. This class gets loaded using the data context class which is currently customermytestentities class.

```
CustomermytestEntities obj = new CustomermytestEntities();
foreach (Customer objCust in obj.Customers)
{}
```

How can we add using EF?

Create the object your entity class, add it to the data context using add object method and then call save changes method.

```
CustomermytestEntities obj = new CustomermytestEntities();
Customer objCust = new Customer();
objCust.CustomerCode = "1001";
obj.Customers.AddObject(objCust);
obj.SaveChanges();
```

If you want to update, select the object and call accept changes.

```
CustomermytestEntities objContext = new CustomermytestEntities();
Customer objCustomer = (Customer)objContext.Customers.FirstOrDefault();
objCustomer.CountryCode = "NEP";
objContext.AcceptAllChanges();
```

If you want to delete call the delete object method as shown in the below code snippet.

```
CustomermytestEntities objContext = new CustomermytestEntities();
Customer objCustomer = (Customer)objContext.Customers.FirstOrDefault();
objContext.DeleteObject(objCustomer);
```

How can we use stored procedures in entity frame work?

You can use the stored procedure mapping details in EDMX as shown in the below figure.

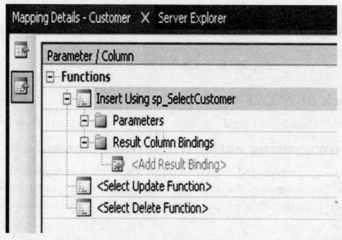

Figure 10.8: Specify stored procedures

What are POCO classes in Entity framework?

POCO means Plain old C# object. When EDMX creates classes they are cluttered with lot of entity tags. For instance below is a simple customer class generated using entity framework. Many times we would like to use simple .NET classes and integrate the same with entity framework.

Entity framework allows the same. In other you can create a simple .NET class and use the entity context object to load your simple .NET classes.

```
[EdmEntityTypeAttribute(NamespaceName="CustomermytestModel",
Name="Customer")]
[Serializable()]
[DataContractAttribute(IsReference=true)]
public partial class Customer: EntityObject
{

     #region Factory Method

     /// <summary>
     /// Create a new Customer object.
     /// </summary>
     /// <param name="id">Initial value of the Id property.</param>
     /// <param name="customerCode">Initial value of the CustomerCode
     property.</param>
     /// <param name="customername">Initial value of the Customername
     property.</param>
     public static Customer CreateCustomer(global::System.Int32 id,
     global::System.String customerCode, global::System.String
     customername)
     {
          Customer customer = new Customer();
          customer.Id = id;
          customer.CustomerCode = customerCode;
          customer.Customername = customername;
          return customer;
     }

     #endregion
     #region Primitive Properties
```

11

Design patterns, UML, Estimation and Project Management

Note: *We have released an exclusive book on 'Architecture Interview questions' which covers architecture in detail. Please email bpb@bol.net.in for details.*

What are design patterns?

Design patterns are recurring solution to recurring problems in software architecture.

Which design patterns have you used in your project?

This question is very subjective as every developer has his own experience. So we will pick up three design patterns i.e. factory, singleton and façade and discuss the same in more depth. In case you are using some other design pattern below is the list with classification, go and pick your best three.

There are three basic classifications of patterns Creational, Structural, and Behavioral patterns.

Creational Patterns

- **Abstract Factory:** Creates an instance of several families of classes
- **Builder:** Separates object construction from its representation
- **Factory Method:** Creates an instance of several derived classes
- **Prototype:** A fully initialized instance to be copied or cloned
- **Singleton:** A class in which only a single instance can exist

Structural Patterns

- **Adapter:** Match interfaces of different classes.
- **Bridge:** Separates an object's abstraction from its implementation.
- **Composite:** A tree structure of simple and composite objects.
- **Decorator:** Add responsibilities to objects dynamically.
- **Façade:** A single class that represents an entire subsystem.
- **Flyweight:** A fine-grained instance used for efficient sharing.
- **Proxy:** An object representing another object.

Behavioral Patterns

- **Mediator:** Defines simplified communication between classes.
- **Memento:** Capture and restore an object's internal state.
- **Interpreter:** A way to include language elements in a program.
- **Iterator:** Sequentially access the elements of a collection.
- **Chain of Resp:** A way of passing a request between a chain of objects.
- **Command:** Encapsulate a command request as an object.
- **State:** Alter an object's behavior when its state changes.
- **Strategy:** Encapsulates an algorithm inside a class.
- **Observer:** A way of notifying change to a number of classes.
- **Template Method:** Defer the exact steps of an algorithm to a subclass.
- **Visitor:** Defines a new operation to a class without change.

Can you explain factory pattern?

Factory pattern is one of the types of creational patterns. You can make out from the name factory itself it's meant to construct and create something. In software architecture world factory pattern is meant to centralize creation of objects. Below is a code snippet of a client which has different types of invoices. These invoices are created depending on the invoice type specified by the client. There are two issues with the code below:

- First we have lots of 'new' keyword scattered in the client. In other ways the client is loaded with lot of object creational activities which can make the client logic very complicated.

- Second issue is that the client needs to be aware of all types of invoices. So if we are adding one more invoice class type called as 'InvoiceWithFooter' we need to reference the new class in the client and recompile the client also.

```
if (intInvoiceType == 1)
{
    objinv = new clsInvoiceWithHeader();
}
else if (intInvoiceType == 2)
{
    objinv = new clsInvoiceWithOutHeaders();
}
```

Figure 11.1: Factory Pattern

Taking these issues as our base we will now look in to how factory pattern can help us solve the same. Below figure 'Factory Pattern' shows two concrete classes 'ClsInvoiceWithHeader' and 'ClsInvoiceWithOutHeader'.

The **first issue** was that these classes are in direct contact with client which leads to lot of 'new' keyword scattered in the client code. This is removed by introducing a new class 'ClsFactoryInvoice' which does all the creation of objects.

The **second issue** was that the client code is aware of both the concrete classes i.e. 'ClsInvoiceWithHeader' and 'ClsInvoiceWithOutHeader'. This leads to recompiling of the client code when we add new invoice types. For instance if we add 'ClsInvoiceWithFooter' client code needs to be changed and recompiled accordingly. To remove this issue we have introduced a common interface 'IInvoice'. Both the concrete classes 'ClsInvoiceWithHeader' and 'ClsInvoiceWithOutHeader' inherit and implement the 'IInvoice' interface.

The client references only the 'IInvoice' interface which results in zero connection between client and the concrete classes ('ClsInvoiceWithHeader' and 'ClsInvoiceWithOutHeader'). So now if we add new concrete invoice class we do not need to change any thing at the client side.

In one line the creation of objects is taken care by 'ClsFactoryInvoice' and the client disconnection from the concrete classes is taken care by 'IInvoice' interface.

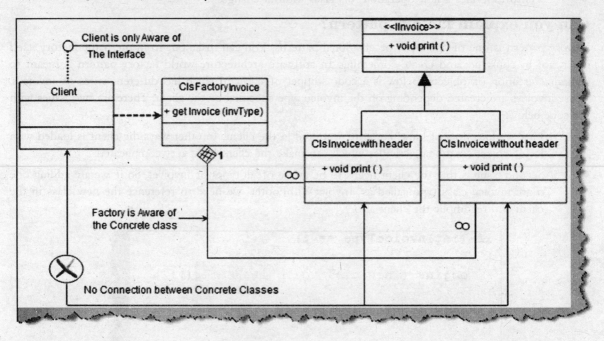

Figure 11.2: ClsFactory Invoice

Below are the code snippets of how actually factory pattern can be implemented in C#. In order to avoid recompiling the client we have introduced the invoice interface 'IInvoice'. Both the concrete classes 'ClsInvoiceWithOutHeaders' and 'ClsInvoiceWithHeader' inherit and implement the 'IInvoice' interface.

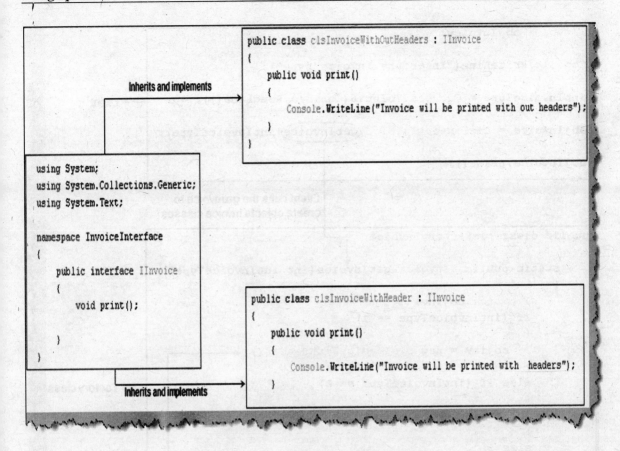

```
public class clsInvoiceWithOutHeaders : IInvoice
{
    public void print()
    {
        Console.WriteLine("Invoice will be printed with out headers");
    }
}
```

Inherits and implements

```
using System;
using System.Collections.Generic;
using System.Text;

namespace InvoiceInterface
{
    public interface IInvoice
    {
        void print();

    }
}
```

```
public class clsInvoiceWithHeader : IInvoice
{
    public void print()
    {
        Console.WriteLine("Invoice will be printed with  headers");
    }
}
```

Inherits and implements

Figure 11.3: ClsInvoice with Header

We have also introduced an extra class 'ClsFactoryInvoice' with a function 'getInvoice()' which will generate objects of both the invoices depending on 'intInvoiceType' value. In short we have centralized the logic of object creation in the 'ClsFactoryInvoice'. The client calls the 'getInvoice' function to generate the invoice classes. One of the most important points to be noted is that client only refers to 'IInvoice' type and the factory class 'ClsFactoryInvoice' also gives the same type of reference. This helps the client to be complete detached from the concrete classes, so now when we add new classes and invoice types we do not need to recompile the client.

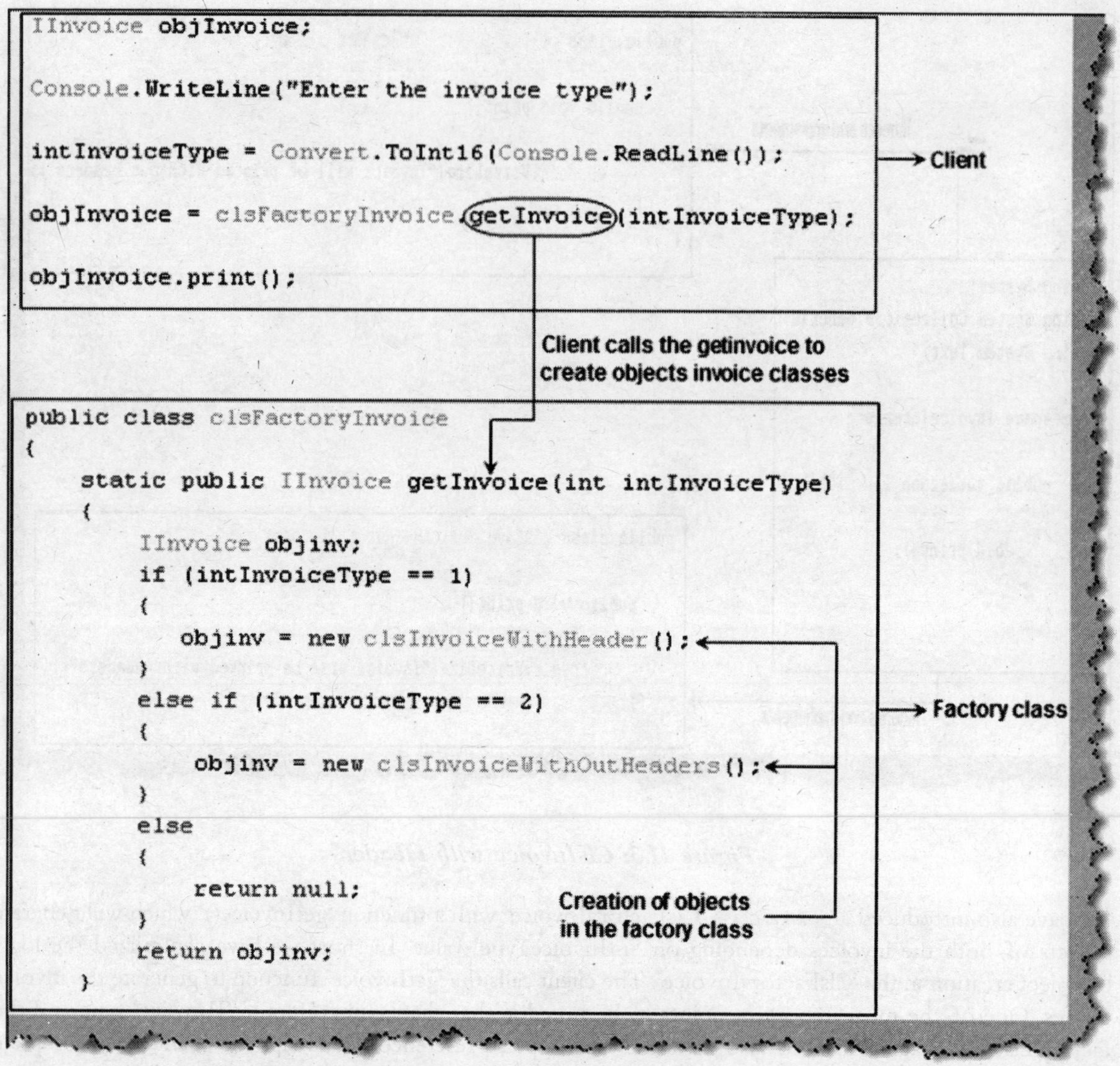

```
IInvoice objInvoice;

Console.WriteLine("Enter the invoice type");

intInvoiceType = Convert.ToInt16(Console.ReadLine());

objInvoice = clsFactoryInvoice.getInvoice(intInvoiceType);

objInvoice.print();
```
→ Client

Client calls the getinvoice to create objects invoice classes

```
public class clsFactoryInvoice
{
    static public IInvoice getInvoice(int intInvoiceType)
    {
        IInvoice objinv;
        if (intInvoiceType == 1)
        {
            objinv = new clsInvoiceWithHeader();
        }
        else if (intInvoiceType == 2)
        {
            objinv = new clsInvoiceWithOutHeaders();
        }
        else
        {
            return null;
        }
        return objinv;
    }
}
```
→ Factory class

Creation of objects in the factory class

Figure 11.4: intInvoice type

Can you explain singleton pattern?

There are situations in a project where we want only one instance of the object to be created and shared between the clients. No client can create an instance of the object from outside. There is only one instance of the class which is shared across the clients. Below are the steps to make a singleton pattern:

- Define the constructor as private.
- Define the instances and methods as static.

Below is a code snippet of a singleton in C#. We have defined the constructor as private, defined all the instance and methods using the **static** keyword as shown in the below code snippet figure 'Singleton in action'. The static keyword ensures that you only one instance of the object is created and you can all the methods of the class with out creating the object. As we have made the constructor private, we need to call the class directly.

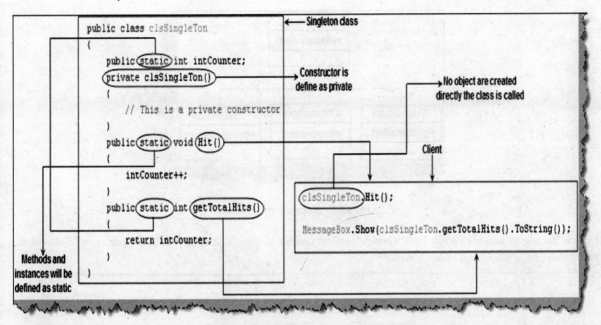

Figure 11.5: Singleton Pattern

Can you explain Façade pattern?

Façade pattern sits on the top of group of subsystems and allows them to communicate in a unified manner.

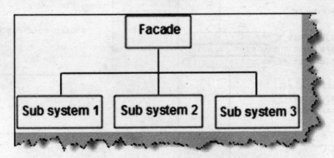

Figure 11.6: Façade Pattern

The above figure shows a practical implementation of the same. In order to place an order we need to interact with product, payment and invoice classes. So order becomes a façade which unites product, payment and invoice classes.

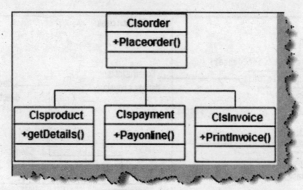

Figure 11.7: Façade in Action

Figure 'façade in action' shows how class 'clsorder' unifies / uses 'clsproduct','clsproduct' and 'clsInvoice' to implement 'PlaceOrder' functionality.

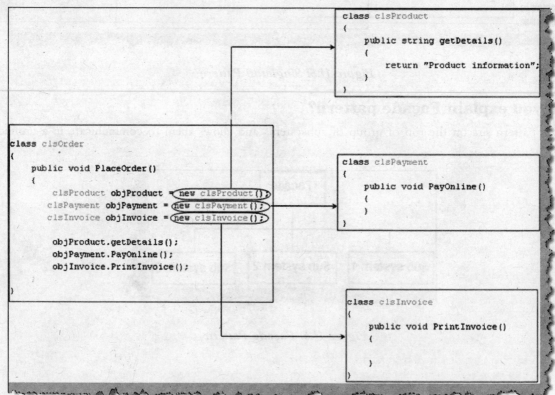

Figure 11.8: Façade code explanation

What is MVC, MVP and MVVM pattern?

All the above design patterns come in presentation pattern category and help to remove any kind of cluttered code in UI like manipulation of user interfaces and maintaining state. Thus keeping your UI code cleaner and better to maintain.

What is MVC pattern?

The main purpose using MVC(model view controller) pattern is to decouple the GUI from the Data. It also gives the ability to provide multiple views for the same Data. MVC pattern separates objects in to three important sections:

- **Model:** This section is specially for maintaining data. It is actually where your business logic, querying database, database connection etc. is actually implemented.

- **Views:** Displaying all or some portion of data, or probably different view of data. View is responsible for look and feel, Sorting, formatting etc.

- **Controller:** They are event-handling section, which affects either the model or the view. Controller responds to the mouse or keyboard input to command model and view to change. Controllers are associated with views. User interaction triggers the events to change the model, which in turn calls some methods of model to update its state to notify other registered views to refresh their display.

How can we implement MVC in ASP.NET?

By using the ASP.NET template provided in visual studio.

What is MVP?

MVP (Model view presenter) has the same goals as MVC i.e separating the UI from the model. It does the same by using a presenter class. The UI talks via an interface to the presenter class and the presenter class talks with the model.

The presenter class contains all the code needed for model communication and synchronization.

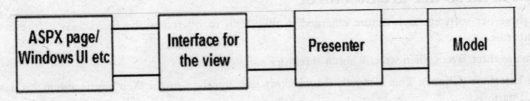

Figure 11.9: MVP

What is MVVM?

Again MVVM is an architectural pattern with the focus of removing UI cluttered code. It does the same by using an extra class called as view model. MVVM is mostly suitable for Silverlight and WPF projects because of the rich bindings provided by the technologies.

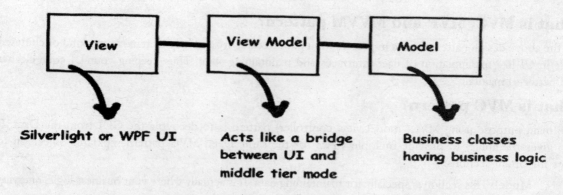

Figure 11.10: MVVM

So UI talks with the view model class and the view model class interacts with the model class.

What is the difference between MVC, MVP and MVVM and when to use what?

MVC: Here the first hit comes to the controller and the controller ties up the view and model and sends the same to the user.

MVP: Here the first hit comes to the UI and the UI interacts with a presenter class who talks with the model.

MVVM: here the first hit comes to UI and the UI talks to the model via a separate class called as view model. Rich bindings are used by the view model class to communicate to the model thus keeping the UI code clean.

MVC is good for web application like ASP.NET, MVP for windows application and MVVM for Silverlight and WPF projects as they have rich bindings.

What is three-tier architecture?

The three-tier software architecture emerged in the 1990s to overcome the limitations of the two-tier architecture.

There are three layers when we talk about three-tier architecture:

User Interface (Client): This is mostly the windows user interface or the Web interface but this has only the UI part.

Mid layer: Middle tier provides process management where business logic and rules are executed and can accommodate hundreds of users (as compared to only 100 users with the two-tier architecture) by providing functions such as queuing, application execution, and database staging.

Data Access Layer: This is also termed by the famous acronym "DAL" component. It has mainly the SQL statement which do the database operation part of the job.

Have you ever worked with Microsoft Application Blocks, if yes then which?

Application Blocks are C# and VB.NET classes distributed as Visual Studio projects that can be downloaded from Microsoft's Web site and used in any .NET application, including ASP.NET Web applications. They are useful and powerful tools that can make applications more maintainable, scalable, and efficient

Secondly, which application blocks have been used depends on really what you have implemented. However, there are two famous MAB, which is making buzz around the industry:

Data access block

Data access block gives us a readymade DAL component.

Exception management block.

This block gives us reusable classes which can reduce exception handling in the project.

What is Service Oriented architecture?

"Services" are components, which expose well-defined interfaces, and these interfaces communicate through XML messages. Using SOA, you can build workflow, which uses interfaces of these components. SOA is typically useful when you are crossing heterogeneous technical boundaries, organizations, domain etc.

In .NET, SOA technically uses Web services to communicate with each service, which is crossing boundaries. You can look SOA, which sits on top of web services and provides a workflow.

SOA uses service components, which operate in their own domain boundary. Let us note some points of service:

- They are independent components and operate in their own boundary and own technology.

- They have well defined interfaces, which use XML and WSDL to describe themselves.

- Services have URL where anyone can find them and clients can bind to theseURL to avail for the service.

- Services have very loosely coupled architecture. In order to communicate to service you only have to know the WSDL. Your client can then generate proxy from the WSDL of the service.

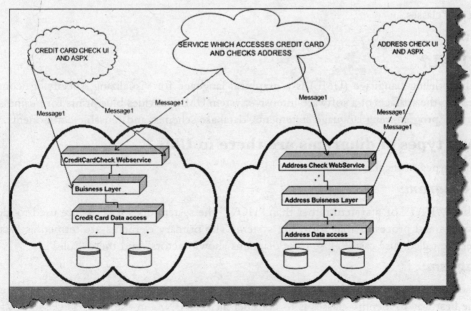

Figure 11.11: SOA Architecture

Above figure describes a broader picture of what service-oriented architecture will look like. The fundamental of SOA is a web service. In above diagram you can see there are two services available. One is the "Credit Card" service and other is "Address Check" web service. Both these services are provided by different company. Now we want to build a functionality, which needs to validate a credit card and check that addresses are proper. In short, we will need functionalities of both the "Credit Card" and "Address Check" service. Also, note the "Credit Card" service has its own business layer and DAL components, which can be in a proprietary language. It is very much possible that the whole Credit card service is made in .NET and the Address check is SAP implementation or JAVA implementation. However, because both the systems provide there functionality using Web services which is nothing but XML message communication. So we have made new service which sits like a FAÇADE on top of both the web service and performs both functionalities in one common service. You will see I have made a third service which sits on top of both the web service and consumes them. Also you can see that the UI part of the systems have access to Business layer and Web service of there system. However, the service which does both these check has only access to the Web service.

> **Note:** *It's beyond the scope of this book to discuss about SOA. However, just to keep you safe during interview this book has tried to clear some basics of SOA. I will really stress you to read WCF chapter of this book, which talks in detail of how Microsoft has visualized SOA.*

What are different ways you can pass data between tiers?

There are many ways you can pass data between tiers:

- Dataset the most preferred one as they maintain data in XML format.
- Data reader
- Custom classes.
- XML

What is UML?

The Unified Modeling Language (UML) is a graphical language for visualizing, specifying, constructing, and documenting the artifacts of a software-intensive system.UML provides blue prints for business process, System function, programming language statements, database schemas and reusable components.

How many types of diagrams are there in UML?

There are nine types of diagrams in UML:

Use case diagram:

They describe "WHAT" of a system rather than "HOW" the system does it. They are used to identify the primary elements and processes that form the system. The primary elements are termed as "actors" and the processes are called "use cases". Use Case diagrams shows "actors" and there "roles".

Class diagram:

From the use case diagram, we can now go to detail design of system, for which the primary step is class diagram. The best way to identify classes is to consider all "NOUNS" in use cases as classes, "VERBS" as methods of classes, relation between actors can then be used to define relation between classes. The relationship or association between the classes can be either an "is-a" or "has-a" relationship which can easily be identified from use cases.

Object diagram:

An object is an instance of a class. Object diagram captures the state of classes in the system and their relationships or associations at a specific point of time.

State diagram:

A state diagram, as the name suggests, represents the different states that objects in the system undergo during their life cycle. Object change in response to certain simulation so this simulation effect is captured in state diagram. Therefore, it has a initial state and final state and events that happen in between them. Whenever you think that some simulations are complicated, you can go for this diagram.

Sequence diagram:

Sequence diagrams can be used to explore the logic of a complex operation, function, or procedure. They are called sequence diagrams because sequential nature is shown via ordering of messages. First message starts at the top and the last message ends at bottom. The important aspect of a sequence diagram is that it is time-ordered. This means that the exact sequence of the interactions between the objects is represented step by step. Different objects in the sequence diagram interact with each other by passing "messages".

Collaboration diagram:

A collaboration diagram groups together the interactions between different objects to fulfill a common purpose.

Activity diagram:

Activity diagram is typically used for business process modeling, for modeling the logic captured by a single use case, or for visualizing the detailed logic of a business rule. Complicated process flows in the system are captured in the activity diagram. Similar to a state diagram, an activity diagram also consists of activities, actions, transitions, initial and final states, and guard conditions. However, difference is state diagrams are in context of simulation while activity gives detail view of business logic.

Deployment diagram:

Deployment diagrams show the hardware for your system, the software that is installed on that hardware, and the middleware used to connect the disparate machines to one another. It shows how the hardware and software work together to run a system. In one, line its shows the deployment view of the system.

Component diagram:

The component diagram represents the high-level parts that make up the system. From .NET angle point of view, they form the "NAMESPACES". This diagram depicts, at a high level, what components form part of the system, and how they are interrelated. Its shows the logical grouping of classes or group of other components.

> **Note:** *The best way to remember all the blocks of UML is "Serve cool SOUP during church ceremony" that covers State chart, Class diagrams, Sequence diagram, Object diagram, Use Case diagram, Package diagram, Deployment diagram, Collaboration diagram, Component diagram.*

What are advantages of using UML?

As the name, suggest UNIFIED MODELING LANGUAGE. Modeling has been around for years, not only in software field but also in other trades like civil, mechanical etc. Example in civil engineering drawing the main architecture built of diagram is a model by itself. Modeling makes complex and huge system to break up in to simple and discrete pieces that can be individually understood. Example simple flowchart drawing is modeling.

There are two main advantages of modeling:

- **Readability:** Representing your whole architecture in flowchart, class diagrams, ER diagrams etc makes your project more readable. Especially when programmer's change jobs handover becomes easier. More the project is not readable more the dependencies.

- **Reusability:** After the system is more readable and broken down to pieces, it becomes easier to identify redundant and similar modules. Thus increasing reusability.

So why UML? Well different languages have different ways of coding and syntaxes. In order to bring all languages in one roof UML is in to picture. As the term comes in UNIFIED, it unifies all disparate languages in one roof so people who are working on some other platforms can understand that.

How did you implement UML in your project?

First let me say, some fact about this question, you cannot implement all the nine diagrams given by UML in one project; you can but can be very rare scenario. The way UML is implemented in project varies from project to project and company to company.

Second very important point to remember is normally all diagrams are not implemented in project, but some basic diagrams are important to have in order that project is readable. When we talk about projects every project have phases example (Requirements phase, design phase, coding phase etc). As every phase of the software cycle proceeds, these diagrams come in picture. Some diagrams span across multiple phases.

> **Note:** *If you want to have a detail about software life cycle look out for chapter "Project Management".*

Normally following are different basic phases:

Requirement phase (Use Case Diagrams, Activity diagrams)

Requirement phase is the phase where you normally gather requirement and Use Cases are the best things to make explanation of the system. In requirement phase, you can further make complicated Use Cases more simple and easy to understand by using activity diagrams, but I do not see it as must in every project. If the Use cases are complicated, go for a Activity diagram. Example CRUD (creates, read, update and delete) operation use cases have no significance for making activity diagrams. So in short, the outcome UML documents from requirement phase will be Use Case and Activity diagram documents (Activity diagram documents will only be there if there are complicated Use Cases to be simplified).

> **Note:** *This question is specially asked to know have you actually used UML. I have seen many guys trying to give some jack of all answers saying "YES". Beware it is a trap.*

Not all diagrams are needed in project example: Activity diagrams will only be needed when you want some simplified look of a complicated use case.

Design phase (Class diagrams, object diagrams, Component diagrams, Collaboration diagrams, Deployment diagrams, Sequence diagrams)

Design phase is the phase where you design your technical architecture of your project. Now again in this you do not use all UML documents of a project.

However, the next document after the Use Case document will be the Component diagram. Component diagrams form a high-level classification of the system. So after "Use Cases" just try to come out with a high-level classification / grouping of related functionalities. This should be compulsory diagram, as outcome of this document will form "NAMESPACES" structure of .NET project.

Ok now once your high-level grouping is done you can go ahead with class diagrams. Especially from Use Case you get the "NOUNS" and "VERBS" which can form the class name and the method name respectively. From my point of view, class diagrams should be compulsory in projects.

Object diagrams are not compulsory it depends on how complicated your project. Object diagrams show the relation between instances of class at runtime. In short, it captures the state and relation of classes at any given moment of time. Example you have class which creates objects of different classes, its like a factory. In class diagram, you will only show that it as a simple class with a method called as "Create Object". However, in object diagrams actually you will show the types of instances create from that object.

Collaboration diagrams mainly depict interaction between object to depict some purpose. I find this diagram to be more useful than Object diagrams as they are addressed for some purpose example "Login Process" which will use "Login object", "User Object" etc to fulfill the login purpose. Therefore, if you find the process very complicated go for this diagram. I see as a thumb rule if there is an activity diagram, which shows some serious complicated scenarios. I will like to go for this diagram in order to simplify the explanation.

State chart diagram is again created if your project requires it. If your project has some complicated start and end states to show then this diagram is most useful. Recently I was making a call center project where the agent phone pickup and hang state has to be depicted. So my first state was when agent picks up the phone and the final stage was when agent hangs the phone, in between process was very complicated, which can only be shown by using state chart diagrams.

Sequence diagrams are needed if some sequence is complicated. Do not confuse sequence diagrams with Activity diagram, Activity diagrams map to a Use Case while sequence diagrams show object interaction in sequence.

Deployment diagrams are again not a compulsory requirement. It will show the hardware and software deployment of your system. If you really have leisure in your project go for it or if you want to make the client smile seeing some diagrams.

Implementation phase / Coding phase (Class diagrams for reverse Engineering, other diagrams for validity check)

In this phase, mostly class diagrams are re-engineered with the source code. However, other diagrams are also present for validity check example state chart diagrams will be used in case to check that the both activity between those states follow the proper logic. If some things have to be changed, then again there is iteration backward to the Requirement phase.

Testing phase

This phase mostly goes for the testing department. I am not talking about preparing UTP plans but SITP plans. Where the testing department will look at all diagrams to prepare a test plan and execute it. Example it will see the Use Case document to see the business rules, it will see the activity diagram and sequence diagrams to see the proper flow of modules. If some things are not proper, there is iteration back to the Design phase.

Roll out and close over phases.

All document just to re-check that things are proper, example all modules deployed according to the deployment diagrams, are all business rules in Use Cases satisfied.

Let us revise the following points:

- Not all diagrams are compulsory
- The minimum diagrams according to software life cycle phases are:
  o **Requirement phase:** Use Case Diagrams
  o **Design Phase:** Component diagrams, Class diagrams
  o **Implementation phase:** All diagrams derived from pervious phases specially class diagram for reverse engineering.
  o **Testing phase:** All diagrams derived from requirement and design phases for verification and preparing test plans.
  o **Roll out and close over phase:** All document derived from Design phase and requirement phases.

Below is a sample figure, which shows all the documents in relevant phases.

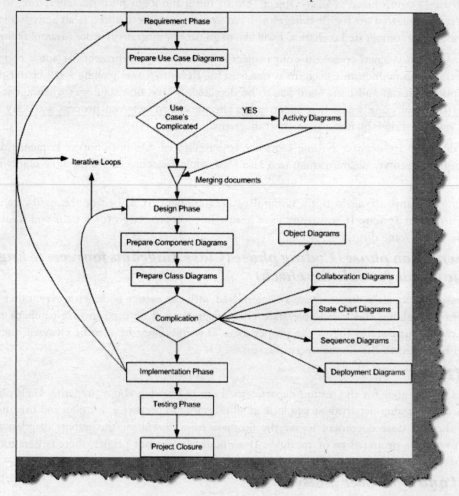

Figure 11.12: Documents in relevant phase

> **Note:** *This book will now attempt to describe every element of a UML diagram. But it is advisable that you should install any decent UML tool and do a small practice of one or two diagrams which will make you comfortable during interview.*

What are different phases in a software life cycle?

There are six phases in software development:

- Requirement
- Design
- Coding and unit testing
- System testing
- Acceptance testing
- Go live

Can you explain different software development life cycles?

SDLC (System Development Life Cycle) is overall process of developing information systems through multi stage process systems from investigation of initial requirements through analysis, design, implementation, and maintenance. The days are gone when one COBOL programmer used to analyze, test, and implement software systems. Systems have become complex, huge team members are involved, architects, analyst, programmers, testers, users etc. To manage this number of SDLC models have been created.

Following are popular models, which are listed:

- Waterfall Model.
- Spiral Model.
- Build and Fix model.
- Rapid prototyping Model.
- Incremental Model.

This section we will go into depth of different SDLC models.

Water Fall Model

This is the oldest model. It has sequence of stages; output of one stage becomes input of other.

Following are stages in Waterfall model:

- **System Requirement:** This is initial stage of the project where end user requirements are gathered and documented.
- **System Design:** In this stage detail requirements, screen layout, business rules, process diagram, pseudo code, and other documentations are prepared. This is first step in technical phase.
- **Implementation:** Depending on the design document, actual code is written here.
- **Integration and Testing:** All pieces are brought together and tested. Bugs are removed in this phase.
- **Acceptance, Installation and Deployment:** This is final stage where software is put in production and runs actual business.

- **Maintenance:** This is least glamorous phase, which runs forever. Code Changes, correction, addition etc are done in this phase.

Waterfall is suited for low risk in areas of User Interface and performance requirements, but high risk in budget and schedule predictability and control. Waterfall assumes that all requirements can be specified in advance. But unfortunately, requirement grows and changes through various stages, so it needs feedback from one stage to other.

Spiral Model

Spiral Model removes the drawback of waterfall model, by providing emphasis to go back and reiterate earlier stages a number of times as project progresses. On broader level, it is a series of short waterfall cycles, each producing an early prototype representing a part of entire project. It also helps demonstrate a Proof of Concept at early software life cycle.

Build and Fix Model

This is the way free-lancers work Write some code and keep modifying it until the customer is happy. This approach can be quite dangerous and risky.

Rapid Prototyping Model

This model is also called as Rapid Application Development. The initial emphasis is on creating prototype that look and acts like the desired product. Prototype can be created by using tools, which is different from those used for final product. Once the prototype is approved, its discarded and real software development is started from scratch. The problem with this model is that sometimes the prototype moves ahead to become the final live product, which can be bad from design point of view. It is a effective model but can have higher costing than other models as you require programmers during the initial phase of the software cycle.

Incremental Model

In this model, we divide products into builds, where section of product are created and tested separately. Here errors are found in requirement phase itself, user feedback is taken for each stage and code is tested after it is written.

What does Agile mean?

Dictionary meaning of Agile is quick moving. Now how does that apply to software? Agile development methodology considers software as the most important entity and accepts user requirement changes. Agile advocates that we should accept changes and deliver the same in small releases. Agile accepts change as a norm and encourages constant feedback from the end user.

Figure 11.13: Agile

Below figure shows how Agile differs in principles from traditional methodologies.

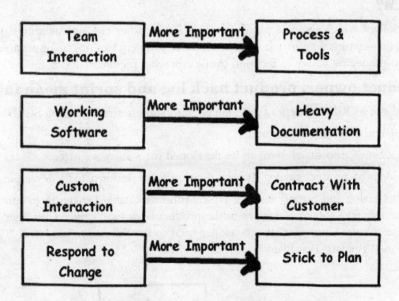

Figure 11.14: Change of Agile thinking

- It's not necessary to have hi-fi tools and process but a good team interaction can solve lot of problems.
- Working software is more important than documentation.
- Management should not pay attention to only customer contract rather interact with customer and analyze the requirements.
- In traditional methodologies we pledge to stick our plans but agile says "If the customer wants to change, analyze and change your plan accordingly".

Now are principles of Agile methodology:

- Welcome change and adapt to changing requirements
- Working software is the main measure of progress.
- Customer satisfaction is the most important thing and that can be attained by rapid, continuous delivery of useful software
- Day to day meetings between business people and development team is a must.
- Business and developers must work together. Face to face to communication is the most important thing.
- Deliver and update software regularly. In Agile we do not deliver software in one go, but rather we deliver frequently and deliver the important features first.
- Build projects around teams of motivated and trustful people.
- Design and execution should be kept simple.
- Strive for technical excellence in design and execution.
- Allow team to organize themselves.

What is SCRUM?

SCRUM is a methodology which believes rapid changes of customer can not be solved by traditional approach. So it adopts an empirical approach where it believes problem can not be understood or defined. Rather concentrate on the team's ability to respond to the emerging requirements.

What does product owner, product back log and sprint mean in SCRUM?

Before we understand the SCRUM cycle let's get familiar with some terms regarding SCRUM.

Product Owner is the end customer or the user.

Product back log is a list of prioritized items to be developed for a software project.

Sprint is the task breakup of product catalog. It's the detail task break down for a development team.

Below figure 'Product Catalog and Sprint' shows a typical product catalog broken in to sprint. In the left hand side of the figure we have shown two items in the product back log "Create Customer" and "Create Supplier". To complete "Create Customer" the developer need to the following sprint task "Code Business Logic", "Design UI" and "Prepare Test Plans".

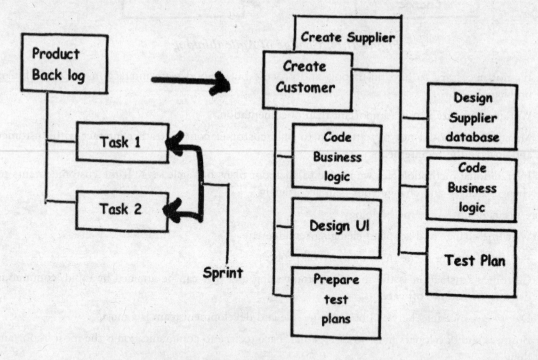

Figure 11.15: Product Catalog and Sprint

Can you explain how SCRUM flows?

Below figure 'SCRUM Flow' shows how the development flow moves in a project. We will understand the SCRUM flow step by step.

Step 1: Product owner (i.e. the customer) creates a list of product log (list of functionalities).

Step 2 and 3: In these phases we sit with the customer and prioritize the product catalog. We discuss with the customer which functionality is must and must be delivered first.

Step 4 and 5: In both these phases we breakdown the product catalog in to tasks called as sprint backlog.

Step 6: We start executing the sprint task and monitoring the sprint activity.

Step 7 and 8: Once we are done with the sprint activity, we take the next sprint / task by again going to the sprint phase.

Step 9: If there are no more sprint / task the product log is completed, which means the project is completed.

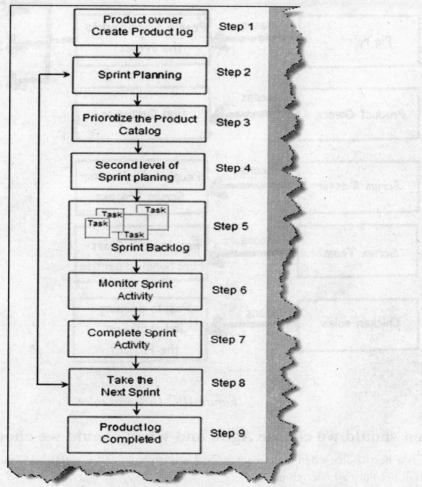

Figure 11.16: Scrum flow

Can you explain different roles in SCRUM?

SCRUM has some different terminologies when it comes to role names in SCRUM. Below is the list of roles with what actually they mean.

People with **pig roles** are those people who are committed to the project. If the project fails it affects these people. So of the pig roles are developer, customer, project manager etc.

Product owner means the end customer or user.

Scrum master is the process driver. These are the people who drive the scrum process. They are consultants for Scrum process.

People with **chicken roles** work indirectly on the project. They do not really benefit from the project but their feedback is valuable to the project. They cannot be held responsible if the project is not successful.

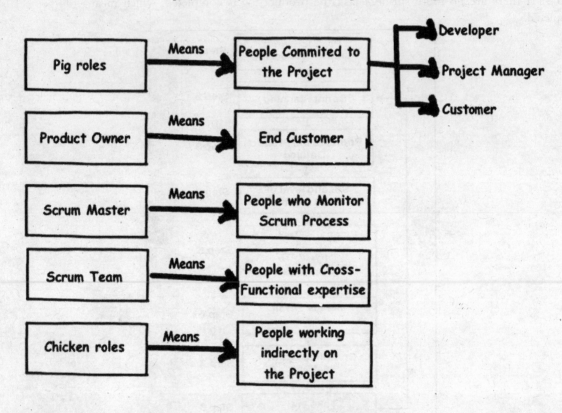

Figure 11.17:Different roles

When should we choose Agile and when should we choose waterfall?

Agile is a best choice when your requirements are evolving and not fixed. If your requirements are fixed waterfall becomes a better choice.

What are some of the important metrics in project?

There are different kinds of metrics but there are 3 prime metrics planned value, earned value and actual cost. These three metrics helps us to understand where the project stands today.

What is effort variance?

Effort Variance = (Actual effort – Estimated Effort) / Estimated Effort.

What is CAR (Causal Analysis and Resolution)?

The basic purpose of CAR is to analyze all defects, problems, and good practices/positive triggers in projects, perform a root cause analysis of the same, identify respective corrective and preventive actions, and track these to closure. The advantage of CAR is that root causes are scientifically identified and their corrective and preventive actions are carried out. CAR needs to be performed at project initiation, all phase and project ends and on a monthly basis. Fishbone diagram is one of the ways you can do CAR.

What is DAR (Decision Analysis and Resolution)?

Decision Analysis and Resolution is to analyze possible decisions using a formal evaluation process that identifies alternatives against established criteria.

Example in a project you are said to use third party tools so you will not depend on only one tool but evaluate three to four more tools so that in case of problems you have alternatives. This is called as DAR

What is a fish bone diagram?

Dr. Kaoru Ishikawa invented the fishbone diagram. Therefore, it can be also referred as Ishikawa diagram.

Fishbone diagram is an analysis diagram, which provides a systematic way of looking at effects and the causes that create or contribute to those effects. Because of the function of the fishbone diagram, it may be referred to as a cause-and-effect diagram. The design of the diagram looks much like the skeleton of a fish. Therefore, it is often referred to as the fishbone diagram.

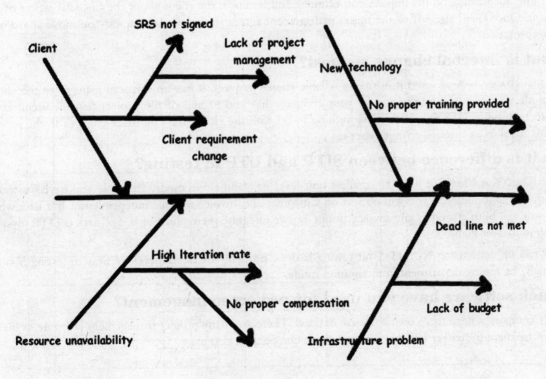

Figure 11.18: Fish bone diagram

Fishbone diagram helps in categorizing potential causes of problems or issues in an orderly way and in identifying root causes.

Below is a sample fish bone diagram, which shows why a project dead line was not met. The middle arrow is the main problem "Deadline not met". Then we start analyzing other problems, which has led to this problem. Example There is client problem — as he is always changing the requirement — this is caused because the company did not sign the SRS — and this happened as proper project management procedures where not at place. So to solve this problem we either appoint a project manager or give training on project management to senior team members.

What is Pareto principle?

Pareto principle also paraphrased as 80/20 principle is simple effective problem tackling way in management. It says that 20% of your problems lead to other 80% of problems. So rather than concentrating on the 80% of problem if you concentrate on 20% of problems you can save lot of trouble. So in pareto you analyze the problems and only concentrate on 20% of your vital problems. In projects, the first 10% and the last 10% of project form the vital part of project.

How do you handle change request?

Normally change request are handled by preparing an Impact analysis document and then doing re-estimation. Example you have an on going project, which has a customer table. Now customer wants to also have addresses assigned to it. Therefore, you normally raise a changerequest and then doan impact analysis of the same. Depending on the impact, you estimate and let know the client about the financial aspect of the project. Once client sign off or the upper management agrees to the change request you move ahead with implementation.

What is internal change request?

Internal change request are not normally billable change request, it has no financial gains from the client. Example your architecture division of your company has said in mid of the project that the architecture has to be modified. Definitely this has nothing to do with the client, but you make changes to the project so this is called as Internal change request.

What is difference between SITP and UTP in testing?

UTP (Unit Test Plan) are done at smallest unit level or stand-alone mode. Example you have Customer and invoicing module. So you will do test on Customer and Invoice module independently. But later when we want test both customer and invoice in one set we integrate them and test it. So that's is SITP (System Integration Test Plan)

UTP can be done using NUNIT. Unit testing is done normally by developers and System testing is done normally by testing department in integration mode.

Which software have you used for project management?

Many companies have there own software defined. There are many project management software available at this moment in market but this can vary from company to company

Worst it can very from project to project. But Microsoft project is the most used software at this moment. So just brush your skills on Microsoft project, its used heavily across industry.

People in your project do not perform, what will you do?

In such kind of question, they want to see your delegation skills. The best answer to this question is a job of a project manager is managing projects and not problems of people, so I will delegate this work to HR or upper authority.... Thanks to my Project Manager for this beautiful answer.

What is black box testing and White box testing?

Black box testing is also termed as functional testing. It ignores how the internal functionality of a system works and depends only what are the outputs on specified inputs. Source code availability is not an important in back box testing. Black box testing is mostly to ensure that it meets the user functionality.

According to IEEE, standards following are characteristics of Black box testing:

● " Testing that ignores the internal mechanism of a system or component and focuses solely on the outputs generated in response to selected inputs and execution conditions,"

● "Testing conducted to evaluate the compliance of a system or component with specified functional requirements."

One of the way of doing black box testing is Manual testing what the tester performs. For instance, you can install the application on a machine and tester starts testing is a type of black box testing. In our case the tester is completely unaware of the how the program logic flows and how its coded etc.

White box testing is opposite to Black box it requires internal know how of how the logic flows. As this testing needs know how of the internal structure it can only be done programmers. Unit testing is one of the ways of doing White box testing in which programmers use NUNIT or JNUIT to test each class individually. White box testing can be done by programmer by either stepping through the code or testing the classes and components in isolation.

What is the difference between Unit testing, Assembly testing and Regression testing?

Unit testing is also termed as Component testing. Unit testing ensures that reliable program unit meets their requirements. Unit testing is normally conducted by programmer under the supervision of the project lead or the team Lead. Main objective of this testing is to test each unit in isolation and individually. This is done by knowing what the inputs to the unit are and what the expected outputs for the same. Unit testing is a white box activity. Unit test normally comes in the implementation phase of the project.

For instance in the below figure we are trying to do unit testing on the customer class. So we create the object of Customer class assign "CustomerCode" and "Age" property and check for the response. For instance, in this condition, we tried to pass a non-numeric value to the "Age" property and the class threw an error saying, "Age should be numeric". So here the basic unit testing entity is your class.

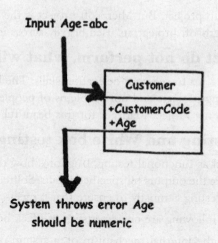

Figure 11.19: unit testing of customer class

However, unit testing is not limited to a component, object, or function. Therefore, definition of a unit testing will depend on the approach. Below are some examples of unit testing:

- Checkpoints in UI like tab orders, error messages, look and feel etc.
- Class, object, component level testing as said previously.

In case of functional programming can be a simple method or function.

- Logic testing for algorithms. Some projects can have some critical algorithm for instance some kind of custom sorting, security implementation etc. Therefore, that logic can be tested independently.

However, the general thumb rule of what is Unit in Unit testing is that the module self-contained and by itself.

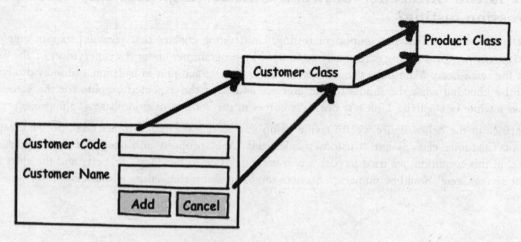

Figure 11.20: Simple Scenario

Assembly testing goes one-step ahead than unit testing. It demonstrates that can the modules interact in a correct, stable, and proper manner as defined by the functional specifications provided by the client. Assembly testing is Black box testing style and also called as Integration testing. For instance in the above unit test of the "Customer" class, testing was done in isolation. But in actually the "Customer" class is not going to be stand alone rather it will be used more in conjunction with the "Product" class and also will have UI to do the same. So in short, the "Customer" class will work with two more entity one is the "UI" and the other is the "Product" class. So normally, assembly testing is done through UI but not necessarily.

The above figure defines a simple scenario for integration testing. The same "Customer" class is now tested with the "UI" and "Product" to see if the interaction between them matches according to functional specifications.

Regression testing ensures that application function properly even if there are changes or enhancements to system. For instance you change the "Product" class still you will run all the test cases for "Product", "Customer" and "UI" just to make sure that any changes in "Product" class does not affect interaction with other entities. So you will see when testers do a regression testing they run all the scripts to ensure that nothing has been affected.

What is V model in testing?

V model maps the type of test to the stage of development in a project. V model stressed the point that every phase in project should have a test phase also.

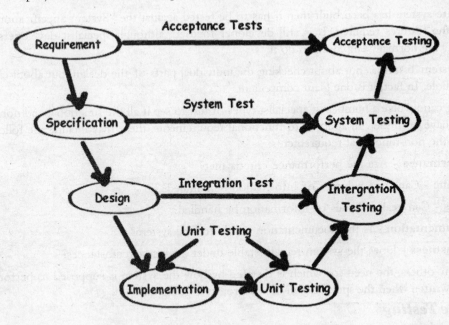

Figure 1!.21: V model

Unit Testing

Starting from the bottom the first test level is "Unit Testing". It involves checking that each feature specified in the "Component Design" has been implemented in the component.

In theory, an independent tester should do this, but in practice, the developer usually does it, as they are the only people who understand how a component works. The problem with a component is that it performs only a small part of the functionality of a system, and it relies on co-operating with other parts of the system, which may not have been built yet. To overcome this, the developer either builds, or uses special software to trick the component into believe it is working in a fully functional system. This test maps with the implementation phase and normally developers do the unit testing for the project.

Integration Testing

As the components are constructed and tested they are then linked together to check if they work with each other. It is a fact that two components that have passed all theirtests independently, when connected to each other produce one new component full of faults. These tests can be done by specialists, or by the developers.

Integration Testing is not focused on what the components are doing but on how they communicate with each other, as specified in the "System Design". The "System Design" defines relationships between components.

The tests are organized to check all the interfaces, until all the components have been built and interfaced to each other producing the whole system. Integration test cases are written when design documents are written.

System Testing

Once the entire system has been built then it has to be tested against the "System Specification" to check if it delivers the features required. It is still developer focused, although specialist developers known as systems testers are normally employed to do it.

In essence, System Testing is not about checking the individual parts of the design, but about checking the system as a whole. In fact, it is one giant component.

System testing can involve a number of specialist types of test to see if all the functional and non-functional requirements have been met. In addition to functional requirements, these may include the following types of testing for the non-functional requirements:

- **Performance -** Are the performance criteria met?
- **Volume -** Can large volumes of information be handled?
- **Stress -** Can peak volumes of information be handled?
- **Documentation -** Is the documentation usable for the system?
- **Robustness -** Does the system remain stable under adverse circumstances?

There are many others, the need for which is dictated by how the system is supposed to perform. System test plans are written when the specification of the project is going on.

Acceptance Testing

Acceptance Testing checks the system against the "Requirements". It is similar to systems testing in that the whole system is checked but the important difference is the change in focus:

Systems testing checks that the system that was specified has been delivered. Acceptance Testing checks that the system will deliver what was requested.

The customer should always do acceptance testing and not the developer. The customer knows what is required from the system to achieve value in the business and is the only person qualified to make that judgment. This testing is more of getting the answer for whether is the software delivered as defined by the customer. It is like getting a green flag from the customer that the software is up to the expectation and ready to be used. Acceptance test plans are written during the requirement phase of the project. In real scenario these test plans should be given by the end customer.

How do you start a project?

Left to the readers

How did you do resource allocations?

Left to the readers

How will you do code reviews?

The way in which code reviews are done change from person to person and also company to company.

However, the normally when a project is started project people define their architecture, coding standards etc in their design document. So before starting the code review you will have go through the standards defined in the project. Reviews are done by two methodologies one is peer review and the other is by external part who is not the member of the project. So we give the standard document to the reviewer he checks it, gives his perspective and logs a review to the development. If the review is critical then the development team can close it or they can wave it off.

What is CMMI?

It is a collection of instructions an organization can follow with the purpose to gain better control over its software development process.

What are the five levels in CMMI?

There are five levels of the CMM. According to the SEI,

Level 1 – Initial

At maturity level 1, processes are usually ad hoc and the organization usually does not provide a stable environment. Success in these organizations depends on the competence and heroics of people in the organization and not on the use of proven processes. In spite of this ad hoc, chaotic environment, maturity level 1 organizations often produce productsand services that work; however, they frequently exceed the budget and schedule of their projects.

Maturity level 1 organizations are characterized by a tendency to over commit, abandon processes in the time of crisis, and not be able to repeat their past successes again.

Level 2 – Repeatable

At maturity level 2, software development successes are repeatable. The organization may use some basic project management to track cost and schedule.

Process discipline helps to ensure that existing practices are retained during times of stress. When these practices are in place, projects are performed and managed according to their documented plans.

Project status and the delivery of services are visible to management at defined points (for example, at major milestones and at the completion of major tasks).

Basic project management processes are established to track cost, schedule, and functionality. The necessary process discipline is in place to repeat earlier successes on projects with similar applications.

Level 3 – Defined

At maturity level 3, processes are well characterized and understood, and are described in standards, procedures, tools, and methods.

The organization has set of standard processes, which is the basis for level 3, is established and improved over time. These standard processes are used to establish consistency across the organization. Projects establish their defined processes by the organization's set of standard processes according to tailoring guidelines.

The organization's management establishes process objectives based on the organization is set of standard processes and ensures that these objectives are appropriately addressed.

A critical distinction between level 2 and level 3 is the scope of standards, process descriptions, and procedures. At level 2, the standards, process descriptions, and procedures may be quite different in each specific instance of the process (for example, on a particular project). At level 3, the standards, process descriptions, and procedures for a project are tailored from the organization's set of standard processes to suit a particular project or organizational unit.

Level 4 – Managed

Using precise measurements, management can effectively control the software development effort. In particular, management can identify ways to adjust and adapt the process to particular projects without measurable losses of quality or deviations from specifications.

Sub processes are selected that significantly contribute to overall process performance. These selected sub processes are controlled using statistical and other quantitative techniques.

A critical distinction between maturity level 3 and maturity level 4 is the predictability of process performance. At maturity level 4, the performance of processes is controlled using statistical and other quantitative techniques, and is quantitatively predictable. At maturity level 3, processes are only qualitatively predictable.

Level 5 – Optimizing

Maturity level 5 focuses on persistently improving process performance through both incremental and innovative technological improvements. Quantitative process-improvement objectives for the organization are established, continually revised to reflect changing business objectives, and used as criteria in managing process improvement. The effects of deployed process improvements are measured and evaluated against the quantitative process-improvement objectives. Both the defined processes and the organization set of standard processes are targets of measurable improvement activities.

Process improvements to address common causes of process variation and measurably improve the organization's processes are identified, evaluated, and deployed.

Optimizing processes that are nimble, adaptable and innovative depends on the participation of an empowered workforce aligned with the business values and objectives of the organization. The organization's ability to rapidly respond to changes and opportunities is enhanced by finding ways to accelerate and share learning.

A critical distinction between maturity level 4 and maturity level 5 is the type of process variation addressed. At maturity level 4, processes are concerned with addressing special causes of process variation and providing statistical predictability of the results. Though processes may produce predictable results, the results may be insufficient to achieve the established objectives. At maturity level 5, processes are concerned with addressing common causes of process variation and changing the process (that is, shifting the mean of the process performance) to improve process performance (while maintaining statistical probability) to achieve the established quantitative process-improvement objectives.

> **Note:** *I am sure during interview specially the SQA guys expect all the different levels of CMMI to be in mind. So below is the figure, which will help you remembering the same.*

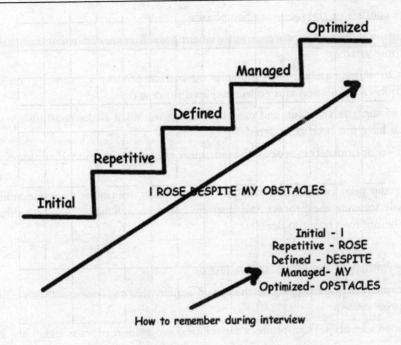

Figure 11.22: CMMI

What is SIX sigma?

Sigma means deviation in Greek language. Deviation means how much variations exist in a set of data. For instance let's say in a software maintenance project out of 100 defects 68 defects are rectified to the mark and remaining bounce back that means your bug fixing process is on "2 Sigma" level. I had described only from bug fixing perspective. But this can be applicable to any process organization.

SIGMA LEVEL	DEFECTS PER MILLION OPPORTUNITIES
1	690,000
2	308,537
3	66,807
4	6,210
5	233
6	3.4

Figure 11.23: Six Sigma

Therefore, I should only have 3.4 defects in a million defects then I can say I am six sigma.

What are DMAIC and DMADV?

Six Sigma has two key methodologies DMAIC and DMADV. DMAIC is used to improve an existing business process. DMADV is used to create new product designs or process designs in such a way that it results in a more predictable, mature and defect free performance.

DMAIC

Basic methodology consists of the following five phases:

- **Define:** formally define the process improvement goals that are consistent with customer demands and enterprise strategy.

- **Measure:** to define baseline measurements on current process for future comparison. Map and measure process in question and collect required process data.

- **Analyze:** to verify relationship and causality of factors. What is the relationship? Are there other factors that have not been considered?

- **Improve:** to optimize the process based upon the analysis using techniques like Design of experiments.

- **Control:** setup pilot runs to establish process capability, transition to production and thereafter continuously measure the process and institute control mechanisms to ensure that variances are corrected before they result in defects.

DMADV

Basic methodology consists of the following five phases:

- **Define:** formally define the goals of the design activity that are consistent with customer demands and enterprise strategy.

- **Measures:** to identify CTQs, product capabilities, production process capability, risk assessment, etc.

- **Analyze:** to develops and design alternatives, creates high-level design and evaluates design capability to select the best design.

- **Design:** to develop detail design, optimize design, and plan for design verification this phase may require simulations.

- **Verify:** to design, setup pilot runs, implement production process and handover to process owners. This phase may also require simulations.

What are the various ways of doing software estimation ?

There are many techniques available for estimating a project:

- Function points
- Use Case points
- WBS etc etc.

What is function point estimation?

In function point we break the application in to smaller pieces called as elementary process and estimate the application.

How did you estimate by using function points ?

Below are the steps in function points:

- First Count ILF, EIF, EI, EQ, RET, DET, FTR and use the rating tables. After you have counted all the elements, you will get the unadjusted function points.

- Put rating values 0 to 5 to all 14 GSC. Adding all total 14 GSC to come out with total VAF. Formula for VAF = 0.65 + (sum of all GSC factor/100).

- Finally, make the calculation of adjusted function point. Formula: Total function point = VAF * Unadjusted function point.

- Make estimation how many function points you will do per day. These is also called as "Performance factor".

- On basis of performance factor, you can calculate Man/Days.

What is the FP per day in your current company?

Left to the readers as every company has his own FP per Day. For .NET its 0.8 FP per day as a general standard.

> **Note:** *There is a free PDF provided "How to prepare Software Quotations?" Please do refer Function point chapter.*

What is SMC approach of estimation?

In this approach we divide the project in to small section and assign complexity factory (simple, medium and complex) to each of those sections. Each of these complexities are assigned man days and the total man days are estimated.

How do you estimate maintenance project and change requests?

Mostly people use Simple, medium and complex approach for change request estimation.

12

Ajax

What problem does Ajax solve?

In order to answer this question first lets understand how does browser and server work when we request any website. Below figure depicts pictorially the web environment. When client sends data to the server it post backs form element data, hidden fields,images,cookie information to the server and server make the page and sends the same information back to the browser. The bad part this happens with every request and response.

Below are the issues:

- **Unnecessary data transfers:** In the below model, unnecessary data is transferred between client and server. For instance, the whole page is posted and refreshed even when we want small data of the page to be refreshed.

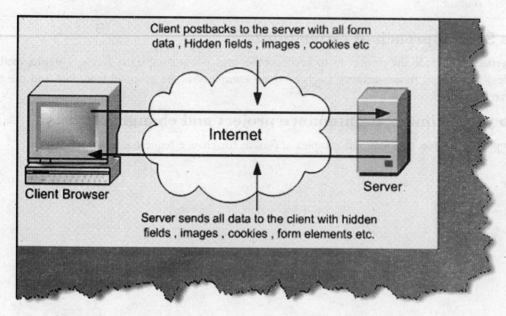

Figure 12.1: The problem

- **Synchronous processing:** When a user requests for a page he has to wait until the complete round trip happens. In short, the request / response work on a synchronous model rather than asynchronous which makes user experience very difficult. How many times it has happened that you are requesting a page and you see the below screen...frustrating right.

Figure 12.2: Synchronous processing

- **Unnecessary processing by server:** Because we are posting unnecessary information to the server, the server is overloaded with unnecessary processing.

What is Ajax?

Ajax is a set of client side technologies that provides asynchronous communication between user interfaces and web server. So the advantages of using Ajax are asynchronous communication, minimal data transfer and server is not overloaded with unnecessary load.

What is the fundamental behind Ajax?

XmlHttpRequest is the fundamental behind Ajax. This allows the browser to communicate to a back end server asynchronously.XmlHttpRequest object allows the browser to communicate with server with out posting the whole page and only sending the necessary data asynchronously.

How do we use XMLHttpRequest object in JavaScript?

Below is a code snippet, which shows how to use XMLHttpRequest object. In this code snippet, we are sending a GET request on the local IIS. Below is the explanation of the code snippet according to the numbers specified in the code snippet?

1,2,3,4 - This is like checking which is this browser and create the objects accordingly. XMLHttpRequest objects have different ways of technical implementation according to different browsers. In Internet explorer it is an activex object but in other browsers its XMLHttpRequest. So if windows.XMLHttpRequest does not return null then we can createXMLHttpRequest object. If it returns null then we can try creating the activex object Microsoft.XMLHttp object. In case it fails probably then probably we have an older version of XML that is MSXML2. So in the error handling we will try to create the MSXML2 object.

5 - In this snippet, we OPEN the connection to the local host server and specify what type of request we are using. In this case, we are using the GET method.

6 - Finally, we make a request to the server.

7 - Here we get the request sent by the server back to the client browser. This is a blocking call as we need to wait to get the request back from the server. This call is synchronous that means we need to wait for the response from the server.

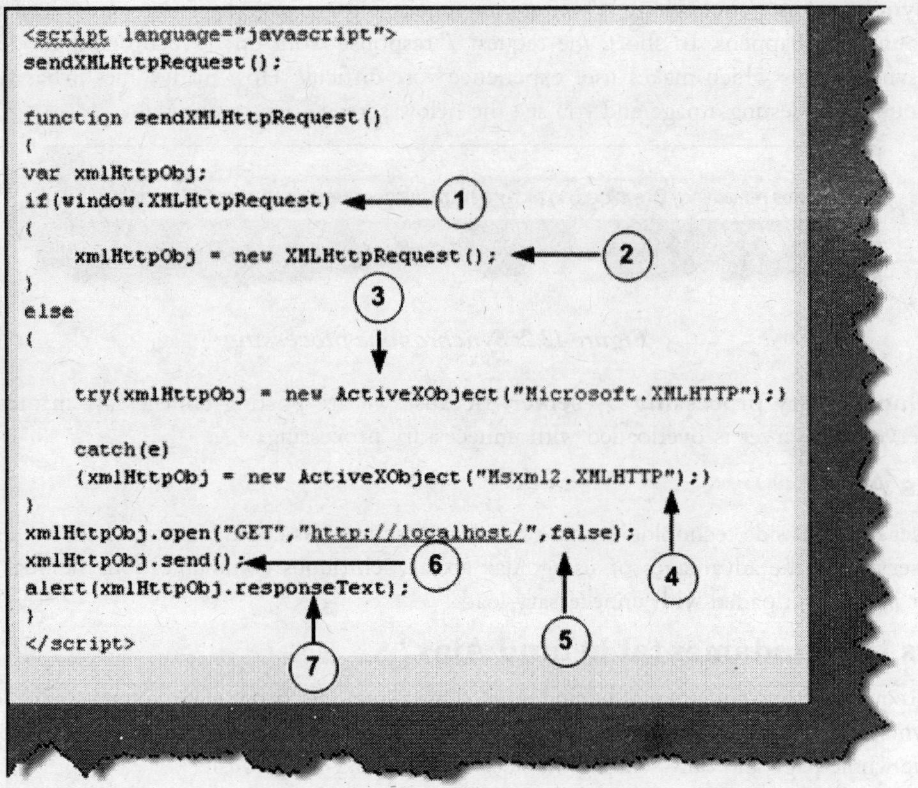

```
<script language="javascript">
sendXMLHttpRequest();

function sendXMLHttpRequest()
{
var xmlHttpObj;
if(window.XMLHttpRequest)      ◄—— ①
{
    xmlHttpObj = new XMLHttpRequest();  ◄—— ②
}
                                   ③
else
{



    try{xmlHttpObj = new ActiveXObject("Microsoft.XMLHTTP");}

    catch(e)
    {xmlHttpObj = new ActiveXObject("Msxml2.XMLHTTP");}
}
xmlHttpObj.open("GET","http://localhost/",false);
xmlHttpObj.send();◄——  ⑥                          ④
alert(xmlHttpObj.responseText);            ⑤
}
</script>
                        ⑦
```

Figure 12.3: XML Httprequest

Can you explain Scriptmanager control in Ajax?

Scriptmanager control is the central heart of Ajax. They manage all the Ajax related objects on the page. Some of the core objectives of scriptmanager control are as follows:

- Helps load core Ajax related script and library.
- Provides access to web services.
- ASP.NET authentication, role and profile services are loaded by scriptmanager control.
- Provided registration of server controls and behaviors.
- Enable full or partial rendering of a web page.
- Provide localization features.

In short, any Ajax enable page should have this control.

What is the use of update panel in Ajax?

Update panel is a component which enables sections of ASP.NET page to be partially rendered without a post back.

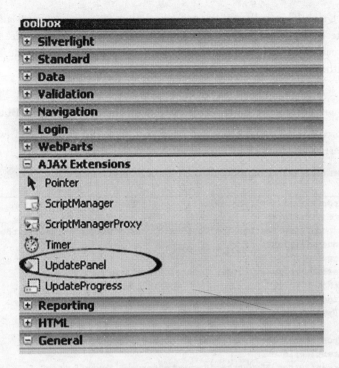

Figure 12.4: Update panel

How do we consume web service in Ajax?

In the script manager tag we need to specify the service reference path of the web service URL.

```
<asp:ScriptManager ID="ScriptManager1" runat="server">
<Services>
<asp:ServiceReference Path="Customer.asmx" />
</Services>
</asp:ScriptManager>
```

We can then call the Customer object in the javascript client as shown in the below code snippet.

```
function LoadAll()
{
      Customer.LoadCustomers(LoadCustomerToSelectOption, ErrorHandler,
      TimeOutHandler);
}
```

Can you explain the concept of triggers in 'UpdatePanel' control?

Triggers are child tags for 'UpdatePanel' tag. Many times we would like to update the panel when some event occurs or a value change on a control. This can be achieved by using triggers. There are two types of triggers **'ControlEventTrigger'** and **'ControlValueTrigger'**. So let's first understand

'ControlEventTrigger'. Using 'ControlEventTrigger' we define on which control and at which event the update panel should refresh. Below is a simple code snippet for 'ControlEventTrigger'. 'ControlEventTrigger' are defined using '<atlas:ControlEventTrigger>' tag. We have numbered the code snippet below so let's understand the same with numbers:

1 → We need to define 'ControlEventTrigger' using '<atlas:ControlEventTrigger>' tag.

2 → In this sample we will link trigger in 'UpdatePanel1' with the click event of 'Button1'.

3 → In the '<atlas:ControlEventTrigger>' tag we need to define the control and event using 'ControlId' and 'EventName' properties respectively.

So now when the button click event happens 'UpdatePanel1' is refreshed.

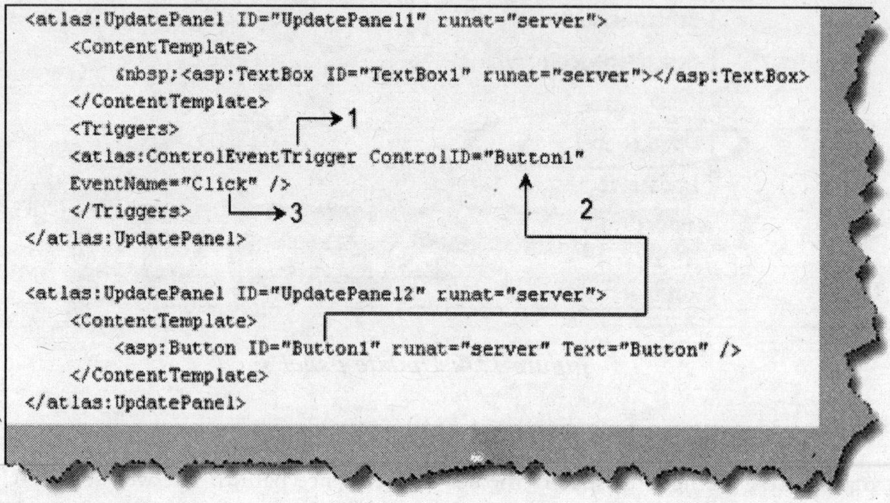

```
<atlas:UpdatePanel ID="UpdatePanel1" runat="server">
    <ContentTemplate>
         <asp:TextBox ID="TextBox1" runat="server"></asp:TextBox>
    </ContentTemplate>
    <Triggers>                      →1
    <atlas:ControlEventTrigger ControlID="Button1"
    EventName="Click" />
    </Triggers>        →3                    2
</atlas:UpdatePanel>

<atlas:UpdatePanel ID="UpdatePanel2" runat="server">
    <ContentTemplate>
        <asp:Button ID="Button1" runat="server" Text="Button" />
    </ContentTemplate>
</atlas:UpdatePanel>
```

Figure 12.5: UpdatePanel control

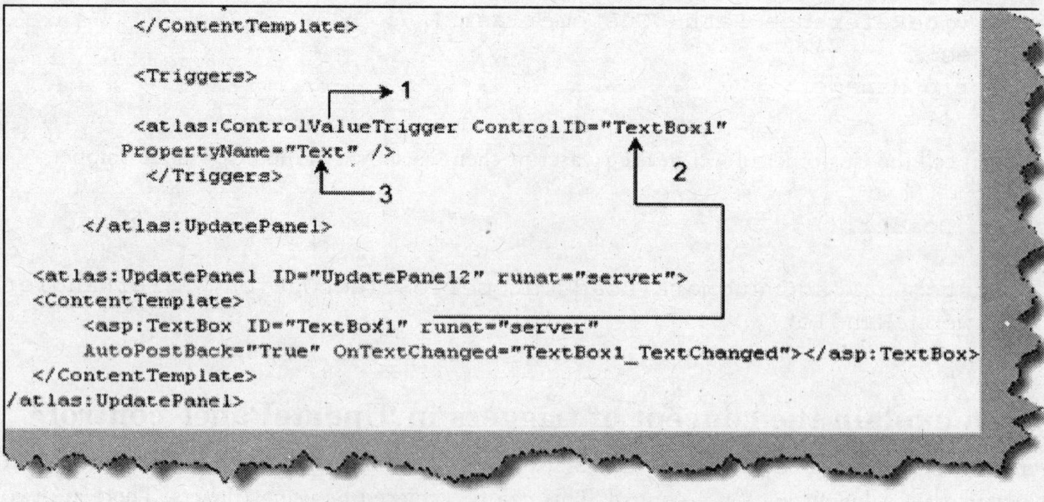

```
    </ContentTemplate>

    <Triggers>                      →1

    <atlas:ControlValueTrigger ControlID="TextBox1"
    PropertyName="Text" />
    </Triggers>      →3                    2

    </atlas:UpdatePanel>

<atlas:UpdatePanel ID="UpdatePanel2" runat="server">
<ContentTemplate>
    <asp:TextBox ID="TextBox1" runat="server"
    AutoPostBack="True" OnTextChanged="TextBox1_TextChanged"></asp:TextBox>
</ContentTemplate>
/atlas:UpdatePanel>
```

Figure 12.6: Control Value Trigger

Using 'ControlValueTrigger' we can update a panel when an external control has reached some value. So again we need to define the same in a 'Triggers' tag. We need to put the 'ControlvalueTrigger' tag with control and property defined using the 'ControlId' property. So according to below code snippet when the value of 'Textbox1' changes we need to update the top panel.

Can you explain the 'UpdateProgress' component?

Some times we have huge task at the back end for processing and we would like to show a user friendly message until the processing finishes. That's where the 'UpdateProgress' control comes in to picture.

To use 'UpdateProgress' control we need to use 'UpdatePanel' tag. 'UpdateProgress' forms the child tag of 'UpdatePanel' control. Until the server processing finishes we can display a message which can be defined in the 'ProgressTemplate' tag which is the child tag of 'UpdateProgress' tag.

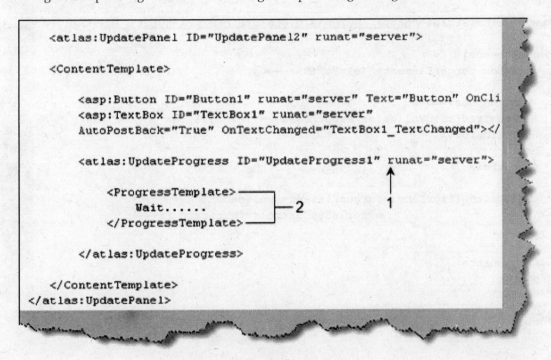

```
<atlas:UpdatePanel ID="UpdatePanel2" runat="server">

<ContentTemplate>

    <asp:Button ID="Button1" runat="server" Text="Button" OnCli
    <asp:TextBox ID="TextBox1" runat="server"
    AutoPostBack="True" OnTextChanged="TextBox1_TextChanged"></

    <atlas:UpdateProgress ID="UpdateProgress1" runat="server">    1

        <ProgressTemplate>
            Wait......                                 2
        </ProgressTemplate>

    </atlas:UpdateProgress>

</ContentTemplate>
</atlas:UpdatePanel>
```

Figure 12.7: Update progress

How can you do validations in Ajax?

We can perform all the necessary validation like required field, type checking, range checking etc using Ajax. Below is a small snippet which shows how to use a required field validator. We have numbered the code snippet to understand the code more proper.

1 → We have defined a text box 'TextBox1' which will be validated for required field.

2 → We have defined a simple '<span>' HTML tag which will display the error message.

3, 4 and 5 → We use the XML declarative Ajax script to define that 'TextBox1' has validators and it's a required field validator. To define the required field validator we need the 'RequiredFieldValidator' controls inside the validators.

6 → We then define where the error should be displayed using the 'ValidationErrorLabel'. In this case we will be displaying error in the span 'Validator1' which was defined previously.

```
<input type="text" id="TextBox1" class="input" /> ─────► 1
<span id="validator1" style="color: red">*</span> ─────► 2
</form>

<script type="text/xml-script">

<page xmlns:script="http://schemas.microsoft.com/xml-script/2005">

 <components>
  <textBox targetElement="TextBox1"> ─────► 3

   <validators> ─────► 4
    <requiredFieldValidator errorMessage="TextBox1 can not be empty." />
   </validators>
                       ↓
                       5

  </textBox>

  <validationErrorLabel targetElement="validator1" ──────┐
                       associatedControl="TextBox1" /> ───┴─ 6


 </components>
</page>
</script>
```

Figure 12.8: Validation in Ajax

Note: *The above sample shows a sample for 'requiredFieldValidator', but we can also use other validators like rangeValidator, typeValidator, rangeValidator and regexValidator.*

How do we do exception handling in Ajax?

Exception handling in Ajax is done using the 'ErrorTemplate' which forms the child tag of 'ScriptManager'. There are three steps to achieve error handling in Ajax. Below figure 'ErrorHandling' in Ajax shows the three steps in a pictorial fashion.

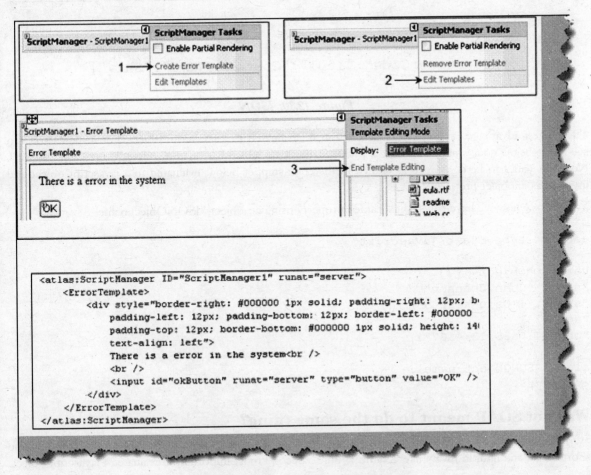

Figure 12.9: exception handling

Step 1 → Right click on the script manager and click 'Create Error Template'.

Step 2 → Once done click on 'Edit Templates'.

Step 3 → Enter which error message you want to display when there is a error and then finally click 'End Template Editing'.

Just click back on the HTML view to see what we have in the HTML. You can see the 'ErrorTemplate' tag is the fundamental driver for handling errors.

What is JSON?

JSON (JavaScript object notation) helps us to present and exchange data in a self-descriptive, independent and light way. This data can then be easily consumed and transformed in to javascript objects.

Below is a simple example of JSON format looks. You can understand from the format how lightweight and easy the format looks.

← → C   🗋 localhost:1402/Myajax/getCustomer

{"CustomerCode":"1001","CustomerName":"Shiv"}

Figure 12.10: JSON

The biggest advantage of JSON format is it can be evaluated to a javascript object. For instance you can see in the below code snippet we have a JSON format data which has "name","street","age" and "phone". Now this data can be consumed as shown in the code snippet below, evaluated to a javascript object and invoked as anobject property.

You can see how we have called the "name" property using an object "JSONObject.name".

```
<script type="text/javascript">

var JSONObject= {
"name":"John Johnson",
"street":"Oslo West 555",
"age":33,
"phone":"555 1234567"};

alert(JSONObject.name);
</script>
```

Was not SOAP meant to do the same thing?

SOAP is heavy due to XML tags. For example a SOAP message "<Name>Shiv</Name>" will become short, sweet and light in JSON like "Name": "Shiv". Second most important it evaluates a javascript object.

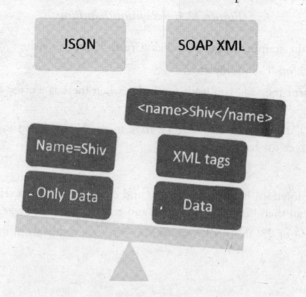

Figure 12.11: SOAP meant to do the same thing

Do all technologies support JSON?

Yes, Almost all technologies who deal with exchange of data support JSON. For instance if you want to that your WCF service should send JSON message rather than SOAP you can set the "ResponseFormat" as "WebMessageFormat.Json" on your operation contract.

```
[OperationContract]
[WebInvoke(Method="GET", UriTemplate="/GetData",
RequestFormat=WebMessageFormat.Json,
        ResponseFormat=WebMessageFormat.Json)]
string GetData();
```

If you want your MVC to emit out JSON data you can return "JsonResult" as shown below. If you call the below action it will emit out Customer objects in Json format.

```
public JsonResult CustomerJson()
{
        List<Customer> obj1 = new List<Customer>();
        Thread.Sleep(5000);
        Customer obj = new Customer();
        obj.CustomerCode = "1001";
        obj1.Add(obj);
        return Json(obj1,JsonRequestBehavior.AllowGet);
}
```

13

Reports

How do we access crystal reports in .NET?

Crystal reports comes with Visual studio setup itself. Right click the solution explorer → add new item and you can see a crystal report template as shown in figure 'Crystal report template'. You can add an '.rpt' file using this template.

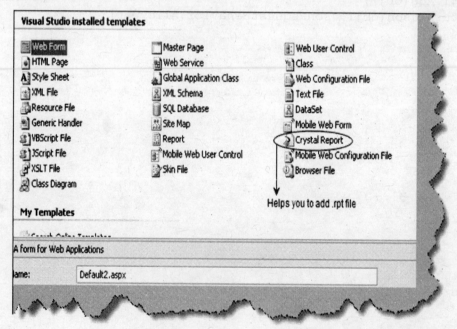

Figure 13.1: crystal report

What are the various components in crystal reports?

There are four major components in crystal reports **Report designer**, **Reports engine**, **Report viewer** and **object models**.

Report designer gives a graphical interface to create and modify reports. To view the designer add a new crystal report file and double click on it you should see the report designer as shown in figure 'Report designer'.

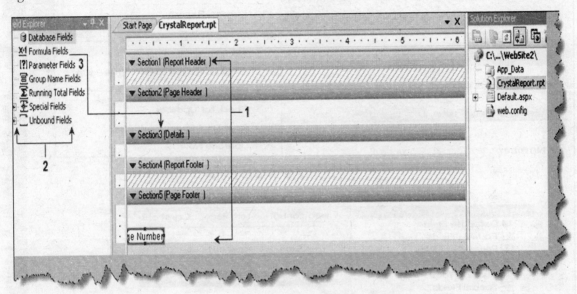

Figure 13.2: various component

Reports engine does the formatting and conversion part of crystal reports. It helps convert the contents of reports in word, excel, PDF, HTML and other formats. **Report viewer**s are controls which you can see on the visual studio tool box; you can drag and drop those controls on an ASPX page or windows application to view reports made using crystal. **Object models** help us manage crystal reports objects during design time and run time.

What basic steps are needed to display a simple report in crystal?

To understand this sample let display a simple report using crystal.

Step1: Create a web application project.

Step2: Add new item and select crystal report from the template. This adds a new RPT file in your solution explorer.

Step3: Double click on the RPT file click on Crystal reports → Field explorer as shown in figure below. You should see the field explorer toolbar.

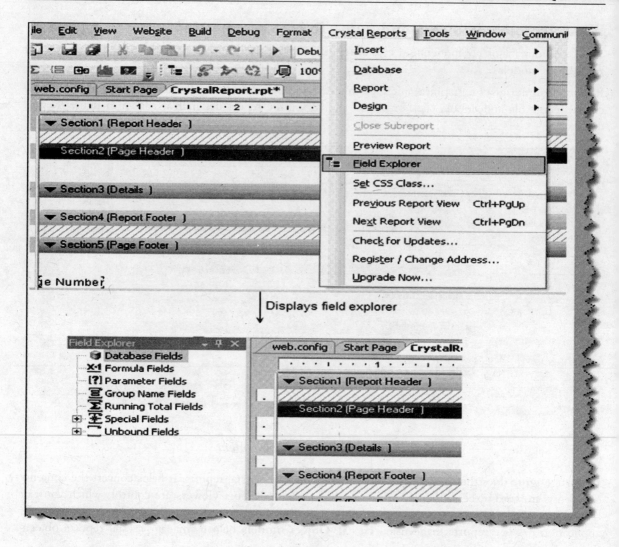

Figure 13.3: basic steps

Step 4 → Right click on 'Database fields' on the field explorer → then click on database expert → Expand create new connection → Expand OLE DB ADO → Select Microsoft OLEDB provider for SQL Server (this depends on what kind of data you want to connect) → Give the server credentials → Click finish and done.

Step5 → Right click on 'Database fields' on the field explorer → then click on database expert → Expand the server, database and select table which you want to add to the report. Below figure 'Table added in reports' shows the right pane showing the table added using database expert.

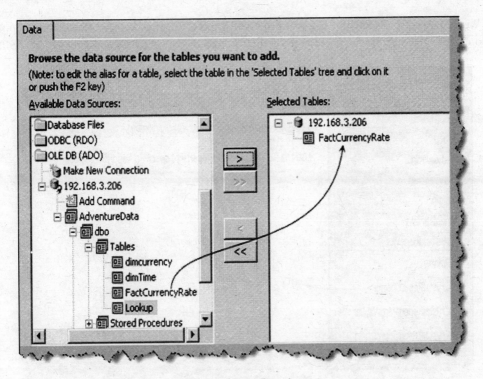

Figure 13.4: Database

Step 6 → Expand database fields → table (in this case it is 'FactCurrencyRate' table). Now you can drag and drop the fields on the report.

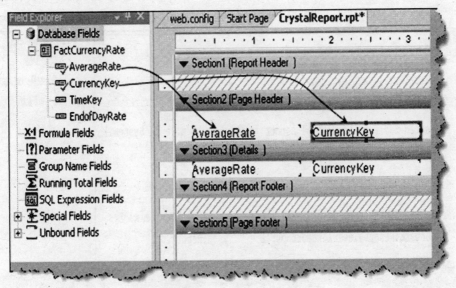

Figure 13.5: Fact Current rate

Step 7 → We now need to display the report on the ASPX page. For that we need the 'CrystalReportViewer' control. So expand the crystal reports section of the toolbar and drag the component on the ASPX page.

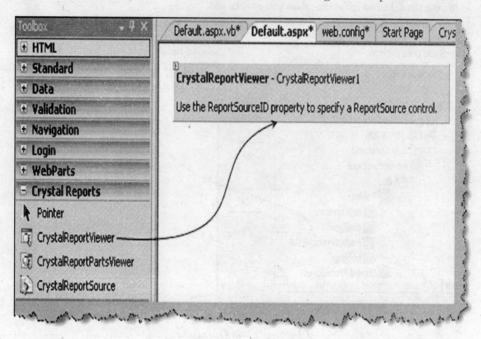

Figure 13.6: crystal report viewer

Step 8: Now we need to go to code behind and specify the report source. That's it now compile and run the project you can see your report live in action.

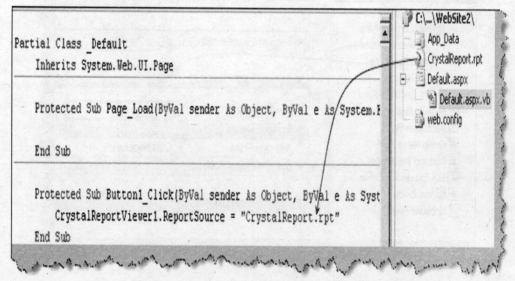

Figure 13.7: compile and run the project

Can crystal reports be published as a web service?

Right click on the 'RPT' file and click 'Publish as web service' as shown in figure 'Publish crystal as web service'.

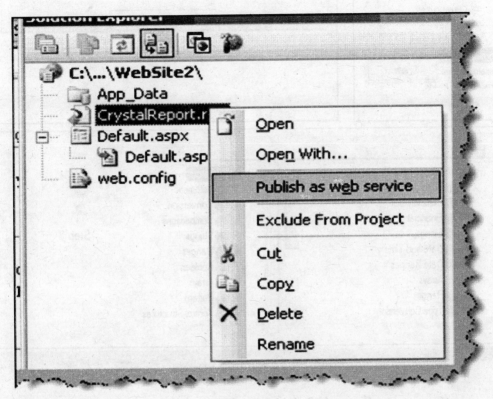

Figure 13.8: publishing crystal reports

How do we invoke the crystal report web service?

We can consume the web service as a normal web service in .NET. The easiest way is by using the 'ReportViewerControl' and specifying the ASMX URL in the report source property.

How do we add formulas using crystal reports?

To add any formula in crystal report is a three step procedure. Below figure 'Add formula in crystal report' shows the three steps in a pictorial format. Step 1 → Go to field explorer and right click and click new formula. Step 2 → Give and name to the formulae and click on 'Use Editor'. Step 3 → You will be presented with UI which has all the formulas and function.

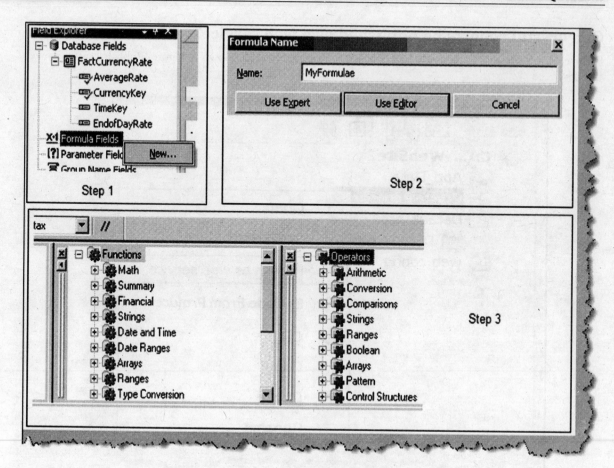

Figure 13.9: Add formula in crystal reports

How do we pass parameters to crystal reports?

Some times we want to accept input parameter and the report works according to the parameter. To add a input parameter go to field explorer, go to parameter fields, right click, create parameter and you should be popped with a dialog box as shown in the figure 'Parameter field'. Give a name to the parameter, type and that's it you are in action.

How do we export from crystal reports?

There are two way of using the export option one is when we display a report using crystal report viewer you can see a export icon as shown in figure 'Export' below. You can the select in which format you want to export.

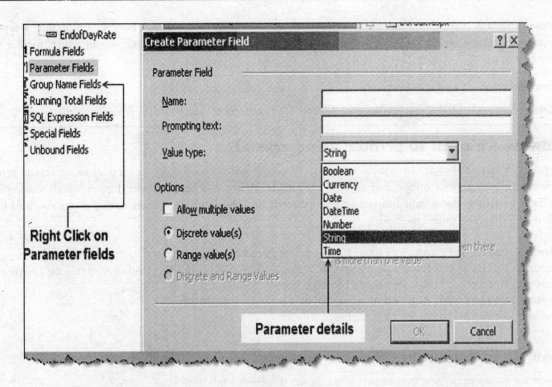

Figure 13.10: pass parameters

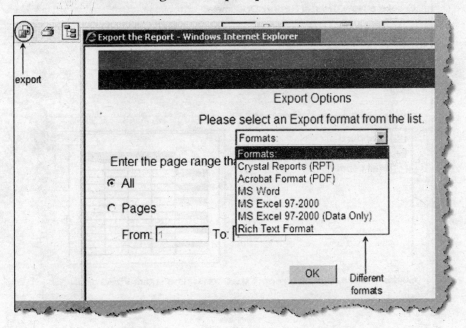

Figure 13.11: export from crystal reports

Second option is through coding. Below is a simple code snippet which shows how we can export a report. Create a object of the crystal report and call the 'ExportToDisk' method specifying in which format you want to export.

Dim Report as New CrystalReport1

Report.ExportToDisk(CrystalDecisions.Shared.ExportFormatType.WordForWindows,"c:\my.doc")

How do we print to printer using crystal?

In print we have two ways by which we can print one is when you display the report using crystal report viewer you have a print option and second is by code. Below is a simple code snippet which shows how we have created a object called as report from the rpt file, specified the printer name, paper size and then called the 'PrintToPrinter' method.

```
Report.PrintOptions.PrinterName = "MyPrinter"
Report.PrintOptions.PaperSize = CrystalDecisions.Shared.PaperSize.PaperA4
Report.PrintOptions.PaperOrientation =
CrystalDecisions.Shared.PaperOrientation.Landscape
Report.PrintToPrinter(1, True, 1, 3)
```

How do we generate cross tab reports?

When we go for creating a new report you can see the cross –tab option.

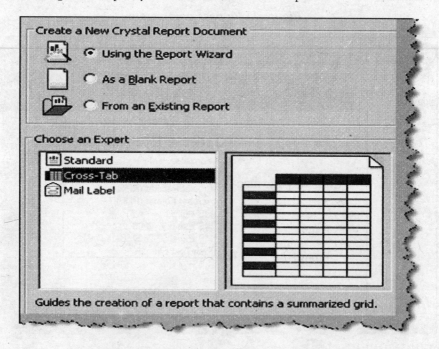

Figure 13.12: cross tab report

How can we do grouping in crystal?

For grouping in crystal you need to use the group expert wizard.

Can you explain three-pass reporting which crystal report uses?

Crystal report uses the three pass method for parsing reports. Before we understand what does it means lets define what is a pass? Pass is a process used by crystal reports to read and manipulate data as per the report format. Below figure 'Three pass method' shows how the parsing happens. Let's understand the same step by step. In **Pre-Pass1** crystal report engine evaluates constants like x=1 and pie=3.14 for a report. **Pass 1** does two important things get data from the database and sort records with given conditions. Once this is done it's saved in memory and given to **pre-pass2** for further parsing and manipulation. **Pre-pass2** is all about grouping and sorting the records according to conditions specified in the crystal report. **Pass 2** formats a report, applies condition and groups them. **Pass 3** is the final tunnel it just counts the pages and generates reports.

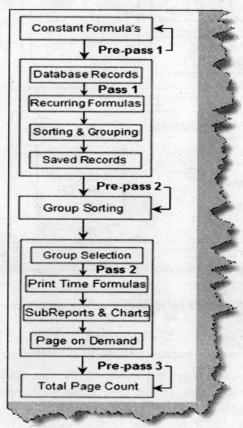

Figure 13.13: three phase reporting

Can you explain reporting services architecture?

Reporting services is mainly used to generate reports. Below are the main components of reporting services as shown in figure 'Reporting Services Architecture'. Reporting services has four major components Client,

Web services, report server/manager and reporting services database. Let's understand all the major components and the sub components of the same.

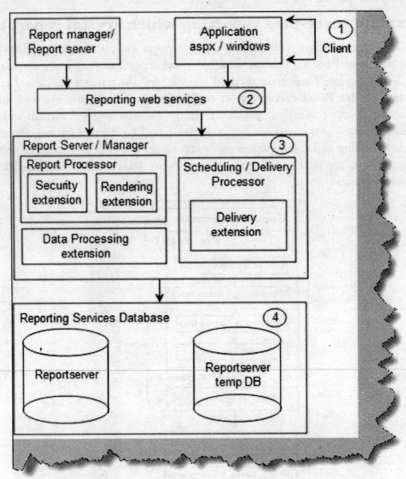

Figure 13.14: reporting service architecture

Client: These are the consumers of reporting services functionality. It can be the report manager or report server (we will discuss report server and manager in more details further) or ASPX and windows application.

Reporting Web service: Microsoft chose XML to expose the functionality of reporting services. So all the functionality is exposed through web services. One of the most important gains for a web service is that it can be platform independent.

Report server / manager: Report server and manager forms the core engine of reporting services. They two important systems one is '**Report processor**' and the other is '**Scheduling and Delivery processor**'. Reporting processor is the main driver to deliver reports. They take request from the end user and process the report and send it to the end client. Figure 'Report Processor' shows how the flow moves. We have seven basic steps which can help us understand in more detail how the report processor works. **Step 1** → Any client like ASPX or windows application will request to the web service for reports.

Step 2 and 3 → Web service will forward the request to the report processor and get the report definition from the report server DB. **Step 4** → Reporting services uses the **security extensions** to authenticate the end user. **Step 5** → **Data processing extension** calls queries the application database to get data. With data processing extension we can connect to standard data sources like SQL Server, ODBC, Oracle etc. You can also extend the data processing extension to adapt it to some custom data processing extension. **Step 6** → **Rendering extension** then renders the report applies format and sends the same to the end client. Using rendering extension you can deliver reports in Excel, PDF, HTML, CSV and XML. You can also extend the rendering extension to deliver in custom formats.

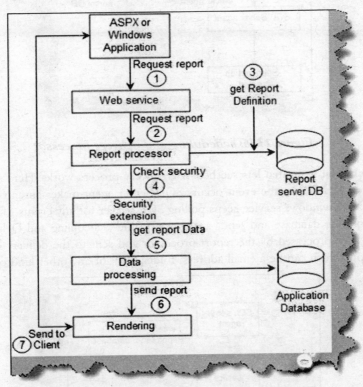

Figure 13.15: Report processor

The second system is 'Scheduling and Delivery processor'. **Delivery extensions** makes reports with the specified format and sends the same to an output target like file, email, FTP etc. Scheduling and delivery processor does two important steps schedules reports and delivers them the same to a output like FTP,Email etc. Schedule and delivery processor using delivery extension to deliver reports to the defined output. So users can subscribe to the reports and depending on these subscriptions the delivery is done by schedule and delivery processor. There are two steps in this one is the subscription process and the other is deliver process. Lets first try to understand the subscription process. There are three steps basically:

Step 1 → First is the requests a subscription to the report.

Step 2 → This subscription is then stored in the report server DB.

Step 3 → A new SQL Server agent is created for this subscription. So we have completed the subscription process.

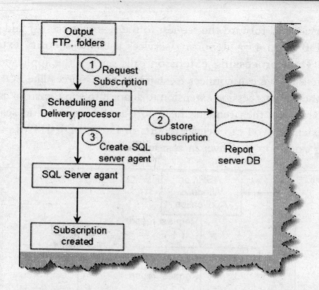

Figure 13.16: scheduling and delivery processor

Now that the subscription is created lets see how the delivery process works. Here are five basic steps in delivery process. Step 1 → When the event occurs SQL Server agent makes an entry in the report server DB. Step 2 and 3 → RS windows service keeps polling SQL Server for any events. If a event has occurred it gets the event from the database and sends a message to the 'Scheduling and Delivery Processor'. Step 4 → The report is then processed by the report processor and sent to the delivery extension who finally delivers it on a output which can be a email address, folder, FTP or any other kind of output.

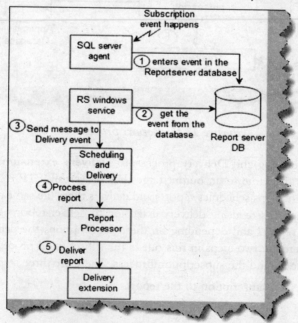

Figure 13.17: delivery process

Reporting Services Database: When you install reporting services you will see two databases 'ReportServer' and 'ReportServerTempDB'.'ReportServer' database contains report definitions, schedule, subscriptions, security details and snapshots. 'ReportServerTempDB' stores temporary information like session state about reports which is needed in between HTTP requests and report cache information. **Please note snapshots are stored in reportserver and not in tempDB**.

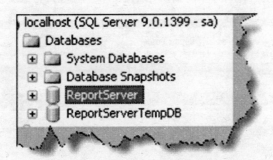

Figure 13.18: install reporting services

We have two IIS application 'Reports' and 'Reportserver' what do they do?

When you install reporting services there are two virtual directories created as shown in the figure below.

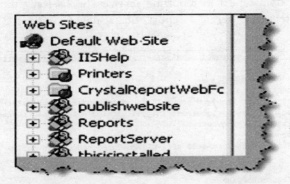

Figure 13.19: two virtual directories

The 'Reports' virtual directory is like an admin. If you browse to http://yourpcname/reports/home.aspx page you can view, edit properties and display reports. We have numbered the below figure. 1 → We can browse reports and see the output of reports. 2 → We can upload a RDL file directly in the report's database. 3 → Using the report builder link we build new reports. 4 → Using the properties we can do role assignment. 5 → Using subscription link we can add new outputs (FTP, Folder etc) to subscribe to the reports. 6 →Site settings help us to decide how many numbers of snapshots we want in the history, report time out execution, report execution logging, scheduling, manage jobs and security settings.

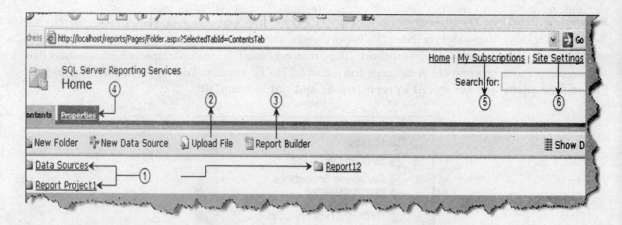

Figure 13.20: reports details

The second virtual directory is the 'ReportServer' this helps us to use browse reports and use the same in ASP.NET code using URL methodology, try browsing to http://yourpcname/reportserver/ you can easily figure out what this virtual directory is all about.

Can you explain Report definition language (RDL) file in reporting services?

RDL is an XML description of a report in reporting services. So basically the RDL file has the XML grammar which describes a reporting services report. Below figure 'Snip of RDL file' shows a simple snippet of a RDL file.

```
<Report xmlns="http://schemas.microsoft.com/sqlserver/reporting/2005/01/reportdefinition"
  <DataSources>
    <DataSource Name="Database123">
      <ConnectionProperties>
        <Prompt>Specify a user name and password for data source Database123</Prompt>
        <ConnectString>Data Source=localhost;Initial Catalog=Database123</ConnectString>
        <DataProvider>SQL</DataProvider>
      </ConnectionProperties>
      <rd:DataSourceID>e3aea286-32e8-4b18-a9f2-214abb87a390</rd:DataSourceID>
    </DataSource>
  </DataSources>
  <BottomMargin>1in</BottomMargin>
  <RightMargin>1in</RightMargin>
  <ReportParameters>
    <ReportParameter Name="Report_Parameter_0">
      <DataType>String</DataType>
      <AllowBlank>true</AllowBlank>
      <Prompt>Report_Parameter_0</Prompt>
    </ReportParameter>
    <ReportParameter Name="custname">
      <DataType>String</DataType>
      <Prompt>custname</Prompt>
    </ReportParameter>
  </ReportParameters>
  <rd:DrawGrid>true</rd:DrawGrid>
  <InteractiveWidth>8.5in</InteractiveWidth>
```

Figure 13.21: report definition language

What is the basic process of making a report in reporting services?

Here are the basic steps which will help you in creating reports in reporting services:

● Open Visual studio 2005 → File → New project → Select 'Business Intelligence Reports' → Select Report Server project.

● When the project is created in the solution explorer you will see two folder 'Shared data resources' (we will come to data sources in the coming questions) and 'Reports'. Right click the 'Reports' folder and click add new reports.

● You need to give credentials in the wizard. Once done it pops up a query builder. Specify the report query in the query builder and go next.

● Wizard then helps you to select the report type and some other features. Next, next and you should see a RDL file in your 'Reports' folder.

● Click on the view menu and select tool box and you should be able to design the report.

● Till now we are only in the design mode of report. As said previously all reports meta-data are stored in SQL Server database 'ReportServer'. In order that the report's meta-data gets saved in database we need to publish the report.

● To publish the report we need to specify the IIS report path. So right click on the report project, select properties and specify the 'TargetServerURL' property.

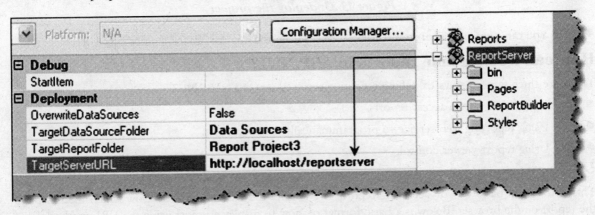

Figure 13.22: reporting services

● Once we have specified the 'TargetServerURL' property we need to deploy the project. So right click on project and click 'Deploy'

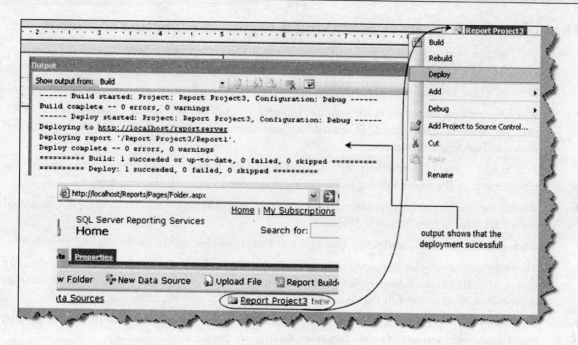

Figure 13.23: deploy the project

- You can now view your report using http://localhost/Reports/Pages/Folder.aspx URL.

How can we consume reports in ASP.NET?

There are three famous ways of calling reporting services report in ASP.NET:

- Using URL way to access reports.
- Using reporting web service to programmatically access reports.
- Using report viewer control.

URL way

This is the most basic way of accessing reports. We specify the URL as shown below which then displays the report on the browser. Below is a basic format of how to display a report using the URL methodology. 1 → This is the IIS report application. 2 → This is the project name or the project folder in which the report resides. 3 → This is the report name. 4 → This is the command to the reporting service of what to do. In this case we are saying render the report.

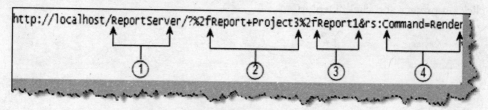

Figure 13.24: URL methodology

If we want to get the report in PDF format we need to use the 'Format' parameter.

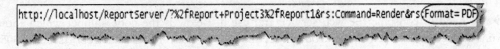

http://localhost/ReportServer/?%2fReport+Project3%2fReport1&rs:Command=Render&rs(Format= PDF)

Figure 13.25: URL for PDF format

If we want to pass parameters to the report we can do something as shown in the figure 'Pass parameters to the report'. In this scenario we have passed the 'Category' parameter.

http://localhost/ReportServer/%2fReport+Project3%2fReport1&rs:Command=Render(&Category=12)

Figure 13.26: Pass parameter to the report

Consuming reporting services web service

If you look at the architecture of reporting service all reports are exposed through XML i.e. Web services. You can see the web service using this URL http://localhost/ReportServer/ReportService2005.asmx. In localhost you need to put the server name or IP address. So below are the steps to display reports using web service.

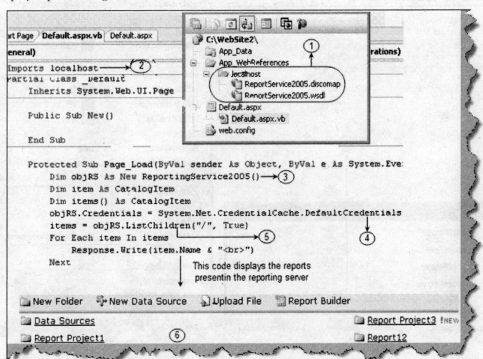

Figure 13.27: consuming report services

Step 1 → First add the web service using http://localhost/ReportServer/ReportService2005.asmx in your ASP.NET project.

Step 2 → We need to consume the web service and use it. Below is the code snippet which shows how the reporting service object is used. 1 → You can see the web service references to 'reportservice2005.asmx'. 2 → We have the named the web service as 'Localhost', so you can see we have imported the web service. 3 → We need to create object of 'ReportingService2005' class. 4 → We need to set the credentials of the reporting object. 5 → In this we will display which reports are present in the reporting server database. So we use the 'ListChildren' method to get the reports from the web service and then loop to display the same. 6 → This sample code should display the reports present in the reporting service.

The above example is a sample of how to use the reporting web service. If you want to get how many input parameters the report has we need to use **'GetReportParameters'** method, if we want to display the report we use the **'Render'** function. There are many other function and methods which we have not discussed to keep the chapter simple and to the point. Please experiment around the reporting web service object for new methods and functions.

Reportviewer control

ASP.NET 2.0 comes with crystal report viewer control. You can drag and drop the control on the ASPX page and set the properties. Below figure shows how the 'ReportviewerControl' looks like and how we can set the properties to view the report.

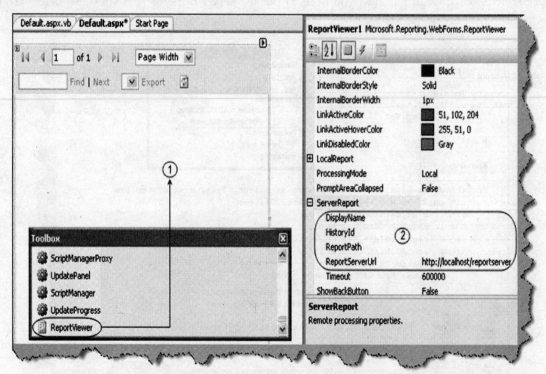

Figure 13.28: report viewer control

Can you explain the difference between private and shared data sources?

Private data source is used by single report only while shared data sources are shared between reports. As a practice it is good to have shared data source so if you want to change anything you need to change only on one data source.

How does reports caching in reporting services work?

As said previously reporting services has two main databases 'ReportServer' and 'ReportServerTempDB'. Below figure 'Reporting Services Caching' shows how caching works in reporting services. Client first sends a request to the reporting service for report. Reporting processor gets data from the database and the report format from the 'reportserver' database. Both these elements are then used to create 'Intermediate report format'. This intermediate format is saved in 'ReportServerTempDB'. This intermediate format is for a particular user and for a session. So if the user generates the same report he will get a cached version. If the report is having parameters then there are different cached versions of report for every parameter combination. Cached versions expire after particular schedule, when reports are modified, deleted or redeployed.

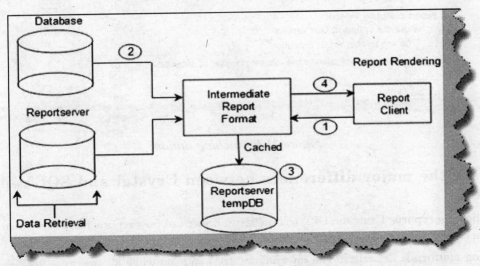

Figure 13.29: reporting services caching

In order to set the caching properties browse to a particular report using http://localhost/reports/ → click on properties → and go to execution tab. Below figure 'Caching options' shows different conditions on which you can define caching strategy.

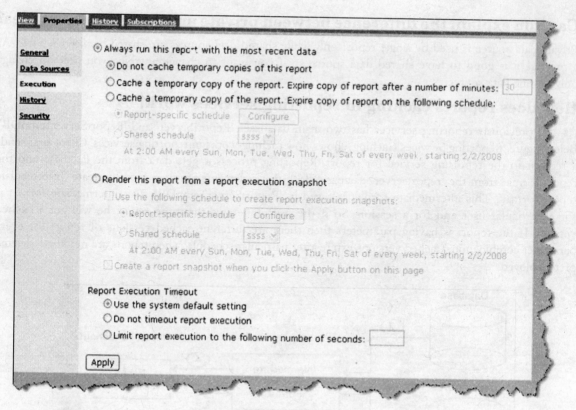

Figure 13.30: caching option

What are the major differences between Crystal and SQL reporting services?

Ease of hosting reports: Using the URL technology in RS we can host reports more easily than in crystal report where we need to make a UI for the same.

Supporting platforms: Crystal can run on windows, IBM and sun while RS (reporting services) can run only on windows environment.

Client tools: In reporting services we have Business intelligence (BI) and development studio while in crystal its Report designer.

Caching: This achieved in crystal by using cache server while in reporting services it's stored as snapshots in Reportserver database.

Export formats: In crystal we have HTML,PDF,Excel,XML,Word, PDF, RTF, CSV, text files while in SQL Server 2005 we have all the formats above it also gives capability to extend custom reporting formats.

Data sources: Crystal support more data sources while RS only supports Microsoft and oracle data sources. Crystal supports ADO, COM, Database excel Access, Exchange, NT, Xbase, JDBC, File system and Paradox. RS supports only SQL Server, Oracle, ODBC, OLEDB and **you can also extend additional data sources** which does not exists in crystal reports.

Version issues: One of the main issues faced in crystal is it have different versions which makes it difficult to use, while RS comes with SQL Server minimizing the version issue.

Web server support: Crystal can run on IIS 5/6, Apache, lotus etc while RS works only with IIS 5.0 and above.

> ***Note:*** *We have also shipped a PDF 'SQLvsCrystal_WP.pdf' which is been published by http:// www.globalknowledge.com/ . This PDF has very precise and detail differences between crystal reports and SQL reporting services.*

14
Threading

What is Multi-tasking?

It is a feature of modern operating systems with which we can run multiple programs at same time example Word, Excel etc.

What is Multi-threading?

Multi-threading forms subset of Multi-tasking. Instead of having to switch between programs, this feature switches between different parts of the same program. Example you are writing in word and at the same time word is doing a spell check in background.

What is a Thread?

A thread is the basic unit to which the operating system allocates processor time.

Did VB6 support multi-threading?

While VB6 supports multiple single-threaded apartments, it does not support a free-threading model, which allows multiple threads to run against the same set of data.

Can we have multiple threads in one App domain?

One or more threads run in an AppDomain. An AppDomain is a runtime representation of a logical process within a physical process. Each AppDomain is started with a single thread, but can create additional threads from any of its threads.

Note: All threading classes are defined in System.Threading namespace.

Which namespace has threading?

'Systems.Threading' has all the classes related to implement threading. Any .NET application who wants to implement threading has to import this namespace.

Note: .NET program always has at least two threads running one is the main program and second is the garbage collector.

Can you explain in brief how can we implement threading?

```
Private Sub Form1_Load (ByVal sender As System. Object, ByVal e as
System.EventArgs) Handles MyBase.Load
Dim pthread1 As New Thread (AddressOf Thread1)
Dim pthread2 As New Thread (AddressOf Thread2)
pthread1.Start ()
pthread2.Start ()
End Sub
Public Sub Thread1 ()
Dim pint count As Integer
Dim pstr As String
Pstr = "This is first thread"
Do Until pint count > 5
lstThreadDisplay.Items.Add (pstr)
Pint count = pint count + 1

Loop
End Sub
Public Sub Thread2 ()
Dim pint count As Integer
Dim pstr As String
Pstr = "This is second thread"
Do Until pint count > 5
lstThreadDisplay.Items.Add (pstr)
Pint count = pint count + 1
Loop
End Sub
```

> *Note: If you run the sample, you will see that sometimes the first thread runs first and then the second thread. This happens because of thread priorities. The first thread is run with highest priority.*

How can we change priority and what the levels of priority are provided by .NET?

Thread Priority can be changed by using

Threadname.Priority = ThreadPriority.Highest

Following are different levels of Priority provided by .NET:

- ThreadPriority.Highest
- ThreadPriority.AboveNormal
- ThreadPriority.Normal
- ThreadPriority.BelowNormal
- ThreadPriority.Lowest

What does Address Of operator do in background?

The AddressOf operator creates a delegate object to the Background Process method. A delegate within VB.NET is a type-safe, object-oriented function pointer. After the thread has been instantiated, you begin the execution of the code by calling the Start () method of the thread

How can you reference current thread of the method?

"Thread.CurrentThread" refers to the current thread running in the method."CurrentThread" is a public static property.

What is Thread.Sleep () in threading?

Thread's execution can be paused by calling the Thread.Sleep method. This method takes an integer value that determines how long the thread should sleep. Example Thread.CurrentThread.Sleep(2000).

How can we make a thread sleep for infinite period?

You can also place a thread into the sleep state for an indeterminate amount of time by calling Thread.Sleep (System.Threading.Timeout.Infinite). To interrupt this sleep you can call the Thread. Interrupt method.

What is Suspend and Resume in Threading?

It is Similar to Sleep and Interrupt Suspend allows you to block a thread until another

Thread calls Thread.Resume. The difference between Sleep and Suspend is that the latter does not immediately place a thread in the wait state. The thread does not suspend until the .NET runtime determines that it is in a safe place to suspend it. Sleep will immediately place a thread in a wait state.

> **Note:** *In threading interviews, most people get confused with Sleep and Suspend. They look very similar.*

What the way to stop a long running thread?

Thread.Abort() stops the thread execution at that moment itself.

How do I debug thread?

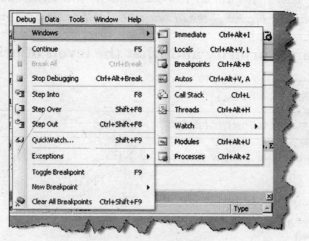

Figure 14.1: debug thread

This window is only seen when the program is running in debug mode. In windows one of the windows is "Threads".

What is Thread.Join () in threading?

There are two versions of Thread join-

- Thread. join ().
- Thread.join (Integer) this returns a Boolean value.

The Thread.Join method is useful for determining if a thread has completed before starting another task. The Join method waits a specified amount of time for a thread to end. If the thread ends before the time-out, Join returns true; otherwise, it returns False. Once you call Join, the calling procedure stops and waits for the thread to signal that it is done.

Example you have "Thread1" and "Thread2" and while executing 'Thread1" you call "Thread2.Join ()".So "Thread1" will wait until "Thread2" has completed its execution and the again invoke "Thread1".

Thread.Join (Integer) ensures that threads do not wait for a long time. If it exceeds a specific time, which is provided in integer the waiting thread will start.

What are Daemon threads and how can a thread be created as Daemon?

Daemon thread's run in background and stops automatically the program is not running. Example of a Daemon thread is 'Garbage collector'. Garbage collector runs until some .NET code is running or else it is idle.

You can make a thread Daemon by

```
Thread.Isbackground=true
```

How is shared data managed in threading?

There are certain situations that you need to be careful with when using threads. If two threads (e.g. the main and any worker threads) try to access the same variable at the same time, you'll have a problem. This can be very difficult to debug because they may not always do it at exactly the same time. To avoid the problem, you can lock a variablebefore accessing it. However, if the two threads lock the same variable at the same time, you will have a deadlock problem. To avoid dead lock we need to use the 'SyncLock' keyword as shown in the code snippet below.

```
SyncLock x
     'Do something with x
End SyncLock
```

Can we use events with threading?

Yes, you can use events with thread; this is one of the techniques to synchronize one thread with other.

How can we know a state of a thread?

"ThreadState" property can be used to get detail of a thread. Thread can have one or a combination of status.'System.Threading.Threadstate' enumeration has all the values to detect a state of thread. Some sample states are Isrunning, IsAlive, suspended etc.

What is use of Interlocked class?

Interlocked class provides methods by which you can achieve following functionalities:

- Increment Values.
- Decrement values.
- Exchange values between variables.
- Compare values from any thread.in a synchronization mode.

Example: System.Threading.Interlocked.Increment(IntA)

What is a monitor object?

Monitor objects are used to ensure that a block of code runs without being interrupted by code running on other threads. In other words, code in other threads cannot run until code in the synchronized code block has finished.

SyncLock and End SyncLock statements are provided in order to simplify access to monitor object.

What are wait handles?

Wait handles sends signals of a thread status from one thread to other thread. There are three kind of wait modes:

- WaitOne.
- WaitAny.
- Wait All.

When a thread wants to release a Wait handle it can call set method. You can use Mutex (mutually exclusive) objects to avail for the following modes. Mutex objects are synchronization objects that can only be owned by a single thread at a time. Threads request ownership of the mutex object when they require exclusive access to a resource. Because only one thread can own a mutex object at any time, other threads must wait for ownership of a mutex object before using the resource.

The WaitOne method causes a calling thread to wait for ownership of a mutex object. If a thread terminates normally while owning a mutex object, the state of the mutex object is set to be signaled and the next waiting thread gets ownership

What is ManualResetEvent and AutoResetEvent?

Threads that call one of the wait methods of a synchronization event must wait until another thread signals the event by calling the Set method. There are two synchronization event classes. Threads set the status of ManualResetEvent instances to signaled using the Set method. Threads set the status of ManualResetEvent instances to no signaled using the Reset method or when control returns to a waiting WaitOne call. Instances of the AutoResetEvent class can also be set to signaled using Set, but they automatically return to nonsignaled as soon as a waiting thread is notified that the event became signaled.

What is Reader Writer Locks?

You may want to lock a resource only when data is being written and permit multiple clients to simultaneously read data when data is not being updated. The ReaderWriterLock class enforces exclusive access to a resource while a thread is modifying the resource, but it allows nonexclusive access when reading the resource. Reader Writer locks are a good alternative to exclusive locks that cause other threads to wait, even when those threads do not need to update data.

How can you avoid deadlock in threading?

A good and careful planning can avoid deadlocks. There are so many ways Microsoft has provided by which you can reduce deadlocks example Monitor, Interlocked classes, Wait handles, Event raising from one thread to other thread and using ThreadState property you can poll and act accordingly.

What is TPL (Task parallel library)?

TPL stands for Task parallel library. Its introduced in .NET 4.0 framework to simplify threading. TPL is set of API's which sits on top of core threading and simplifies threading. When we use threading API directly you need to take care of pooling, ensure that thread executes on multiple processors, data and task parallelism etc. When you use TPL all these things are taken care of so that you concentrate on the work rather than these lower level technical details.

TPL simplifies the following things from development aspect:

- Thread pooling is taken care internally.
- TPL ensures that threads will execute on multiple processors.
- Cancellation of threads made easier.
- State management simplified as compared to core threading.

All components of TPL (task parallel library) exists in the below namespace.

```
using System.Threading.Tasks;
```

To invoke a thread using TPL we need to use the below syntax. We need to create the object of task object to invoke a thread.

```
Task tsk = new Task(MyTask); // Run the task.
tsk.Start();
```

What is the difference between thread and process?

A thread is a path of execution that run on CPU, a process is a collection of threads that share the same virtual memory. A process has at least one thread of execution, and a thread always run in a process context.

> **Note:** *Its difficult to cover threading interview question in this small chapter. These questions can take only to a basic level. If you are attending interviews where people are looking for threading specialist, try to get deeper in to synchronization issues, as that is the important point they will stress.*

15

XML

What is XML?

XML (Extensible markup language) is all about describing data. Below is a XML, which describes invoice data.

```
<?xml version="1.0" encoding="ISO-8859-1"?>
<invoice>
<productname>Shoes</productname>
<qty>12</qty>
<totalcost>100</totalcost>
<discount>10</discount>
</invoice>
```

An XML tag is not something predefined but it is something you have to define according to your needs. For instance in the above example of invoice all tags are defined according to business needs. The XML document is self-explanatory; any one can easily understand looking at the XML data what exactly it means.

What is the version information in XML?

"Version" tag shows which version of XML is used.

What is ROOT element in XML?

In our XML sample given previously <invoice></invoice> tag is the root element. Root element is the top most elements for a XML.

If XML does not have closing tag will it work?

No, every tag in XML, which is opened, should have a closing tag. For instance in the top if I remove </discount> tag that XML will not be understood by lot of application.

Is XML case sensitive?

Yes, they are case sensitive.

What is the difference between XML and HTML?

XML describes data while HTML describes how the data should be displayed. Therefore, HTML is about displaying information while XML is about describing information.

Is XML meant to replace HTML?

No, they both go together one is for describing data while other is for displaying data.

Can you explain why your project needed XML?

> **Note:** *This is an interview question where the interviewer wants to know why you have chosen XML.*

Remember XML was meant to exchange data between two entities as you can define your user-friendly tags with ease. In real world scenarios, XML is meant to exchange data. For instance, you have two applications who want to exchange information. However, because they work in two complete opposite technologies it is difficult to do it technically. For instance, one application is made in JAVA and the other in .NET. However, both languages understand XML so one of the applications will spit XML file, which will be consumed and parsed by other applications

You can give a scenario of two applications, which are working separately and how you chose XML as the data transport medium.

What is DTD (Document Type Definition)?

It defines how your XML should structure. For instance in the above XML we want to make it compulsory to provide "qty" and "total cost", also that these two elements can only contain numeric. Therefore, you can define the DTD document and use that DTD document with in that XML.

What is well formed XML?

If a XML document is confirming to XML rules (all tags started are closed, there is a root element etc) then it is a well-formed XML.

What is a valid XML?

If XML is confirming to DTD rules then it is a valid XML.

What is CDATA section in XML?

All data is normally parsed in XML but if you want to exclude some elements, you will need to put those elements in CDATA.

What is XSL?

XSL (the extensible Style sheet Language) is used to transform XML document to some other document. Therefore, its transformation document which can convert XML to some other document. For instance, you can apply XSL to XML and convert it to HTML document or probably CSV files.

What is element and attributes in XML?

In the below example invoice is the element and the in number the attribute.

<invoice in number=1002></invoice>

Which are the namespaces in .NET used for XML?

"System.xml.dll" is the actual physical file, which has all XML implementation. Below are the commonly used namespaces:

- System.Xml
- System.Xml.Schema
- System.Xml.XPath
- System.Xml.Xsl

What are the standard ways of parsing XML document?

XML parser sits in between the XML document and the application who want to use the XML document. Parser exposes set of well-defined interfaces, which can be used by the application for adding, modifying, and deleting the XML document contents. Now whatever interfaces XML parser exposes should be standard or else that would lead to different vendors preparing there own custom way of interacting with XML document.

There are two standard specifications, which are very common and should be followed by a XML parser:

DOM: Document Object Model.

DOM is a W3C recommended way for treating XML documents. In DOM, we load entire XML document into memory and allows us to manipulate the structure and data of XML document.

SAX: Simple API for XML.

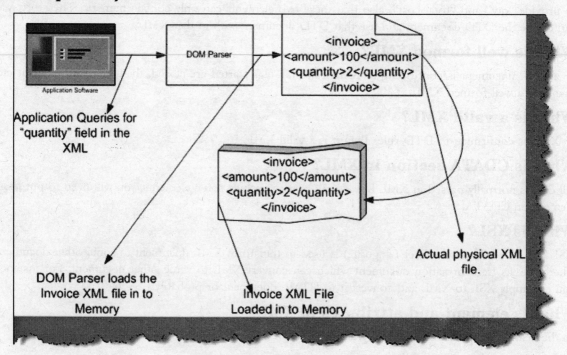

Figure 15.1: Simple API for XML

SAX is event driven way for processing XML documents. In DOM, we load the whole XML document in to memory and then application manipulates the XML document. However, this is not always the best way to process large XML documents, which have huge data elements. For instance, you only want one element from the whole XML document or you only want to see if the XML is proper which means loading the whole XML in memory will be quiet resource intensive. SAX parsers parse the XML document sequentially and emit events like start and end of the document, elements, text content etc. Therefore, applications who are interested in processing these events can register implementations of callback interfaces. SAX parser then only sends those event messages, which the application has demanded.

Above is a pictorial representation of how DOM parser works. Application queries the DOM Parser for "quantity" field. DOM parser loads the complete XML file in to memory.

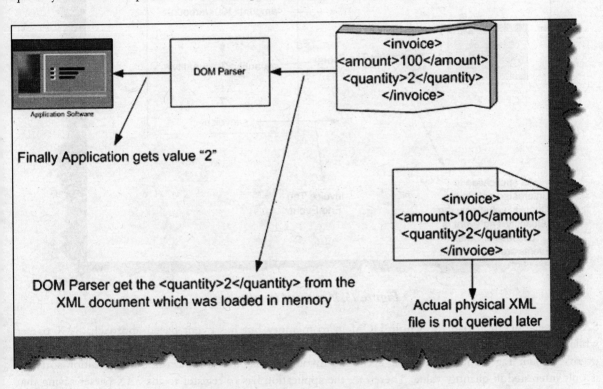

Figure 15.2: Memory loaded XML file

DOM parser then picks up the "quantity" tag from the memory loaded XML file and returns back to the application.

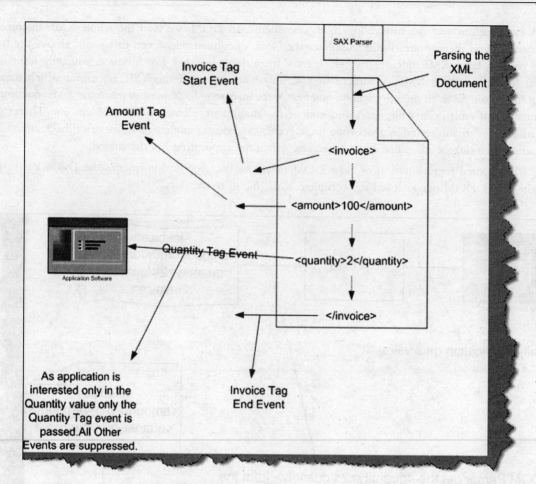

Figure 15.3: emitted invoice tag

SAX parser does not load the whole DOM in to memory but has event based approach. SAX parser while parsing the XML file emits events. For example in the above figure its has emitted Invoice tag start event, Amount Tag event, Quantity tag event and Invoice end tag event. However, our application software is only interested in quantity value. Therefore, the application has to register to the SAX parser saying that he is only interested in quantity field and not any other field or element of the XML document. Depending on what interest the application software has SAX parser only sends those events to the application the rest of events is suppressed. For instance in the above figure only quantity tag event is sent to the application software and the rest of the events are suppressed

In What scenarios will you use a DOM parser and SAX parser?

• If you do not need all the data from the XML file then SAX approach is much preferred than DOM as DOM can be quiet memory intensive. In short, if you need large portion of the XML document its better to have DOM.

• With SAX parser, you have to write more code than DOM.

• If you want to write the XML in to a file, DOM is the efficient way to do it.

●   Some time you only need to validate the XML structure and do not want to retrieve any Data
        for those instances SAX is the right approach.

How was XML handled during COM times?

During COM, it was done by using MSXML 4.0. So old languages like VB6, VC++ used MSXML 4.0,
which was shipped with SP1 (Service Pack 1).

> **Note:** *This book will not show any samples as such for MSXML 4.0. So if anyone interested please do
> refer the same in MSDN and try to compile some sample programs.*

What is the main difference between MSML and .NET Framework XML classes?

MSXML supports XMLDOM and SAX parsers while .NET framework XML classes support XML DOM
and XML readers and writers.

MSXML supports asynchronous loading and validation while parsing. For instance, you can send synchronous
and asynchronous calls to a remote URL. However, as such there is not direct support of synchronous
and asynchronous calls in .NET framework XML. However, it can be achieved by using "System.Net"
namespaces.

What are the core functionalities in XML .NET framework? Can you explain in detail those functionalities?

The XML API for the .NET Framework comprises the following set of functionalities:

XML readers

With XML readers, the client application gets reference to instance of reader class. Reader class allows
you to scroll forward through the contents like moving from node to node or element to element. You
can compare it with the "SqlDataReader" object in ADO.NET, which is forward only. In short, XML
reader allows you to browse through the XML document.

XML writers

Using XML writers, you can store the XML contents to any other storage media. For instance, you want
to store the whole in memory XML to a physical file or any other media.

XML document classes

XML documents provides a in memory representation for the data in an XMLDOM structure as defined
by W3C. It also supports browsing and editing of the document. Therefore, it gives you a complete memory
tree structure representation of your XML document.

What is XSLT?

XSLT is a rule-based language used to transform XML documents in to other file formats. XSLT are
nothing but generic transformation rules, which can be applied to transform XML document to HTML,
CS, Rich text etc.

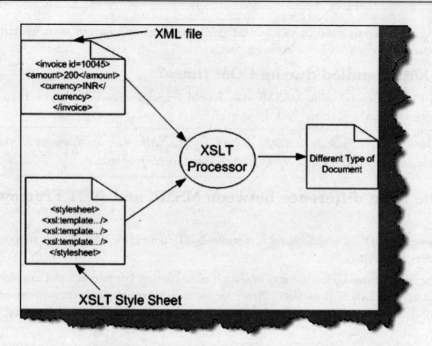

Figure 15.4: XSLT Processor in Actions

You can see in the above figure how the XSLT processor takes the XML file and applies the XSLT transformation to produce a different document.

Define XPATH?

It is an XML query language to select specific parts of an XML document. Using XPATH, you can address or filter elements and text in a XML document. For instance a simple XPATH expression like "Invoice/Amount" states find "Amount" node that are children of "Invoice" node.

What is the concept of XPOINTER?

XPOINTER is used to locate data within XML document. XPOINTER can point to a particular portion of a XML document, for instance

```
address.xml#xpointer (/ descendant::streetnumber[@id=9])
```

So the above XPOINTER points street number=9 in "address.xml".

What is an XMLReader Class?

It is an abstract class available from System.XML namespace. XML reader works on a read-only stream browsing from one node to other in a forward direction. It maintains only a pointer to the current node but has no idea of the previous and the next node. You cannot modify the XML document, you can only move forward.

What is XMLTextReader?

The "XmlTextReader" class helps to provide fast access to streams of XML data in a forward-only and read-only manner. It also checks if the XML is well formed. However, XMLTextReader does not validate against a schema or DTD for that you will need "XmlNodeReader" or "XmlValidatingReader" class.

Instance of "XmlTextReader" can be created in number of ways. For example if you want to load file from a disk you can use the below snippets.

```
XmlTextReader reader = new XmlTextReader (filename);
```

To loop through all the nodes you need to call the "read ()" method of the "XmlTextreader" object. "read()" method returns "true" if there are records in the XML document or else it returns "false".

```
//Open the stream
XmlTextReader reader = new XmlTextReader (file);
While (reader. Read())
{
      // your logic goes here
      String pdata = reader. Value
}
// Close the stream
Reader. Close ();
```

To read the content of the current node on which the reader object is you use the "value" property. As shown in the above code "pdata" gets the value from the XML using "reader. Value".

How do we access attributes using "XmlReader"?

Below snippets shows the way to access attributes. First in order to check whether there any attributes present in the current node you can use "HasAttributes" function and use the "MoveToNextAttribute" method to move forward in attribute. In case you want to move to the next element use "MoveToElement ()".

```
if (reader.HasAttributes)
{
      while(reader.MoveToNextAttribute())
      {
          // your logic goes here
          string pdata = reader.Value
      }
}
reader.MoveToElement();
```

Explain simple Walk through of XmlReader.

In this section, we will do a simple walkthrough of how to use the "XmlReader" class. Sample for the same is available in both languages (C# and VB.NET) which you can find in

"WindowsApplicationXMLVBNET" and "WindowsApplicationCSharp" folders. Task is to load "TestingXML.XML" file and display its data in a message box. You can find "TestingXML.XML" file in "BIN" directory of both the folders. Below is the display of "TestingXML.XML" file and its content.

```
<invoice id="100">
<amount>200</amount>
<currency>Rupees</currency>
<productname>Interview Question Series</productname>
<authorname>Shivprasad Koirala</authorname>
</invoice>
```

Figure 15.5: Testing.XML Data

Both the projects have command button "CmdLoadXML" which has the logic to load the XML file and display the data in message box. I have pasted only the "CmdLoadXML" command button logic for simplicity. Following are the basic steps done:

● Declared the "XMLTextReader" object and gave the XML filename to load the XML data.

● Read the "XMLTextReader" object until it has data and concatenate the data in a temporary string.

● Finally display the same in a message box.

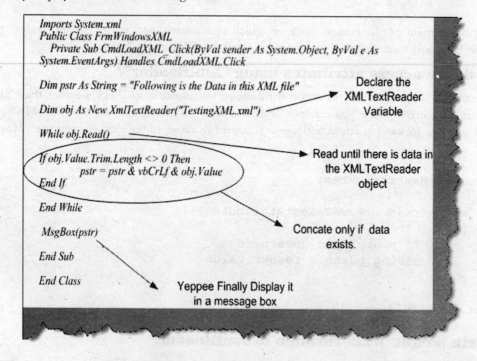

Figure 15.6: Displaying message

It holds true for C# code as shown below.

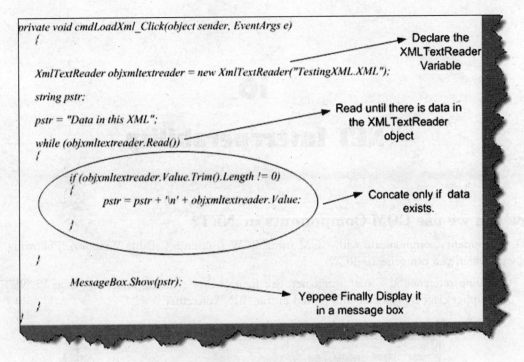

Figure 15.7: Message display with C# code

Figure 15.8: Final Message box display

What does XmlValidatingReader class do?

XmlTextReader class does not validate the contents of an XML source against a schema. The correctness of XML documents can be measured by two things is the document well formed and is it valid. Well-formed means that the overall syntax is correct. Validation is much deeper which means is the XML document is proper w.r.t schema defined.

Therefore, the XmlTextReader only checks if the syntax is correct but does not do validation. There is where XmlValidatingReader class comes in to picture. Therefore, this again comes at a price as XmlValidatingReader have to check for DTD and Schema's that's the reason they are slower compared to XmlTextReader.

16

NET Interoperability

How can we use COM Components in .NET?

.NET components communicate with COM using RCW (Runtime Callable Wrapper). Following are the ways with which you can generate RCW:

● Adding reference in Visual Studio.net. See figure below (Adding reference using VS.NET 2005). Wrapper class is generated and placed in the "BIN" directory.

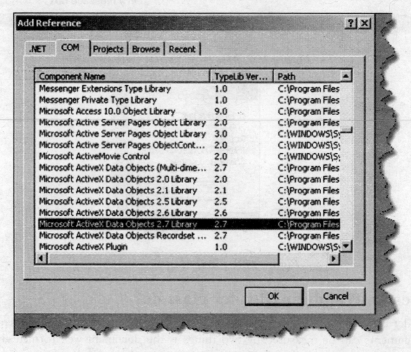

Figure 16.1: Adding reference

● Using Type library import tool. Tlbimp.exe yourname.dll.

o Using interopservices.System.runtime.Interopservices namespace contains class TypeLib Converter that provides methods to convert COM classes and interface in to assembly metadata.

o   Make your custom wrappers. If your COM component does not have type library then the only way to communicate is writing custom wrappers. That means communicating directly with COM components.

We have developed the COM wrapper do we have to still register the COM?

Yes.

How can we use .NET components in COM?

.NET components cannot be used in a straightforward way with COM. You will need to create CCW in order that COM components communicate with .NET assemblies. Following are the different approaches to implement it:

● Explicitly declare interfaces..

```
Public Interface ICustomer
Property CustomerName() As String
Property CustomerCode() As String
Sub AddCustomer()
End Interface
Public Class Customer
Implements ICustomer
Private PstrCustomerName As String
Private PstrCustomerCode As String


Public Sub AddCustomer() Implements ICustomer.AddCustomer
Try
' addin of database code can go here
Catch ex As Exception
Throw ex
End Try
End Sub
Public Property CustomerCode() As String Implements ICustomer.CustomerCode
Get
Return PstrCustomerCode
End Get
Set(ByVal value As String)
PstrCustomerCode = value
End Set
End Property
Public Property CustomerName() As String Implements ICustomer.CustomerName
Get
Return PstrCustomerName
End Get
Set(ByVal value As String)
PstrCustomerName = value
End Set
```

```
End Property
Public Sub New()

End Sub
End Class
```

The above customer class is going to be used by COM components so all the properties and methods are declared in interface and implemented in the customer class. Customer Name.Customer Code and AddCustomer are first declared in ICustomer and then implemented in Customer Class. Also, note that the class must have a default constructor.

> **Note:** *All source code in this book is provided in VB.NET that does not mean that author of the book does not like C#. In fact, the main programming language of author is C#. In order to keep things small I have only used one language. However, the conversion is so seamless that it is of least matter.*

- The second way to create CCW is by using InteropServices attributes. Here interfaces are created automatically.

Following are different type of class attributes:

None: No class interface is generated for the class. This is default setting when you do not specify anything.

AutoDispatch: Interface that supports IDispatch is created for the class. However, no type information is produced.

Auto Dual: A dual interface is created for the class. Type information is produced and made available in the type library.

Below in the source code we have used the third attribute.

```
Imports System.Runtime.InteropServices
<ClassInterfaceAttribute (ClassInterfaceType.AutoDual)> _
PublicClass ClsCompliant
EndClass
```

Other than class, attributes defined up there are other attributes with which you can govern other part of assembly. Example "GuidAttribute" allows you to specify the GUID, "ComVisibleAttribute" can be used to hide .NET types from COM etc. All attributes are not in scope of the book as this is a interview questions book refer MSDN for more details.

- Once .NET assembly is created using either interface or using interopservices method we need to create a COM type library using Type library export tool.

    Tlbexp (Assembly Name)
- The final thing is registering the CCW in registry using regasm tool.

    regasm Assembly Name [Options]
- Finally refer the TLB in your COM IDE Below is figure showing VB6 IDE referencing the DLL

> **Note:** DLL and TLB should be in same directory where the application is executed.2..NET Interoperability

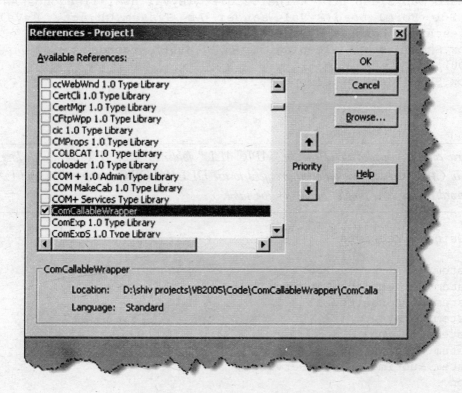

Figure 16.2: Referencing the DLL

How can we make Windows API calls in .NET?

Windows API calls are not COM based and they are invoked through Platform Invoke Services.

> *Declare StringConversionType (Function | Sub) MethodName Lib "DllName"*
>
> *([Args]) As Type*

- StringConversionType is for what type of conversion should take place. Either we can specify Unicode to convert all strings to Unicode values, or Auto to convert strings according to the .NET runtime rules.

- MethodName is the name of the API to call.

- DllName is the name of the DLL.

- Args are any arguments to the API call.

- Type is the return type of the API call.

Below is a sample code for VB.NET, which uses Sleep windows API for delaying.

```
Public Class Form1
Declare Auto Sub Sleep Lib "kernel32.dll" (ByVal dwMilliseconds As Long)
Private Sub Form1_Load(ByVal sender As System.Object, ByVal e As
System.EventArgs) Handles MyBase.Load
MessageBox.Show(" start sleeping for 5000 Milli seconds.....")
Sleep(5000)
MessageBox.Show(" end of sleeping.....")
End Sub
End Class
```

> **Note:** *Source code is provided in DVD in "APICALL" folder.In VB.NET we use declare keyword but in C# it goes little bit different, we need to use DLLIMPORT,interopservices and EXTERN keyword. Below is a simple sample for the same.*

```
#region Using directives

using System;
using System.Collections.Generic;
using System.ComponentModel;
using System.Data;
using System.Drawing;
using System.Windows.Forms;
using System.Runtime.InteropServices;
#endregion
namespace CSharpCode
{
        partial class Form1: Form
        {
               [DllImport("Kernel32.dll")]
               static extern int Sleep(long dwMilliseconds);
               public Form1()
               {
                      InitializeComponent();
               }
               private void Form1_Load(object sender, EventArgs e)
               {
                      MessageBox.Show("Starting of 5000 ms...");
                      Sleep(5000);
                      MessageBox.Show("End of 5000 ms...");
               }
        }
}
```

When we use windows API in .NET is it managed or unmanaged code?

Windows API in .NET is unmanaged code.

> **Note:** *Even though VB6 and VC++ has gone off still many people do ask these old questions again and again. Still there are decent old application which are working with COM very much fine. So interviewer still asks you these questions so that those application's can be ported to .NET. So let's play some old music... By the way my favourite music is Kishore, what's yours???*

What is COM?

Microsoft's COM is a technology for component software development. It is a binary standard, which is language independent. DCOM is a distributed extension of COM.

What is Reference counting in COM?

Reference counting is a memory management technique used to count how many times an object has a pointer referring to it. The first time it is created, the reference count is set to one. When the last reference to the object is nulled, the reference count is set to zero and the object is deleted. Care must be exercised to prevent a context switch from changing the reference count at the time of deletion. In the methods that follow, the syntax is shortened to keep the scope of the discussion brief and manageable.

Can you describe IUKNOWN interface in short?

Every COM object supports at least one interface, the IUnknown interface. All interfaces are classes derived from the base class IUnknown. Each interface supports methods access data and perform operations transparently to the programmer. For example, IUnknown supports three methods, AddRef, Release(), and QueryInterface(). Suppose that pinterf is a pointer to an IUnknown. pinterf->AddRef() increments the reference count. pinterf->Release() decrements the reference count, deleting the object when the reference count reaches zero. pinterf->QueryInterface (IDesired,pDesired) checks to see if the current interface (IUnknown) supports another interface, IDesired, creates an instance (via a call to CoCreateInstance ()) of the object if the reference count is zero (the object does not yet exist), and then calls pDesired->AddRef () to increment the reference count (where pDesired is a pointer to IDesired) and returns the pointer to the caller.

Can you explain what DCOM is?

DCOM differs from COM in that it allows for creating objects distributed across a network, a protocol for invoking that object's methods, and secures access to the object. DCOM provides a wrapper around COM, hence it is a backwards compatible extension. DCOM uses Remote Procedural Calls (RPC) using Open Software Foundation's Distributed Computing Environment.

These RPC are implemented over TCP/IP and named pipes. The protocol, which is actually being used, is registered just prior to use, as opposed to being registered at initialization time. The reason for this is that if a protocol is not being used, it will not be loaded.

In order to inform an object that the client is still alive, periodic pinging is used. Hence, when the client has died and no ping has been received (to refresh it) before the expiration time, the server object will perform some clean up tasks (including decrementing its reference count).

Since RPC across a network are typically slow (compared to processes residing on the same machine), DCOM sends multiple requests in the same call. For example, in COM, the program performs a

QueryInterface, one interface at a time. In DCOM, multiple QueryInterfaces are all clustered into one call.

This clustering optimization trick is also used when creating an instance of the object and serializing it with data. Since these two operations usually occur together, DCOM allows one method, which will perform both operations in one call without waiting for an acknowledgment from the first task before performing the second one.

Similarly, when a client pings its server object, he can do it in one call. Moreover, if there are multiple clients sending pings to multiple servers, an optimization is made where the multiple pings going to the same object are consolidated into just one ping. This is to cut down on the use of precious bandwidth used only for pinging.

The client has the control to set the computer, which will be responsible for the lifetime of the object. That is to say, these objects are not created just somewhere where the system resources and access privileges allow for it.

Call security is implemented in all four ways: authentication (to prevent false clients from impersonating the true client), authorization (to insure that a client only does what it is authorized to do), data integrity (to insure that data was not tampered with during transit), and data privacy (to insure that only designated sources can read it). The security issues are handled as they are on operating systems. The client gives the server various access privileges to access memory or disk space

How do we create DCOM object in VB6?

Using the CreateObject method, you can create a DCOM object. You have to put the server name in the registry.

How to implement DTC in .NET?

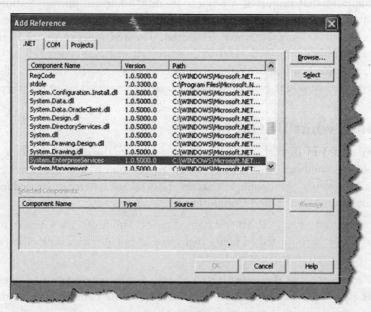

Figure 16.3: BCP in action

DTC is implemented using COM+.

Following are the steps to implement COM + in .NET:

- "EnterpriseService" namespace has all the classes by which we can implement DTC in .NET. You have to add reference "EnterpriseService" namespace.

- You class must derive from "Serviced Component" object.

- Then you have to define your class with the transaction attribute

  (For all transaction attribute look the down question)

[Transaction (TransactionOption.RequiresNew)]

After the class level, transaction type is defined. Its time to define at the method level the AutoComplete attribute. Autocomplete attribute says that if no exception is thrown then mark its part of the transaction as being okay. This helps cut down on the amount of code required. If the implementation sets AutoComplete to false, or omits it all together, then we would need to manage the transaction manually. To manually, control the transaction you will need to use the ContextUtil class and its static members. Following is small snippet of ContextUtil:

```
public void SampleFunction()
{
    try
    {
        // Do something to a database
        // ...
        // Everything okay so far Commit the transaction

        ContextUtil.SetComplete();
    }
    catch(Exception)
    {
        // Something went wrong Abort and Rollback the Transaction.
        ContextUtil.SetAbort();
    }
}
```

- Component derived from "ServicedComponent" should be strong named as they run under COM+.

- Once the classes are compiled using the string name. Register the Component in COM+ services using

---
regsvcs c:\DllPath\TransactionComponent.dll

- You can see that the component is registered using the COM+ explorer.

How many types of Transactions are there in COM + .NET?

5 transactions types can be used with COM+. Whenever an object is registered with COM+, it has to abide either to these 5 transaction types.

Disabled: There is no transaction. COM+ does not provide transaction support for this component.

Not Supported: Component does not support transactions. Hence even if the calling component in the hierarchy is transaction enabled this component will not participate in the transaction.

Supported: Components with transaction type support will be a part of the transaction. This will be only if the calling component has an active transaction. If the calling component is not transaction enabled this component will not start a new transaction.

Required: Components with this attribute require a transaction i.e. either the calling should have a transaction in place else, this component will start a new transaction.

Required New: Components enabled with this transaction type always require a new transaction. Components with required new transaction type instantiate a new transaction for themselves every time.

How do you do object pooling in .NET?

COM+ reduces overhead by not creating object from scratch. So in COM+ when object is activated it's activated, from pool and when it has deactivated it's pushed back to the pool. Object pooling is configures by using the "ObjectPoolingAttribute" to the class.

> **Note:** *When a class is marked with objectpooling attribute it can not be inherited.*

```
ObjectPooling(MinPoolSize:= 2, MaxPoolSize:= 5, CreationTimeout:= 20000)>
_
Public Class testingclass
Inherits ServicedComponent
Public Sub DoWork()
' Method contents go here.
End Sub
End Class
```

Above is a sample code, which has the "Object Pooling" attribute defined. Below is a sample code, which uses the class.

```
Public Class App
Overloads Public Shared Sub Main(args() As String)
Dim xyz As New TestObjectPooling()
xyz.doWork()
ServicedComponent.DisposeObject (xyz)
End Sub
End Class
```

Above is a sample code, which uses the object pooled object. Note the Dispose Object () This ensures its safe return to the object pool.

What are types of compatibility in VB6?

There are three possible project compatibility settings:

- No Compatibility
- Project Compatibility
- Binary Compatibility

No Compatibility

With this setting, new class ID's, new interface ID's and a new type library ID will be generated by VB each time the ActiveX component project is compiled. This will cause any compiled client components to fail (with error 429!) and report a missing reference to the 'VB ActiveX Test Component' when a client project is loaded in the VB IDE.

> **Note:** *Use this setting to compile the initial release of a component to other developers.*

Project Compatibility

With this setting, VB will generate new interface ID's for classes whose interfaces have changed, but will not change the class ID's or the type library ID. This will still cause any compiled client components to fail (with error 429!) but will not report a missing reference to the 'VB ActiveX Test Component' when a client project is loaded in the VB IDE. Recompilation of client components will restore them to working order again.

> **Note:** *Use this setting during the initial development and testing of a component within the IDE and before the component is released to other developers.(A)How many types of Transactions are there in COM + .NET ?*

Binary Compatibility

VB makes it possible to extend an existing class or interface by adding new methods and properties etc. and yet still retain binary compatibility. It can do this, because it silently creates a new interface ID for the extended interface and adds registration code to register the original interface ID but with a new Forward key containing the value of this new interface ID. COM will then substitute calls having the old ID with the new ID and hence applications built against the old interface will continue to work (assuming the inner workings of the component remain backward compatible!).

With this setting, VB will not change any of the existing class, interface or type library ID's, however in order that it can do so, VB requires the project to specify an existing compiled version that it can compare against to ensure that existing interfaces have not been broken

What is equivalent for regsvr32 exe in .NET?

Regasm

17

Windows Workflow Foundation

What is Windows Workflow Foundation?

WWF is a programming model for building workflow-enabled applications on windows. System. Workflow namespace has all the necessary modules to develop any type of workflow.

What is a Workflow?

A Workflow is a set of activities, which is stored as model and they depict a process. Below figure depicts clearly the difference between Workflow and Activity. Every task is an activity and group of activity depicts a complete workflow. Workflow is run by the Workflow runtime engine.

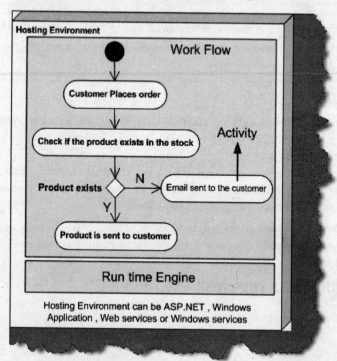

Figure 17.1: Diff. between Workflow and Activity

Workflow model can be written in pure .NET code, pure XAML or Mix of XAML and .NET Code. A workflow model is compiled and can execute under windows, ASP.NET, Web services or windows services application.

What are different types of Workflow in Windows Workflow foundation?

There are two basics type of workflow Sequential Workflow and State machines workflow.

A sequential workflow has clear start and finish boundaries. Workflow controls execution in Sequential workflow. In sequential execution, one task is executed after other. Sequential workflow is more rigid in format and execution path has a determistic nature.

A State machine workflow is more dynamic in nature. Workflow has states and the state waits for events to help it move to next state. In State machine execution path is undetermestic nature.

Below figure shows visual conceptualization of fundamentals. You can see in Sequential workflow the execution path is very determent. Shiv performs the entire task sequentially and these tasks are very determent. Now have a look at the second workflow. Every state goes to other state when it receives some external events. For instance when Shiv is seeing star trek there is an event of flashing news which triggers him to see the flashing new.

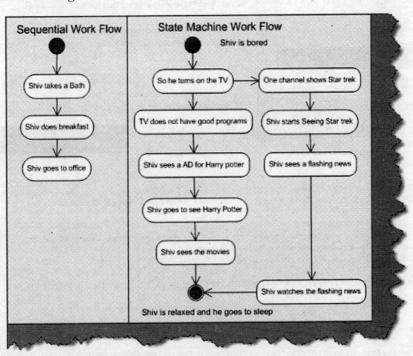

Figure 17.2: visual conceptualization of fundamentals

When should we use a sequential workflow and when should we use state machines?

If the workflow is very rigid then you go for sequential workflow and if the workflow is dynamic then go for State machine workflow. For instance you have placed an order and the order will not pass until your supervisor approves is a rigid flow. Because your order has to be approved by, a supervisor or else it will not be approved. But what if your order moves from one place to other place. For instance, it moves from approval to waiting and then clarification a state machine workflow model is more appropriate.

Below is a simple code snippet which shows practically how to use sequential workflow. Let try to understand step by step as marked in the figure:

1 - First you need to select System. Workflow namespace.

2, 3, and **4 -** In these three steps we created code object and linked them with activity.

5, 6, 7, and **8 -** We start the workflow and create workflow instance object to run the sequential workflow. You can see the output in 8. Depending on how you add the activity in section 3, it executes sequentially. Because we have added codeactivity1, first it executes the first activity first. The sequence on how you add the activity to the activities collection the activities are run.

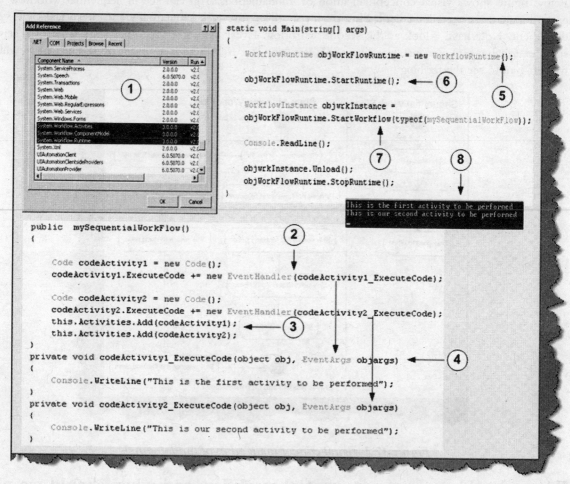

Figure 17.3: sequential workflow

> **Note:** *The above code snippet was developed with out using designer. The whole point was to make you understand what happens behind the scenes. In real projects you will be dependent on designer rather than coding manually. You can find the above code in SimpleWorkFlowSampleManual folder.*

How do we create workflows using designer?

As said previously it is very easy to design workflows using designer. So we will answer this question by actually doing a small sample. Below is the code snippet and image snapshot which shows how we can use the designer to create workflows. So lets understand all the below numbered snapshot.

1 - First select a sequential workflow project. In this case, we have selected Sequential workflow console application to keep the sample simple.

2 - When you are done with creating the project you will see the solution explorer as shown in the second snapshot. There are two files one the WorkFlow1.cs and the other Workflow1.designer.cs.If you click on the WorkFlow1.cs you will get a designer pane as shown in snapshot 3. If you double click on Workflow1.designer.cs, you will get behind code as shown in snapshot 4.

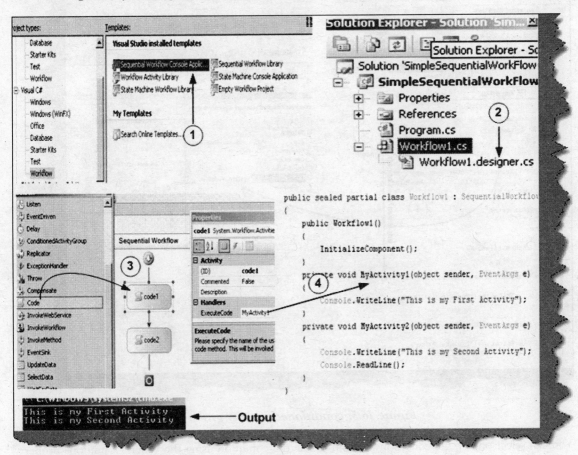

Figure 17.4: designer to create to workflows

3 - So let us drag drop a code activity on the workflow designer and associate this activity with a method called as MyActivity1. This association is done by entering the method name in Execute Code property. In MyActivity1, we have just displayed in the console that this is my first activity. Again, we have added one more code activity, which points to MyActivity2. If you see the designer pane we have sequenced code1 first and code2 next. So in short, code1 will execute first and the code2. This is clear from the output displayed below.

4 - This is the behind code of the workflow.

How do we specify conditions in Work flow?

Yes, you can define conditions in workflow by using conditionedActivitygroup. Below is the numbered snapshot, which shows how to use conditionedActivitygroup.

1 - You can see in this snapshot we have defined a conditionedActivitygroup with two conditions. The two boxes inside the group define two conditions.

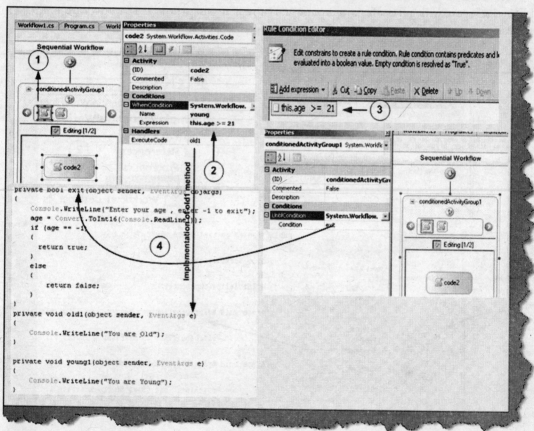

Figure 16.5: conditioned activity group

2 - You can select one of the condition box and define the condition using the When Conditions property. If this condition is true you need to specify in the execute code which method to execute. For instance in the current snapshot we have said that old1 method should execute if age > 21. The same procedure we need to follow for the second condition box. In the second condition box we have specified to execute young1 method if age < 21. Currently the second condition is not visible in the below snapshot.

3 - Workflow editor also provides a cool interface called as Rule Condition Editor, which can be used to specify conditions. Age is a public property in the behind code. You can also get the Age in the intelligence of rule condition editor.

4 - Both the condition will execute inside the condition activity group. We need to also specify when this conditionactivitygroup should exit. Therefore, we have made a function called as exit. If the user inputs age as -1 it will exit from the loop or else it will take inputs from user and continue evaluating depending on the two conditions.

> **Note:** *During interview the interviewer will not like to hear the complete story what we have said above. He needs only a small sentence conditionedActivityGroup is used to specify conditions in workflow. The above story is just in case you also want to do some hands on practical. If you want to explore further you can get the above sample code in SequentialWorkFlowConditions folder.*

How do you handle exceptions in workflow?

Exception handling in Workflow is somewhat different than how we do in normal .NET application. Below is the numbered snapshot of how we can handle exceptions in Workflow.

1 - We have small tab, which says view exceptions. If you click on view exception, you will be redirected to a workflow design only for exception as shown in numbered snapshot 2.

2 - This is the workflow which will execute incase we have exceptions. We have put a code activity, which points to a method called as raise Exception. Incase of exception in the workflow this path will be followed.

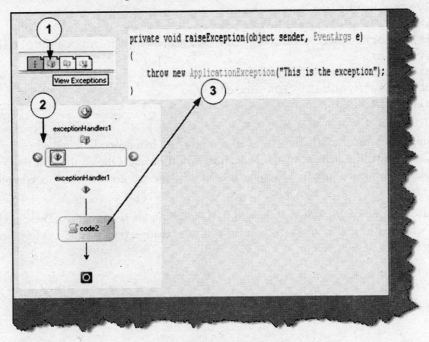

Figure 17.6: handle exception in workflow

What is the use of XOML files?

Windows Workflow Foundation gives developers a declarative way to create workflows by using XAML. See WPF chapter for more details about XAML. These markup files are Stored with XOML (Extensible Object Markup Language) extension. In the below snapshot you can see Workflow1.xoml file created by designer. Markup file can also have code behind. The whole concept of having code behind for XOML file is to separate the presentation from logic files.

In the below code snapshot we have made a simple XOML sample. Below is the explanation number wise:

1 – In order to create a XOML file you need to add sequential workflow with separation. Which means that XOML file will be created with a behind code.

2 – Currently we have two activity code3 and code1. Below is the XOML file contents

```
<?Mapping XmlNamespace="ComponentModel"
ClrNamespace="System.Workflow.ComponentModel"
Assembly="System.Workflow.ComponentModel" ?>
<?Mapping XmlNamespace="Compiler"
ClrNamespace="System.Workflow.ComponentModel.Compiler"
Assembly="System.Workflow.ComponentModel" ?>
<?Mapping XmlNamespace="Activities"
      ClrNamespace="System.Workflow.Activities"
Assembly="System.Workflow.Activities" ?>
<?Mapping XmlNamespace="RuleConditions"
ClrNamespace="System.Workflow.Activities.Rules"
Assembly="System.Workflow.Activities" ?>
<SequentialWorkflow x:Class="WorkflowSeq.Workflow1"
x:CompileWith="Workflow1.xoml.cs" ID="Workflow1" xmlns:x="Definition"
xmlns="Activities">
<Code ExecuteCode="Mycode3" ID="code3" />
<Code ExecuteCode="Mycode1" ID="code1" />
</SequentialWorkflow>
```

See the above snippet of the XOML file. You can see how the behind code is linked using the Compile With attribute. Code forms the element of the Sequential Workflow tag. One of the best thing with Markup is we can change the sequence just by changing the XOML file we do not need to compile the whole application again.

In the above snapshot, one of the things to now is 3, 4, and 5 numbered sections. These sections are not linked with the sample. But just to make you aware you can create serialize any workflow and deserialize them again using the text writer object.

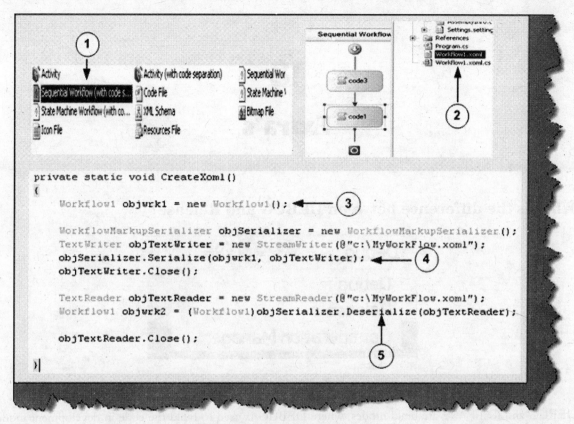

Figure 17.7: sequential workflow

How can we pass parameters to workflow?

When you call the start workflow function, you can pass as name / value pairs using the dictionary object.

```
WorkflowRuntime workflowRuntime = new WorkflowRuntime();
workflowRuntime.StartRuntime();

workflowRuntime.WorkflowCompleted += OnWorkflowCompleted;

Type type = typeof(SequentialWorkFlowConditions.Workflow1);
workflowRuntime.StartWorkflow(type,);
```

```
▲ 2 of 5 ▼  WorkflowInstance WorkflowRuntime.StartWorkflow (Type workflowType,
                                          Dictionary<string,object>
                                          namedArgumentValues)
```

Figure 17.8: pass parameters to workflow

18

Extra's

What is the difference between DEBUG and Release?

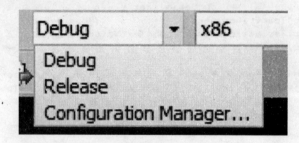

Figure 18.1: DEBUG vs RELEASE

DEBUG and RELEASE are build modes, where DEBUG is used to build the code in development mode and RELEASE is for production / go liveenvironment.

In RELEASE mode the code is more optimized and any debugging related code or debug constants are removed before going to production.

What is the use of DEBUG directive?

#Debug is a preprocessor directive. Now many times you want some code to run while you are debugging but you do want those code shipped to production environment.

For instance in the below code we want todisplay operating system onlyduring debugging but this code we do not want in to be pushed to production server.To achieve this we can use the DEBUG directive.

You can see the below code we have wrapped display operating version code in #if DEBUG condition.This code will be excluded when release compiling happens.

```
#if DEBUG
// This code will not be shipped to production.
Console.WriteLine(System.Environment.OSVersion);
#endif

// This code will be shipped to production.
for (int i = 0; i < 5 ; i++)
```

```
{
        Console.WriteLine(i);
}
```

What does the word scalability, scale-up and scale-out means?

Scalability is the ability of a system to handle growing amount of load without degrading performance. Consider you have system which runs with 100 users efficiently. Let's say over a period of time your load increases to 500 users, your system still has the ability to handle the load and provide the same efficiency.

You can achieve scalability by two ways either you can Scale-up or Scale-out. In scale-up we have only one machine and we increase the processing power of the machine by adding more processor, more ram, more hard disk etc. So if your load increases you add more ram, more processor etc, but you do not add extra physical machines.

In Scale-out, as your load increases you add more computers and you have load balancers in front of those machines to distribute load appropriately.

Can you write a simple c# code to display Fibonacci series?

These are some strange questions which are asked in big companies to test your logical thinking ability. Before we move ahead lets first to understand what exactly is Fibonacci series. Fibonacci series are nothing but series of numbers 0,1,1,2,3,5 and so on.

The specialty of this series is that next number is addition of previous two numbers. Below figure explains how Fibonacci series works. We first start with 0 and 1. The next number is addition of "0 + 1" which will give us "1". The next number will be again addition of previous value which is "1" and the current value which is "1" which will give us "2" and so on.

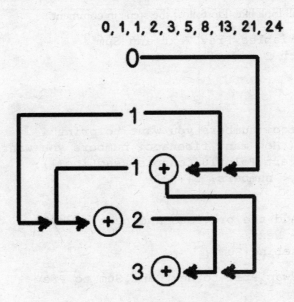

Figure 18.2: What is FB series?

Implementing Fibonacci series in c# is a 4 step process. Below image shows the same in a pictorial format.

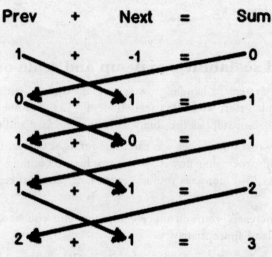

Figure 18.3: Logic of how to code FB series

Step 1: Define 3 variables "Prev","Next" and "Sum". Initialize these variable with "Prev=1", "Next = -1" and "Sum=0".

Step 2: Add "Prev" and "Next" variable to get the Sum. Display the "Sum" variable.

Step 3: Swap "Prev" value to "Next" and "Sum" to "Previous".

Step 4: Execute "Step 2" and "Step 3" again for the next Fibonacci value.

Below is how the code will look like. Do follow the steps in comment.

```
//Step 1 Three variables Prev,Next and Sum
// initialized with 1 and -1 values
int Prev = 1;
int Next = -1;
int Sum = 0;

// How many fibonacci numbers you want to print
Console.WriteLine("How many fibonacci numbers you want to print ?");
int numbers = Convert.ToInt16(Console.ReadLine());
for (int i = 0; i < numbers; i++)
{

    // Step 2: Add the previous and next numbers
    Sum = Prev + Next;
    Console.WriteLine(Sum);

    // Step 3: Swap Prev to next and Sum to Prev
    Next = Prev;
    Prev = Sum;
    // Step 4: Run Step 2 and Step 3 again
}
```

19

Learn .NET in 60 Days

Every time I update my edition, I always want to do something crazy for my readers. Here's one awesome gift you get with this book. Learn .NET for free. With this book you will get a DVD which has the below 32 videos which help you to learn .NET absolutely free. So enjoy the video series created by me personally. Below is the complete list of video index.

Learn .NET in 60 days.	
(Day 1)Lab 1: - Creating your first program	(Day 10) Lab 20: - Creating a web application
(Day 1)Lab 2: - Creating your first program	(Day 10) Lab 21: - Connect app to DAL
(Day 1)Lab 3: - Integer DataType	(Day 11 & 12) Lab 22: - Insert, Update & Delete
(Day 1)Lab 4: - Exception Handling	(Day 13) Lab 23: - Implementing 3 Tier Architecture
(Day 1)Lab 5: - IF Condition, Return Try/Catch	(Day 14) Lab 24: - Security
(Day 2)Lab 6: - Commenting	(Day 15) Lab 25: - Web Security
(Day 2)Lab 7: - For Loop	(Day 16) Lab 26: - REGEX
(Day 2)Lab 8: - Simple calculator program	(Day 17) Lab 27: - Improving Database Design
(Day 3)Lab 9: - Creating your 1st Application	(Day 18)Lab 28: - 1 to many relationship
(Day 3)Lab 10: - Creating the Customer Screen	(Day 19)Lab 29: - 1 to Many (Insert)
(Day 4)Lab 11: - Displaying Customer Screen	(Day 20)Lab 30: - 1 to Many(Select & Delete)
(Day 4)Lab 12: - Multiple Document Interface(MDI)	(Day 21)Lab 31: - 1 to Many(Update)
(Day 5)Lab 13: - Classes & Objects	(Day 22)Lab 32: - Stored Procedure
(Day 6)Lab 14: - Getting Data from SQL Server	Day 23 to Day 60: - Project
(Day 7)Lab 15: - Inserting data into SQL Server	
(Day 7) Lab 16: - Connection string in App.config	
(Day 8) Lab 17: - Delete Functionality	
(Day 9) Lab 18: - Update Functionality	
(Day 9) Lab 19: - 2 Tier Architecture	

20

Invoicing Application End to End

In this book we have a provided a complete invoicing application end to end. The complete application is created demonstrating full SDLC end to end with full video explanation. We suggest everyone to go through the videos for better understanding. The project starts from a simple code to a full blown three tier reusable architecture.

> **Note:** *If you are looking for how big multinationals approach to complete software projects then buy my book "C# and ASP.NET Projects" from BPB publications. It has projects like chat application, job site, accounting application with full project life cycle and estimation. Mail bpb@vsnl.com for more details.*

Software Company hierarchy

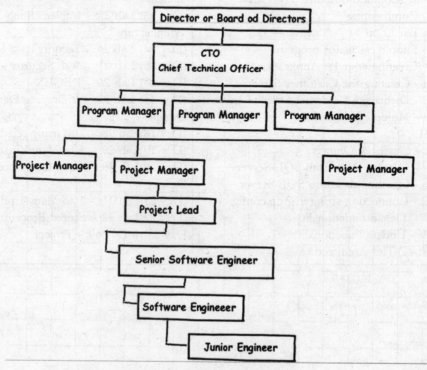

Figure 20.1: Company Hierarchy

It's very important during interview to be clear about what position you are targeting. Depending on what positions you are targeting the interviewer shoots you questions. Example if you are looking for a project manager position you will be asked around 20% technical questions and 80% management.

> *Note: In small scale software house and mid scale software companies there are chances where they expect a PM to be very much technical. But in big software houses the situations are very much different, interview are conducted according to positions.... Unless the interviewer changes the rule.*

Above is a figure of a general hierarchy across most IT companies.

> *Note: There are many small and medium software companies which do not follow this hierarchy and they have there own adhoc way of defining positions in the company.*

So why is the need of hierarchy in a interview.

> *"Interview is a contract between the employer and candidate to achieve specific goals."*

So employer is looking for a suitable candidate and candidate looks for a better career. Normally in interviews, the employer is very clear about what type of candidate he is looking for. However, 90% times the candidate is not clear about the positions he is looking for.

How many times it has happened with you that you have given a whole interview and when you mentioned the position you are looking for...pat comes the answer, " we do not have any requirements for this position". So be clarified about the position right from when you start the interview.

Following are the number of years of experience according to position.

● Junior engineers are especially freshers and work under software engineers.

● Software engineers have around 1 to 2 years of experience. Interviewer expects software engineers to be technically at a medium level.

● Senior Software Engineers have around 2 to 4 years of experience. Interviewer expects them to technically be very strong.

● Project leads should handle majority technical aspect of project and should have around 4 to 8 years of experience. They are also indirect architect of the project. Interviewer expects them to be technically strong so that they can drive the architecture part of the project. Interviewer also expects them to have people management skills.

● Project Manager are expected to be around 40% technically strong and should have experience above 10 years plus. But they are more interviewed from aspect of project management, client interaction, people management, proposal preparation etc.

So now judge where you stand, and where you want to go..........

Resume Preparation Guidelines

> *First impression the last impression*

> *Note: A sample resume is provided in "SampleResume" folder.*

Before even the interviewer meets you he will first meet your resume. Interviewer looking at your resume is almost a 20% interview happening with out you knowing it. I was always a bad guy when it comes to resume preparation. But when I looked at my friends resume they where really good. Now that I am writing series of book on interviews I thought this will be a good point to put in. You can happily skip it if you are confident about your resume. There is no hard and fast rule that you have to follow the same pattern but just see if these all check list are attended.

- Use plain text when you are sending resumes through email. For instance you sent your resume using Microsoft word and what if the interviewer is using Linux he will never be able to read your resume. You can not be sure both wise, you sent your resume in Word 2000 and the guy has Word 97...uuhhh.

- Attach a covering letter it really impresses and makes you look traditionally formal. Yes, even if you are sending your CV through email send a covering letter.

Check list of content you should have in your resume:

- Start with an objective or summary, for instance, "Working as a Senior Database administrator for more than 4 years. Implemented quality web based application. Follow the industry's best practices and adhered and implemented processes, which enhanced the quality of technical delivery. Pledge to deliver the best technical solutions to the industry."

- Specify your Core strengths at the start of the resume by which the interviewer can make a quick decision are you eligible for the position. For example:

  o   Looked after data mining and data warehousing department independently. Played a major role in query optimization.

  o   Worked extensively in database design and ER diagram implementation.

  o   Well versed with CMMI process and followed it extensively in projects.

  o   Looking forward to work on project manager or senior manager position.

This is also a good position to specify your objective or position which makes it clear to the interviewer that should he call you for an interview. For instance, if you are looking for senior positions specify it explicitly 'looking for this job profile'. Any kind of certification like MCP, MCSD etc you can make it visible in this section.

Once you have specified briefly your goals and what you have done its time to specify what type of technology you have worked with. For instance RDBMS, TOOLS, Languages, Web servers, process (Six sigma, CMMI).

- After that you can make a run through of your experience company wise that is what company you have worked with, year / month joining and year / month left. This will give an overview to the interviewer what type of companies you have associated your self.

Now its time to mention all your projects you have worked till now. Best is to start in descending order that is from your current project and go backwards. For every project try to put these things:

- Project Name / Client name (It's sometimes unethical to mention clients name; I leave it to the readers).

- Number of team members.

- Time span of the project.

- Tools, language, RDBMS and technology used to complete the project.
- Brief summary of the project.

Senior people who have huge experience will tend to increase there CV with putting in summary for all project. Best for them is to just put description of the first three projects in descending manner and rest they can say verbally during interview. I have seen CV above 15 pages... I doubt who can read it.

- Finally comes your education and personal details.
- Trying for onsite, do not forget to mention your passport number.
- Some guys tend to make there CV large and huge. I think an optimal size should be not more than 4 to 5 pages.
- Do not mention your salary in CV. You can talk about it during interview with HR or the interviewer.
- When you are writing your summary for project make it effective by using verbs like managed a team of 5 members, architected the project from start to finish etc. It brings huge weight,
- This is essential very essential take 4 to 5 Xerox copies of your resume you will need it now and then.
- Just in case take at least 2 passport photos with you. You can escape it but many times you will need it.
- Carry all your current office documents specially your salary slips and joining letter.

Salary Negotiation

Ok that's what we all do it for MONEY... not everyone but still money means a lot. This is probably the weakest area for techno savvy guys. They are not good negotiators. I have seen so many guys at the first instance they will smile and say "NEGOTIABLE SIR".

So here are some points:

- Do a study of what is the salary trend? For instance have some kind of baseline. For example what is the salary trend on number of year of experience? Discuss this with your friends out.
- Do not mention your expected salary on the resume?
- Let the employer first make the salary offer. Try to delay the salary discussion till the end.
- If they say what you expect? Come with a figure with a little higher end and say negotiable. Remember never say negotiable on something which you have aimed, HR guys will always bring it down. So negotiate on AIMED SALARY + some thing extra.
- The normal trend is that they look at your current salary and add a little it so that they can pull you in. Do your home work my salary is this much and I expect this much so whatever it is now I will not come below this.
- Do not be harsh during salary negotiations.
- It's good to aim high. For instance I want 1 billion dollars / month but at the same time be realistic.
- Some companies have those hidden cost attached in salary clarify it rather to be surprised at the first salary package.

- Many of the companies add extra performance compensation in your basic which can be surprising at times. So have a detail break down. Best is to discuss on hand salary rather than NET or CTC.

- Talk with the employer in what frequency does the hike happen.

- Take everything in writing, go back to your house and have a look once with a cool head is the offer worth it of what your current employer is giving.

- Do not forget once you have job in hand you can come back to your current employer for negotiation.

- Remember the worst part is cribbing after joining the company that your colleague is getting more. So be careful while interview or be sportive to be a good negotiator in the next interview.

- One very important thing is that the best negotiation ground is not the new company where you are going but the old company which you are leaving. So once you have offer on hand get back to your old employee and show them the offer and then make your next move. It's my experience that negotiating with the old employer is easy than the new one....Frankly if approached properly rarely any one will say no as you have spent quiet a amount of time with them. Just do not be aggressive or egoistic that you have an offer on hand.

- Top of all some time some things are worth above money: JOB SATISFACTION. So whatever you negotiate if you think you can get JOB SATISFACTION aspect on higher grounds go for it. I think its worth more than money.

Applicable to Only India	
Years of experience	Amount in Rupees CTC (Monthly)
Freshers	15000 to 20000
1 to 2 yrs	25000 to 30000
4 to 6	40000 to 60000
6 to 8 yrs	60000 to 70000
8 to 10 yrs	70000 to 90000
10 to 15 yrs	90000 to 110000
15 yrs and above	110000 and above. Mostly depends on negotiations.

Table: Salary Card for India

Note: *The indian salary card is as per India mega cities like Mumbai, Pune, Banglore, Chennai, Hyderabad, Delhi etc . For mid size cities like Lucknow, Nagpur, Ahmedabad, Amritsar etc the CTC will be 15% less.*

Applicable to US Only	
Years of experience	**Amount in Dollars (Yearly)**
Fresher's	45000 to 55000
2 to 4 yrs	55000 to 60000
4 to 6 yrs	60000 to 65000
6 to 8 yrs	70000 to 80000
8 to 12 yrs	80000 to 90000
12 and above	Depends on negotiations

Table: US Salary Card

Note: *For big cities like NY, Chicago, California state and down town cities the US rated card will be 10% higher.*

The score card shown above is completely derived from author's experience and interaction he had in his circle. It is not an approved score card by any authorized body as such and should be taken only has bench mark to measure your success. Also note that these rates are applicable for medium and large software companies. Small company rate cards are very irregular and governed by a single owner of the company. So the above rate card is not applicable for small company. Many people do get mind blowing salaries even with small experience which again the score card does not reflect.

Points to Remember

- One of the first questions asked during interview is "Can you say something about yourself"?
- Can you describe about your self and what you have achieved till now?
- Why do you want to leave the current company?
- Where do you see yourself after three years?
- What are your positive and negative points?
- How much do you rate yourself in .NET and SQL Server in one out of ten?
- Are you looking for onsite opportunities? (Be careful do not show your desperation of abroad journeys)
- Why have you changed so many jobs? (Prepare a decent answer do not blame companies and individuals for your frequent change).
- Never talk for more than 1 minute straight during interview.
- Have you worked with previous version of SQL Server?
- Would you be interested in a full time Database administrator job?
- Do not mention client names in resume. If asked say that it's confidential which brings ahead qualities like honesty
- When you make your resume keep your recent projects at the top.
- Find out what the employer is looking for by asking him questions at the start of interview and best is before going to interview. Example if a company has projects on server products employer will be looking for BizTalk, CS CMS experts.
- Can you give brief about your family background?
- As you are fresher do you think you can really do this job?
- Have you heard about our company? Say five points about our company? Just read at least once what company you are going for?
- Can you describe your best project you have worked with?
- Do you work on Saturday and Sunday?
- Which is the biggest team size you have worked with?
- Can you describe your current project you have worked with?
- How much time will you need to join our organization? What's notice period for your current company?
- What certifications have you cleared?

- Do you have pass port size photos, last year mark sheet, previous companies employment letter, last month's salary slip, pass port and other necessary documents.

- What is the most important thing that motivates you?

- Why you want to leave the previous organization?

- Which type of job gives you greatest satisfaction?

- What is the type of environment you are looking for?

- Do you have experience in project management?

- Do you like to work as a team or as individual?

- Describe your best project manager you have worked with?

- Why should I hire you?

- Have you been ever fired or forced to resign?

- Can you explain some important points that you have learnt from your past project experiences?

- Have you gone through some unsuccessful projects, if yes can you explain why did the project fail?

- Will you be comfortable with location shift? If you have personal problems say no right at the first stage.... or else within two months you have to read my book again.

- Do you work late nights? Best answer if there is project deadline yes. Do not show that it's your culture to work during nights.

- Any special achievements in your life till now...tell your best project which you have done best in your career.

- Any plans of opening your own software company...Beware do not start pouring your bill gate's dream to him.....can create a wrong impression.

Other Interview Questions Books by Shivprasad Koirala

Note: *Below are questions from my 3 books project interview questions , SQL Server interview question and architecture interview questions.*

Project Management Interview Questions

Basics of Project Management

- Define project?
- Who is a stakeholder?
- Can you explain Scope triangle?
- Can you explain what are a vision and a goal?
- What is ROI?
- Can you explain project life cycle?
- You have people in your team who do not meet there deadlines or do not perform what actions you will take?
- Are risk constant through out the project?
- Explain SDLC (Software development Life Cycle) in detail?
- Can you explain waterfall model?
- Can you explain big-bang waterfall model?
- Can you explain phased waterfall model?
- Explain Iterative model, Incremental model, Spiral model, Evolutionary model and VModel?
- Explain Unit testing, Integration tests, System testing and Acceptance testing?
- what's the difference between system and acceptance testing?
- Which is the best model?
- What is CAR (Causal Analysis and Resolution)?
- What is DAR (Decision Analysis and Resolution)?
- Can you explain the concept of baseline in software development?
- What is the software you have used for project management?
- What does a project plan consist?
- When do you say the project has finished?
- Can you explain what a PMO office is?
- How many members in your team you have handled?

- Is GANTT chart a project plan?
- Two resources are having issues how do you handle the same?
- What is a change request?
- How did you manage change request in your project?
- Can you explain traceability matrix?
- what is configuration management?
- What is CI?
- Define stakeholders?
- Can you explain versioning?
- Can you explain the concept of sign off?
- How will you start a project?
- what is an MOU?
- What where the deliverables in your project?
- Can you explain your project?
- Do you also participate in technical activities?
- How did you manage code reviews?
- you have team member who does not meets his deadlines how do you handle it?
- did you have project audits if yes how was it handled?
- What is a non-conformance report (NCR)?
- How did you estimate your project?
- How did you motivate your team members?
- did you create leaders in your team if yes how?
- how did you confirm that your modules are resource independent?
- Was your project show cased for CMMI or any other project process standardization?
- what are the functions of the Quality Assurance Group (QAG)?
- Can you explain milestone?
- How did you do assessme nt of team members?
- What does entry and exit criteria mean in a project?How much are you as leader and how much are you as PM ?
- How can he handle the conflicts between peers and subordinates?
- In your team you have highly talented people how did you handle their motivation ?
- How can you balance between underperforming and outperforming people ?
- You need to make choice between delivery and quality what's your take ?

Risk Management
- Define risk?
- What is risk break down structure?
- How did you plan your risk?
- What is DR, BCP and contingency planning?
- Schedule Management
- Can you explain WBS?

- Can you explain WBS numbering?
- How did you do resource allocation?
- Can you explain the use of WBS?
- Can you explain network diagram?
- What are the different types of network diagram?
- What is the advantage of using network diagrams?
- Can you explain Arrow diagram and Precedence diagram?
- What are the different types of Network diagrams?
- Can you explain Critical path?
- Can you define EST, LST, EFT, LFT?
- Can you explain Float and Slack?
- Can you explain PERT?
- Can you explain GANTT chart?
- What is the disadvantage of GANTT chart?
- What is Monte-Carlo simulation?

CMMI

- What is CMMI?
- What's the difference between implementation and Institutionalization?
- What are different models in CMMI?
- Can you explain staged and continuous models in CMMI?
- Can you explain the different maturity levels in staged representation?
- Can you explain capability levels in continuous representation?
- Which model should we use and under what scenarios?
- How many process areas are present in CMMI and in what classification do they fall in?
- What the difference between every level in CMMI?
- what different sources are needed to verify authenticity for CMMI implementation?
- Can you explain SCAMPI process?
- How is appraisal done in CMMI?
- Which appraisal method class is the best?
- Can you explain the importance of PII in SCAMPI?
- Can you explain implementation of CMMI in one of the Key process areas?
- Explanation of all process areas with goals and practices?
- Can you explain the process areas?

Six Sigma

- What is six sigma?
- Can you explain the different methodology for execution and design process in SIXsigma?
- What does executive leaders, champions, Master Black belt, green belts and black beltsmean?
- What are the different kinds of variations used in six sigma?
- Can you explain the concept of standard deviation?
- Can you explain the concept of fish bone/ Ishikawa diagram?

- What is Pareto principle?
- Can you explain QFD?
- Can you explain FMEA?
- Can you explain X bar charts?
- Can you explain Flow charting and brain storming?

Costing

- Can you explain PV, AC and EV?
- Can you explain BCWS, ACWS and BCWP?
- What are the derived metrics from Earned Value?
- Can you explain earned value with a sample?
- Estimation, Metrics and Measure
- What is meant by measure and metrics?
- Which metrics have you used for tracking purpose?
- What are the various common ways of estimation?
- Can you explain LOC method of estimation?
- How do we convert LOC in to effort?
- Can you explain COCOMO?
- Can you explain Intermediate COCOMO and COCOMO II?
- How do you estimate using LOC?
- Can you explain in brief Function points?
- Can you explain the concept Application boundary?
- Can you explain the concept of elementary process?
- Can you explain the concept of static and dynamic elementary process?
- Can you explain concept of FTR, ILF, EIF, EI, EO , EQ and GSC ?
- How can you estimate number of acceptance test cases in a project?
- Can you explain the concept of Use Case's?
- Can you explain the concept of Use case points?
- What is a use case transaction?
- How do we estimate using Use Case Points?
- Can you explain on what basis does TPA actually work?
- How did you do estimation for black box testing?
- How did you estimate white box testing?
- Is there a way to estimate acceptance test cases in a system?
- Can you explain Number of defects measure?
- Can you explain number of production defects measure?
- Can you explain defect seeding?
- Can you explain DRE?
- Can you explain Unit and system test DRE?
- How do you measure test effectiveness?
- Can you explain Defect age and Defect spoilage?

Agile Development

- What does Agile mean?
- Can you explain Agile modelling?
- What are core and supplementary principles in Agile modeling?
- What is the main principle behind Agile documentation?
- What are the different methodologies to implement Agile?
- What is XP?
- What are User Stories in XP and how different are they from requirement?
- Who writes User stories?
- When do we say a story is valid?
- When are test plans written in XP?
- Can you explain the XP development life cycle?
- Can you explain how planning game works in Extreme Programming?
- How do we estimate in Agile?
- On What basis can stories be prioritized?
- Can you point out simple differences between Agile and traditional SDLC?
- Can you explain the concept of refactoring?
- What is a feature in Feature Driven Development?
- Can you explain the overall structure of FDD project?
- Can you explain the concept of time boxing?
- When to choose FDD and when to choose XP?
- What is SCRUM?
- What does product owner, product back log and sprint mean in SCRUM?
- Can you explain how SCRUM flows?
- Can you explain different roles in SCRUM?
- Can you explain DSDM?
- Can you explain different phases in DSDM?
- Can you explain in detail project life cycle phase in DSDM?
- Can you explain LSD?Can you explain ASD?

SQL Server Interview Questions

Database Concepts

- What is database or database management systems (DBMS)?
- What is difference between DBMS and RDBMS?
- What are CODD rules?
- Is access database a RDBMS?
- What is the main difference between ACCESS and SQL SERVER?
- What is the difference between MSDE and SQL SERVER 2000?
- What is SQL SERVER Express 2005 Edition?
- What is SQL Server 2000 Workload Governor?

- What is the difference between SQL SERVER 2000 and 2005?
- What are E-R diagrams?
- How many types of relationship exist in database designing?
- What is normalization?
- What are different types of normalization?
- What is denormalization?
- Can you explain Fourth Normal Form?
- Can you explain Fifth Normal Form?
- Have you heard about sixth normal form?
- What is Extent and Page?
- What are the different sections in Page?
- What are page splits?
- In which files does actually SQL Server store data?
- What is Collation in SQL Server?
- Can we have a different collation for database and table?.

NET Integration

- What are steps to load a .NET code in SQL SERVER 2005?
- How can we drop an assembly from SQL SERVER?
- Are changes made to assembly updated automatically in database?
- Why do we need to drop assembly for updating changes?
- How to see assemblies loaded in SQL Server?
- I want to see which files are linked with which assemblies?
- Does .NET CLR and SQL SERVER run in different process?
- Does .NET controls SQL SERVER or is it vice-versa?
- Is SQLCLR configured by default?
- How to configure CLR for SQL SERVER?
- How does SQL Server control .NET run-time?
- In previous versions of .NET it was done via COM interface"ICorRuntimeHost"
- What is a "SAND BOX" in SQL Server 2005?
- What is an application domain?
- How is .NET Appdomain allocated in SQL SERVER 2005?
- What is Syntax for creating a new assembly in SQL Server 2005?
- Do Assemblies loaded in database need actual .NET DLL?"?
- You have an assembly, which is dependent on other assemblies; will SQL Serverload the dependent assemblies?
- Does SQL Server handle unmanaged resources?
- What is Multi- tasking?
- What is Multi-threading?
- What is a Thread?
- Can we have multiple threads in one App domain?

- What is Non-preemptive threading?
- What is pre-emptive threading?
- Can you explain threading model in SQL Server?
- How does .NET and SQL Server thread work?
- How is exception in SQLCLR code handled?
- Are all .NET libraries allowed in SQL Server?
- How many types of permission level are there for an assembly?
- In order that an assembly gets loaded in SQL Server what type of checks aredone?
- Can you name system tables for .NET assemblies?
- Are two version of same assembly allowed in SQL Server?
- How are changes made in assembly replicated?
- Is it a good practice to drop a assembly for changes?
- In one of the projects following steps where done, will it work?
- What does Alter assembly with unchecked data signify?
- How do I drop an assembly?
- Can we create SQLCLR using .NET framework 1.0?
- While creating .NET UDF what checks should be done ?
- How do you define a function from the .NET assembly?
- Can you compare between T-SQL and SQLCLR?
- With respect to .NET is SQL SERVER case sensitive?
- Does case sensitive rule apply for VB.NET?
- Can nested classes be accessed in T-SQL?
- Can we have SQLCLR procedure input as array?
- Can object data type be used in SQLCLR?
- How is precision handled for decimal data types in .NET?
- How do we define INPUT and OUTPUT parameters in SQLCLR?
- Is it good to use .NET data types in SQLCLR?
- How to move values from SQL to .NET data types?
- What is System.Data.SqlServer?
- What is SQLContext?
- Can you explain essential steps to deploy SQLCLR?
- How do create function in SQL Server using .NET?
- How do we create trigger using .NET?
- How to create User Define Functions using .NET?
- How to create aggregates using .NET?
- What is Asynchronous support in ADO.NET?
- What is MARS support in ADO.NET?
- What is SQLbulkcopy object in ADO.NET?
- How to select range of rows using ADO.NET?
- What are different types of triggers in SQl SERVER 2000?

- If we have multiple AFTER Triggers on table how can we define the sequence of the triggers ?
- How can you raise custom errors from stored procedure?

XML Integration
- What is XML?
- What is the version information in XML?
- What is ROOT element in XML?
- If XML does not have closing tag will it work?
- Is XML case sensitive?
- What is the difference between XML and HTML?
- Is XML meant to replace HTML?
- Can you explain why your project needed XML?
- What is DTD (Document Type definition)?
- What is well formed XML?
- What is a valid XML?
- What is CDATA section in XML?
- What is CSS?
- What is XSL?
- What is Element and attributes in XML?
- Can we define a column as XML?
- How do we specify the XML data type as typed or untyped?
- How can we create the XSD schema?
- How do I insert in to a table that has XSD schema attached to it?
- What is maximum size for XML data type?
- What is Xquery?
- What are XML indexes?
- What are secondary XML indexes?
- What is FOR XML in SQL Server?
- Can I use FOR XML to generate SCHEMA of a table and how?
- What is the OPENXML statement in SQL Server?
- I have huge XML file, which we want to load in database?
- How to call stored procedure using HTTP SOAP?
- What is XMLA?

Integration Services / DTS
- What is Integration Services import / export wizard?
- What are prime components in Integration Services?
- How can we develop a DTS project in Integration Services?

Replication
- Whats the best way to update data between SQL Servers?
- What are the scenarios you will need multiple databases with schema?

- How will you plan your replication?
- What are publisher, distributor and subscriber in "Replication"?
- What is "Push" and "Pull" subscription?
- Can a publication support push and pull at one time?
- What are different models / types of replication?
- What is Snapshot replication?
- What are the advantages and disadvantages of using Snapshot replication?
- What type of data will qualify for "Snapshot replication"
- What is the actual location where the distributor runs?
- Can you explain in detail how exactly "Snapshot Replication" works?
- What is merge replication?
- How does merge replication works?
- What are advantages and disadvantages of Merge replication?
- What is conflict resolution in Merge replication?
- What is a transactional replication?
- Can you explain in detail how transactional replication works?
- What are data type concerns during replications?

Reporting Services

- Can you explain how can we make a simple report in reporting services?
- How do I specify stored procedures in Reporting Services?
- What is the architecture for "Reporting Services "?

Transaction and Locks

- What is a "Database Transactions" ?
- What is ACID?
- What is "Begin Trans", "Commit Tran", "Rollback Tran" and "Save Tran"?
- What are "Checkpoint's" in SQL Server?
- What are "Implicit Transactions"
- Is it good to use "Implicit Transactions"?
- What is Concurrency?
- How can we solve concurrency problems?
- What kind of problems occurs if we do not implement proper locking strategy?
- What are "Dirty reads"?
- What are "Unrepeatable reads"?
- What are "Phantom rows"?
- What are "Lost Updates"?
- What are different levels of granularity of locking resources?
- What are different types of Locks in SQL Server?
- What are different Isolation levels in SQL Server?
- What are different types of Isolation levels in SQL Server?
- If you are using COM+, what "Isolation" level is set by default?

- What are "Lock" hints?
- What is a "Deadlock"?
- What are the steps you can take to avoid "Deadlocks"?
- How can I know what locks are running on which resource?

SQL

- Revisiting basic syntax of SQL?
- What are "GRANT" and "REVOKE' statements?
- What is Cascade and Restrict in DROP table SQL?
- How to import table using "INSERT" statement?
- What is a DDL, DML and DCL concept in RDBMS world?
- What are different types of joins in SQL?
- What is "CROSS JOIN"?
- You want to select the first record in a given set of rows?
- How do you sort in SQL?
- How do you select unique rows using SQL?
- Can you name some aggregate function is SQL Server?
- What is the default "SORT" order for a SQL?
- What are Wildcard operators in SQL Server?
- What is the difference between "UNION" and "UNION ALL"?
- What are cursors and what are the situations you will use them?
- What are the steps to create a cursor?
- What is a self-join?
- What are the different Cursor Types?
- What are "Global" and "Local" cursors?
- What is "Group by" clause?
- What is ROLLUP?
- What is the difference between DELETE and TRUNCATE?
- What is CUBE?
- What is the difference between "HAVING" and "WHERE" clause?
- What is "COMPUTE" clause in SQL?
- What is "WITH TIES" clause in SQL?
- What does "SET ROWCOUNT" syntax achieves?
- What is a Sub-Query?
- What is "Correlated Subqueries"?
- What is "ALL" and "ANY" operator? or
- What is a "CASE" statement in SQL? or
- What does COLLATE Keyword in SQL signify? or
- What is CTE (Common Table Expression)?
- Select addresses which are between '1/1/2004' and '1/4/2004'?
- What is TRY/CATCH block in T-SQL?

- What is UNPIVOT?
- What are RANKING functions?
- Why should you use CTE rather than simple views?
- What is RANK ()?
- What is ROW_NUMBER()?
- What is DENSE_RANK()?
- What is NTILE()?
- What is SQl injection?
- What (is PIVOT feature in SQL Server?

ADO.NET

- Which are namespaces for ADO.NET?
- Can you give a overview of ADO.NET architecture?
- What are the two fundamental objects in ADO.NET?
- What is difference between dataset and data reader?
- What are major difference between classic ADO and ADO.NET?
- What is the use of connection object?
- What are the methods provided by the command object?
- What is the use of "Data adapter"?
- What are basic methods of "Data adapter"?
- What is Dataset object?
- What are the various objects in Dataset?
- How can we connect to Microsoft Access, FoxPro, Oracle etc?
- What is the namespace to connect to SQL Server?
- How do we use stored procedure in ADO.NET?
- How can we force the connection object to close?
- Can we optimize command object when there is only one row?
- Which is the best place to store connection string?
- What are steps involved to fill a dataset?
- What are the methods provided by the dataset for XML?
- How can we save all data from dataset?
- How can we check for changes made to dataset?
- How can we add/remove row is in "DataTable" object of "Dataset"?
- What is basic use of "Data View"?
- What is difference between "Dataset" and "Data Reader"?
- How can we load multiple tables in a Dataset?
- How can we add relation' s between table in a Dataset?
- What is the use of Command Builder?
- What is difference between "Optimistic" and "Pessimistic" locking?
- How many way's are there to implement locking in ADO.NET?
- How can we perform transactions in .NET?

- What is difference between Dataset?
- Clone and Dataset. Copy?
- What's the difference between Dataset and ADO Record set?

Notification Services

- What are notification services?
- What are basic components of Notification services?
- Can you explain architecture of Notification Services?
- Which are the two XML files needed for notification services?
- What is Nscontrols command?
- What are the situations you will use "Notification" Services?

Service Broker

- What do we need Queues?
- What is "Asynchronous" communication?
- What is SQL Server Service broker?
- What are the essential components of SQL Server Service broker?
- What is the main purpose of having Conversation Group?
- How to implement Service Broker?
- How do we encrypt data between Dialogs?

Data Warehousing / Data Mining

- What is "Data Warehousing"?
- What are Data Marts?
- What are Fact tables and Dimension Tables?
- What is Snow Flake Schema design in database?
- What is ETL process in Data warehousing?
- How can we do ETL process in SQL Server?
- What is "Data mining"?
- Compare "Data mining" and "Data Warehousing"?
- What is BCP?
- How can we import and export using BCP utility?
- During BCP we need to change the field position or eliminate some fields howcan we achieve this?
- What is Bulk Insert?
- What is DTS?
- Can you brief about the Data warehouse project you worked on?
- What is an OLTP (Online Transaction Processing) System?
- What is an OLAP (On- line Analytical processing) system?
- What is Conceptual, Logical and Physical model?
- What is Data purging?
- What is Analysis Services?
- What are CUBES?

- What are the primary ways to store data in OLAP?
- What is META DATA information in Data warehousing projects?
- What is multi-dimensional analysis?
- What is MDX?
- How did you plan your Data warehouse project?
- What are different deliverables according to phases?
- Can you explain how analysis service works?
- What are the different problems that "Data mining" can solve?
- What are different stages of "Data mining"?
- What is Discrete and Continuous data in Data mining world?
- What is MODEL is Data mining world?
- How are models actually derived?
- What is a Decision Tree Algorithm?
- Can decision tree be implemented using SQL?
- What is Naïve Bayes Algorithm?
- Explain clustering algorithm?
- Explain in detail Neural Networks?
- What is Back propagation in Neural Networks?
- What is Time Series algorithm in data mining?
- Explain Association algorithm in Data mining?
- What is Sequence clustering algorithm?
- What are algorithms provided by Microsoft in SQL Server?
- How does data mining and data warehousing work together?
- What is XMLA?

Database Optimization

- What are indexes?
- What are B-Trees?
- I have a table which has lot of inserts, is it a good database design to createindexes on that table?
- What are "Table Scan's" and "Index Scan's"?
- What are the two types of indexes and explain them in detail?
- What is "FillFactor" concept in indexes?
- What is the best value for "FillFactor"?
- What are "Index statistics"?
- How can we see statistics of an index?
- How do you reorganize your index, once you find the problem?
- What is Fragmentation?
- How can we measure Fragmentation?
- How can we remove the Fragmented spaces?
- What are the criteria you will look in to while selecting an index?
- What is "Index Tuning Wizard"?

- What is an Execution plan?
- How do you see the SQL plan in textual format?
- What is Nested join, Hash join and Merge join in SQL Query plan?
- What joins are good in what situations?
- What is RAID and how does it work?